PRODUCTION MANAGEMENT AND INVENTORY CONTROL

OTHER BOOKS ON

M-BAsic Series ...

- ★ Management Principles and Basic Functions
- ★ Personnel Management and Productivity Factors
- ★ International Business Management and Corporate Profitability
- ★ Financial Management and Cost Control
- ★ Management Policy and New Technology
- ★ Organisation Behaviour : Design and Systems for Successful Management
- ★ Business Environment : Public Policy Perspectives and Corporate Management
- ★ Business Policy and Planning
- ★ Marketing and Sales Management
- ★ Production Management and Inventory Control
- ★ Management Information System and Corporate Communications
- ★ Entrepreneur and Enterprise Management

M-BAsic Series

Production Management and Inventory Control

Edited by :
Raj K. Wadhwa
Jimmy Davar
P. Bhaskara Rao

KANISHKA PUBLISHERS, DISTRIBUTORS
NEW DELHI-110 002

KANISHKA PUBLISHERS, DISTRIBUTORS
4697/5-21A, Ansari Road, Darya Ganj
New Delhi-110 002
Phones: 327 0497, 328 8285
Fax : 011-328 0028 (Kanishka)

First Published 1998

ISBN 81-7391-223-8

PRINTED IN INDIA

Published by Madan Sachdeva for Kanishka Publishers, Distributors, 4697/5-21A, Ansari Road, Darya Ganj, New Delhi-110 002; Typesetting by Heart Data Processing, Delhi-31, and Printed at Nice Printing Press Delhi.

Preface

The most dynamic feature of the discipline of management may be assumed to be its constant evolution along with people, institutions, ideas and technological advancement. Management is at once a science and an art. It is precise in its approaches to technical and technological innovation and egalitarian in its principles of application, optimisation of human talents and skills, and adaptation of concepts and practices. Management also encompasses a cultural component as it is about human attitudes, capabilities and behaviour in varying circumstances. Management also incorporates the most crucial components of philosophy, because the successful manager is expected to possess keen insight into people and problems, is detached enough to acquire that essential overview of the organisation he serves, performs to the best of his ability without being obsessed with the expectation of high rewards, and experience concerns large enough to include the present and future of mankind worldwide. While the true manager seeks excellence in his own line of work, yet he pursues and conceives distant goals and fruitful human endeavours. Thus, the management professional of today would be expected to inculcate a scientific approach, an egalitarian attitude, a philosophical nature, a humanistic world-view and a liberal outlook. Above all, the genuine management professional loves people but hates politics.

The present series of publications has been conceived and put together as insightful readings for the benefit of students of management and business administration, as also aspiring professionals who seek a panoramic window onto the management landscape. M. BAsic Series provides overviews in that the materials brought together combine usefulness with readability, depth as well as perception, and practical value with conceptual appeal. The papers, articles, essays, abstracts and discussion notes are drawn from several countries and diverse contexts—mainly with the purpose of affording the management student and aspiring professional the contoured picture of globalisation of management principles and practices. A series has limitations and the present publication would also have the same flaw, yet it is a firm hope, even a belief, that together the materials presented here serve a valuable and necessary purpose.

The compilation that follows is offered as a valuable aid in the study of production and productivity management, including several technical and technological aspects that modern business firms and manufacturing units are required to cope with. Of special interest is the materials on inventory control and production planning, as also modernisation of the workshop, including robotisation.

EDITORS

Contents

1

Production Functions and Effective Management

The key concept is accuracy of quantity, quality and production time. It is not possible to specify any exact pattern of production in an industrial undertaking. The size of the undertaking, the company policy, nature and range of product, size and frequency of orders, extent of changes of product specification, number of manufacturing stages and the nature of the manufacturing methods all influence the final pattern. For example, it may be the policy to manufacture to order only. Here each product is a special item and the production problems would be different from those encountered by a company producing articles whose style, colour and size present a long production line. Again, the nature of the products to be made must be reflected in the production organisation. This is immediately apparent on contrasting a simple unit such as a cooking utensil with a complicated adding machine. Similarly, there will be marked differences arising from manufacturing methods. Production planning and control methods for one-off or jobbing work, for batch production and flow production must of necessity vary. The continuous processing in chemical industries presents less of a production problem than does the intermittent type of manufacture associated with machine tool fabrication. These factors affecting production have not been introduced to confuse the fundamental issues, but rather to find some common meeting ground.

The major problem confronting the production specialist in a company is to secure the maximum utilisation of productive resources and to direct those resources so as best to meet the needs of various consumers. The task is complicated by the almost unlimited types of industry manufacturing processes and final products.

Modern Production Planning and Control

To narrow the field and in the interests of standardisation, it has seemed advisable to adhere to the recommendations of the *British Standard* 1100, Part I, from which the explanatory chart (Fig. 1.1) is reproduced, by kind permission of the British Institute of Management.

It will be seen that production planning and control consists of determining the plan of how the manufacturing objective is to be achieved, where, when and by whom the work is to be done, and the subsequent control of the work after it has been started to ensure maintenance of the predetermined programme.

No procedure or system can be expected to operate satisfactorily unless the stages which precede it are carefully considered. These preliminary stages may be grouped as—

1. Sales forecasting.
2. Specification of the product.
3. Operation specification.

Sales Forecasting Methodology

It is obviously necessary to know the company's general sales programme; some engineers state that sales forecasting is 90 per cent of production control and that the remainder is purely mechanical. Here it is possible to comment only briefly on the major problems of sales forecasting which will involve analysis of the following factors :

1. What has been the trend of total sales of the industry? For example, have they been increasing or decreasing?

2. What are the prospects for customers of the industry? In the case of aircraft instrument makers, for example, what is the outlook for aircraft production?
3. What is the general economic outlook? What about consumer purchasing power?
4. What is the trend for related competitor industries? For example, what is the effect of plastic floor coverings on the sales of linoleum?
5. What will be the effect of competition from unrelated industries? For example, between television and electric washing machines?

The foregoing are by no means all the factors to be considered, but they indicate the complexity of sales forecasting. The importance of developing and passing on this type of information to the production department cannot be overestimated.

Explanatory Chart

Production control is the means by which a manufacturing plan is determined, information issued for its execution and data collected and recorded which will enable the plan to be controlled through all its stages.

Information On

Sales or contract programme.
Approval and modification of design for manufacture.
Specification, drawings and material schedules.
Jig, tools and test gear design and manufacture.
Rate fixing and time study.
Estimating.
Routing and processing.
Inspection.
Labour analysis.
Budgetary control.
Costs.

Coming from the

Production Engineering Department	Works Department	Cost Department	Sales or Contracts Department

provides the basis for

Production Control
sub-divided into

—Scheduling	The means by which the production plan is presented to all concerned to provide for the commencement and completion of work in all stages of manufacture.
—Machine and Labour Utilisation	The means by which the maximum use of machines and labour is co-ordinated in the production plan.
—Stock Control	The means by which the correct quantity and quality of material and components are made available according to the production plan.
—Manufacturing Order Control	The means by which authority is given to all concerned to produce according to plan.
—Progressing	The means by which the execution of the production plan is co-ordinated so as to reveal, and as far as possible to eliminate or correct, any variations from the plan.

in order to formulate

The Production Plan

Fig. 1.1

Specification of the Product

Specifications for the products to be manufactured set out the "what" of manufacture and may be grouped under three main headings :

1. *Parts List*: Such a list shows the names of the parts and sub-assemblies, and the quantities required for the manufacture of a completed unit. The use of such a list is to extend the requirements for a given number of assemblies into the requirements for the parts which make up the assembly.

   In some cases a parts list may not be required. In the manufacture of a spool of camera film a parts list does not have the same significance as it does for the camera. The parts list may, in certain instances, be replaced by a materials specification giving the quantity of ingredients for a given batch size of, for example, a pharmaceutical preparation.

2. *Drawings and Descriptions* : Without a detailed description of each piece, part and sub-assembly, a product specification is incomplete. These drawings should show the required form, shape, dimensions, tolerances and material to be used. Not only are such drawings and descriptions necessary for the preparation of tools, jigs and fixtures, but they also form the basis for control of quality.
3. *Materials* : Product specification is obviously incomplete without correct descriptions of the material to be used. This is usually shown on the drawings. The purpose of such material description is to provide sufficient identification for co-ordination of raw material requirements with production plans to be easily and successfully made.

Operation Specification

The lack of sufficient information concerning processing operations is a frequent point of failure for production control systems. Yet nothing is more important than basing controls on information developed by careful study. The first step in such a study is to decide what parts will be bought from outside suppliers and what will be made within the plant. Again, it will have to be decided what parts have to be purchased in a fully fashioned state. Such parts as springs, bearings, washers; in fact, any item for which specialised manufacturing methods have been established. The volume of production will determine in each case the decision to buy or make. Thus it is economical for Kodak Ltd. to make and print their own cartons, and for the Ford Company to manufacture their own pig iron, whereas in most companies these items would be purchased. Another factor which determine the decision to make or buy is the availability of machines. A company with several automatic screw machines may on occasion decide to manufacture a part and on another to purchase the same part.

When it is decided what items have to be manufactured, it is then necessary to specify the machines to be used. This activity is termed "routing" and in general defines the "where" of manufacture. The results of routing are customarily summarised on a form termed a route sheet or an operation sheet. A routing may be prepared by any of a number of different individuals depending on the processes involved. In chemical industries the laboratory may be responsible for the job, while in metal-working plants the production engineering department may handle the work. Whoever may be responsible for this task, a properly recorded master routing form is fundamental to good production planning.

Preceding production control should be the determination of manufacturing methods. This is the description of the "how" of manufacture. It is essential to lay down manufacturing methods in order that production standards may be established, the correct grade of labour employed and the loading of machine tools be done to best advantage. The "how" of manufacture is often inadequate or insufficiently detailed for those who have to interpret it. As a consequence, the establishment of production standards is delayed until work commences on the shop floor and time studies are made of worker interpretations of how to manufacture. It is true that some method improvement, dependent upon the amount of time a foremen may have to spare from his other duties or the imagination of the time study man, may in certain instances be made before detailed time studies, and hence production standards are established, but this is not enough. The establishment of manufacturing methods must be as complete in detail as practicable *before* a job is issued to the shops. This implies the closest liaison between the planning and methods engineering departments.

The *methods engineering* department is responsible for the application of the techniques charted in Figure 1.2. This chart shows both the scope and the techniques of methods engineering. Only an outline of the major techniques as they apply to production in this profile has been given. To decide which of the techniques to apply it is necessary to consider—*(a)* the repetitiveness of the activity, *(b)* its labour content, and *(c)* its anticipated life. It would be both wasteful and unnecessary to bring all the techniques into operation on every occasion—a micrometer is not used if a foot rule will do

Under the first major sub-division—Ananysis—are listed the means whereby an investigation into methods may be undertaken. Mental analysis is rapid but can be unsystematic, and there is no permanent record of the findings. The process questionnaire, on the other hand while quite simple, is a written analysis designed to ensure that none of the factors which should be considered in making a thorough analysis of an operation will be neglected.

In the *operation process chart* are recorded the stages at which materials are introduced into a process, the sequence of operations and inspections, and the various times for each of these activities.

The *flow process chart* is somewhat more detailed and includes, in addition to the information shown on an operation process chart, transportations, delays, storages and distances travelled. In order to avoid confusion, such a record should refer either to the operator or the material, but not to both simultaneously. In a man-machine chart, the relation between the man operating time and the machine or process time in a full work cycle is recorded. The desirable condition is to have man and machine fully occupied if possible during the operation cycle.

In order to show at a glance the classification of every activity, yet at the same time ensure careful analysis, certain distinguishing symbols are employed for every major type of activity.

These symbols and their interpretation are shown below, in Figure 1.3. These charts are a means to an end and not an end in themselves. They do not of themselves solve problems but, by assisting in visualizing a procedure, they suggest to an investigator improvements which might not otherwise have been considered.

Assuming a more intensive investigation is justified, then one of the secondary analyses may be employed. In motion study a conscious study is made of the body movements in a complete work cycle in terms of the basic divisions of accomplishment. Subsequently, these are re-arranged into what is considered to be the most practical sequence. The conception of the basic divisions was due to Frank Bunker Gilbreth (1868-1924) who, with the collaboration of his wife (Lillian M. Gilbreth),

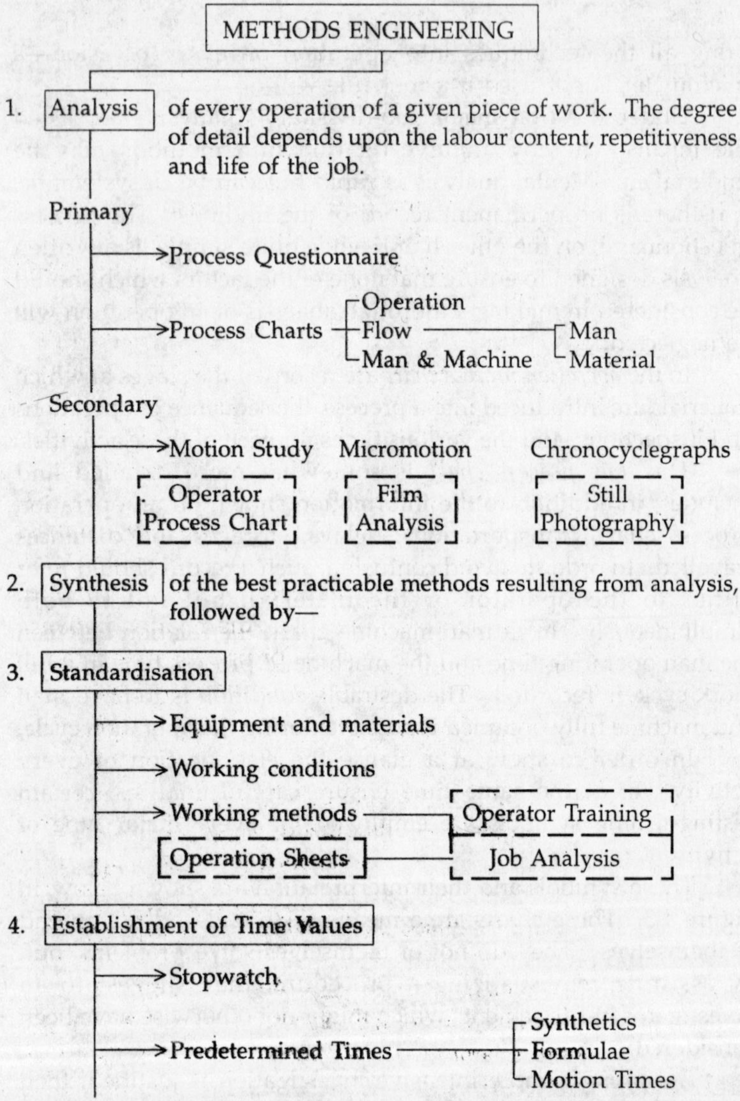

Fig. 1.2 : Methods engineering, as here visualized, precedes actual production and has as its main objective the engineering of effective work methods rather than the rapid establishment of time values which are to form the basis of a financial incentive.

developed motion study as a primary tool for managers. The American Society of Mechanical Engineers standardised these divisions, and their groupings with accepted abbreviations are :

Physical Basic Elements

Reach	R	*Hold	H
Move	M	Release Load	RL
*Change Direction	CD	*Preposition	PP
Grasp	G	Disengage	D

Semi Mental Basic Elements

*Position	P	*Search	S	*Select	SE

Mental Basic Elements

*Plan	PL	*Examine	E

Objective Basic Elements

DO DO

Delay Basic Elements

*Avoidable Delay	AD	Rest to Overcome Fatigue	F
*Unavoidable Delay	UD	*Balancing Delay	BD

All work from the simplest to the most complex consists of these elements in varying sequence and repetition. Those marked * are considered to be ineffective, and wherever they occur an attempt should be made to eliminate them. With a clear understanding of these basic elements the methods engineer can prepare a *Two Handed Operator Process Chart* by observing the operation, and he has a sound basis for judging the effectiveness of any operation. Essentially such a chart is an analysis of the movements or motions of both the operator's arms and hands in terms of the basic elements. In micromotion study a similar but more detailed analysis is carried out by a frame by frame examination of a film of the operation cycle. The result when charted is known as a Simultaneous Motion or Simo Chart. To study the actual path of motions, by far the most important aspect of motion study, cyclegraphs or chrono-cyclegraphs are used. These are special types of still photographs which are often dismissed as laboratory extravagances by those who have not the imagination to visualise their usefulness.

As a result of the various analyses , it is possible to synthesize an effective method of work. But this is of small avail unless measures are taken to standardise the factors listed in the chart.

Symbol	*Activity*	*Predominant Result*
○	Operation	Accomplishes
⇨	Transport	Moves
□	Inspection	Verifies
D	Temporary Storage or Delay	Interferes
▽	Permanent Storage	Keeps

Fig. 1.3

Once this has been done it becomes possible to establish time values for an operation. When a stopwatch is used for this purpose the essential stages are :

1. A task is subdivided into convenient activities termed "elements"
2. Each element is described fully. The beginning and ending points of each element particularly are stated clearly.
3. The elements are listed on an observation or time-study sheet.
4. The time taken for the performance of each element is then noted with the aid of a stopwatch. The method of doing this may vary : some observers use the instantaneous or fly-back method and some the continuous-reading method. Again, various types of stopwatches are used for timing.
5. Each element is timed repeatedly to get what is considered to be a representative sample.
6. The operator's performance is then assessed; this may be done in two ways :

(a) *Rating* : The operator's pace or speed in performing each element, or over the entire study, is estimated numerically. This assessment is made simultaneously with the timing and recorded on the observation sheet.

(b) *Levelling* : The operator's skill and effort in performing the work are assessed individually in accordance with established definition. Consistency and working conditions are also assessed. The four factors are expressed numerically, by reference to a standardised scale, and constitute "the levelling factor".

Both these processes are entirely subjective, but it is claimed by time-study engineers that remarkable consistency in their assessments is achieved.

7. The actual time values are now RATED OR LEVELLED.
   Rated Time : A representative rating is applied to a *selected* elemental time to give what are termed the Normalised times for each element.
   Levelled Time : The *average* elemental times are multiplied by the levelling factor to give what are termed the LEVELLED times for each element.
8. After consideration has been given to the frequency with which any particular element is performed, the normalised or levelled elemental times are totalled and certain allowances added to get the STANDARD time for the task.

In a later technique of establishing time values, the stopwatch was dispensed with and times arrived at by motion analysis of the operation and then applying the times for these motions from a series of tables. This method ensures consistency between observers, provides an accurate record of method, and obviates assessment of the operator's performance.

An important part of setting operation specifications is the determination of the proper quantities to manufacture at one time. Some balance must be maintained in the economic operation of a factory between the utilisation of labour and production facilities, levels of stock, and the meeting of delivery dates. The more important factors to consider are :

1. Those costs which are fixed regardless of the quantity produced. An example would be the "setting up" charges for a machine tool.
2. Costs such as labour and material which vary with the quantity produced.
3. Other charges, such as interest on capital invested in stock, or costs arising from possible obsolescence or deterioration.
4. Storage costs.
5. The rate at which the product is expected to sell.
6. The time required to produce a unit quantity of the product.

With knowledge of the above facts it is not a difficult matter to establish the most economical batch size for production.

Production Endorsement

There should be a systematic authorisation of production, otherwise there may be either excessive stock or shortages of critical items. As a company's manufacturing programme must be geared to its sales budget, it is essential that the sales department have a say in stipulating what is to be made and when. This apparent conflict of interests can be resolved by delegating production authorisation to the production department within agreed limits. Before considering various methods of authorising production, a consideration of the following general requirements is necessary:

1. A description of the product to be produced, the quantity required and the time limit allowed.
2. The production authorised should be related to the overall sales and production budgets so that any variation can be investigated immediately.
3. It should be checked by the production control department to determine the possibility of meeting the requirements in the time specified.

In authorising production to cover a long-term forecast, the first step could be the determination of sales by individual items for the next twelve months. These sales are then broken down into months by applying percentages which represent the estimated sales of the months in relation to the annual sales. Following this, the monthly sales can be adjusted to conform to the economic lot sizes. For example if 10,000 packages are to be produced in each of the three months March, April, May, and the economic lot size is 15,000, the production will be re-scheduled to 15,000 in the months of March and April and none in May. After this step has been taken, the company can calculate an estimated stock of each item at the end of each month. This is done by knowing the stock in hand at the start of the year and by knowing the production and estimated sales by months. These stocks are checked against an allowed maximum and should the forecast position exceed this maximum, re-scheduling is effected to ensure that the capital tied up in stock is not excessive.

Where production authorisation is to be based on short-term forecasts, the responsibility is generally vested in the sales department. In such cases the sales department will give the production department authority to make up the quantity they believe necessary to cover their immediate requirements. Short-term budgets may be made for a period of one, two or three months into the future. The length of time to be covered will depend to a large degree upon the length of the manufacturing cycle.

In manufacturing against stock control limits, authorisation for production is automatic. An estimate is made of the stock to be carried in anticipation of customer orders. The sales figures used in estimating these amounts may be either forecast or based on previous experience. The minimum stocks to be permitted would be established by knowing the manufacturing intervals for the products. The difference between the minimum and maximum stock then becomes the manufacturing quantity. If this quantity is greater than an economic manufacturing lot, some reduction in the maximum could be made or the amount to manufacture may be split into several different lots. Records are kept of the stock on hand and as this decreases to the minimum point a manufacturing order is put through for the appropriate quantity. This method is well adapted to a lengthy product line in that the authorisation of production is theoretically automatic. This feature is a result of having the system tied closely with accurate perpetual inventory records.

In the production of non-standard items, it is generally accepted that the authorisation of production should originate from the customer's order. The exact procedure used varies, but generally follows this pattern :the customer's order is entered in the usual order department routine and is then passed to the production control group after the necessary approval has been secured. The production control department then issues the manufacturing order. It will be appreciated that production authorised in this manner is based strictly on the sales results of the company. There is little that can be done in laying out a balanced programme of manufacture for a long period. However, in many cases it is possible to manufacture certain of the sub-assemblies or piece parts for a given product. This system of partially manufacturing up to the point where specialisation in the product occurs is widely used in all companies manufacturing to customer order.

Requirements Checklist and Documentation

Let us consider a product consisting of several parts and sub-assemblies, under circumstances where various models are made with certain piece parts which are interchangeable between models.

The determination of requirements entails the extension of the product parts list, previously mentioned, into a requirements of piece parts. For example, if authorisation has been made for 1,000 engines, reference to the parts list may show that 1,000 crankshafts, 4,000 connecting rods, and 8,000 link rods are required. To these quantities must be added a percentage for estimated scrap. A similar procedure must be followed for all the items shown on the parts list so that when the extension is completed the total number of parts to be manufactured will be known. At this stage, the piece parts will fall into one of three categories. The first class will include those which are to be manufactured, the second class those which are to be purchased, and the third those on which a decision must be made at that time as to whether to purchase or produce. This decision will naturally be based on the availability of machines within the company to produce the required items in the time schedule which has been imposed.

If we assume that it is decided that a given part is to be manufactured, the order authorising production has to be issued. The form of order used will vary as between companies, but in general will give the following information :

1. Part number, description.
2. Quantity to be produced.
3. Manufacturing order number.
4. Date of completion of order.
5. Materials required.
6. Needed operations.

One copy of the manufacturing order will be used to determine raw material requirements. By sending this copy to the raw material stock control section the possible need for additional amounts of raw material can be determined quickly. In this way it is ensured that no machines are set up for jobs for which material is not available.

Scheduling

This is the determination of the "when" of manufacture. It has as its objectives :

1. The preparation of delivery time-tables to ensure that customers receive their goods at the desired time.
2. The insurance that all items in a product are available at the time of assembly.
3. The determination of the adequacy of existing equipment and personnel.
4. The balancing of machine loads.

To accomplish these objectives it is essential that the time-table be based on facts concerning:

1. Quantities of the various items which are to be produced.
2. Required delivery dates of these items.
3. Available machines and their interchangeability.

4. Machines over which each of the items must be routed to complete its production.
5. The time requirements per piece for each of these operations.

From the manufacturing order, a copy of which should have been passed to the scheduling section, it is possible to calculate the machine hours for producing a given lot size. It is then possible to prepare what may be termed machine load cards. These cards will show in respect of a particular machine its load commitments. To determine the sequence and dates for the commencement of work on any machine the calculations can be done by working backwards from the desired date for completion of the final product. Thus the date for starting the assembly work would be obtained by deducting the required assembly time from the desired final date, and the date for the commencement of the last operations on each of the piece parts by deducting the time required for those operations from the desired assembly date. In a similar manner the dates for the start of each of the operations for each of the piece parts may be calculated. In all the foregoing instances suitable allowances for transfer of semi-finished parts from one department to another and for contingencies must be made.

Progressing

It is of little use to do a comprehensive job of planning and scheduling production if some means is not provided for ensuring the accomplishment of the plan. This co-ordination and follow-up of the production plans is known as progressing. There are naturally many ways by which this control may be assured, and what is satisfactory in one works may not meet the requirements of another. Most of the systems would, however, be operated in conjuction with the forms and procedures already described.

Thus on the progress section's copy of the manufacturing order the daily production on any operation can be posted from the daily time tickets. Any significant variation from scheduled dates is thus immediately brought to attention and the necessary revisions can be made. Sometimes the postings are made only when the operations are complete. This obviates daily postings but does not give the day-to-day production position. The decision as to which method to follow depends a great deal upon the length of the manufacturing cycle. Where this is short and the operations follow each other in rapid sequence the control of individual operations is impracticable and is best based on final completion.

Again, with the aid of the machine loading cards, an adaptation sui able for progressing can readily be made. Space could be provided on the card for a comparison of actual with scheduled accomplishment. As with the manufacturing order, the machine loading card may be posted from daily time tickets or completed notifications.

Another method for progressing machine loadings is by means of the Gantt Chart. This is an excellent graphic means of control. The chart is made by listing the machines down the left-hand margin or vertical axis. The horizontal axis is divided into a suitable time scale. A mark (⌈) is placed on the line for a job under the date on which production is to begin. Another mark (⌉) is placed on the same line under the expected completion date. A line is then drawn between the beginning and closing marks ⌈——⌉. As work proceeds a heavier line or one drawn in a different colour is plotted in line with the specific job and below the previous line. Thus a job on which a quarter of the total production has been completed would look like Job No. 3248 on the chart below.

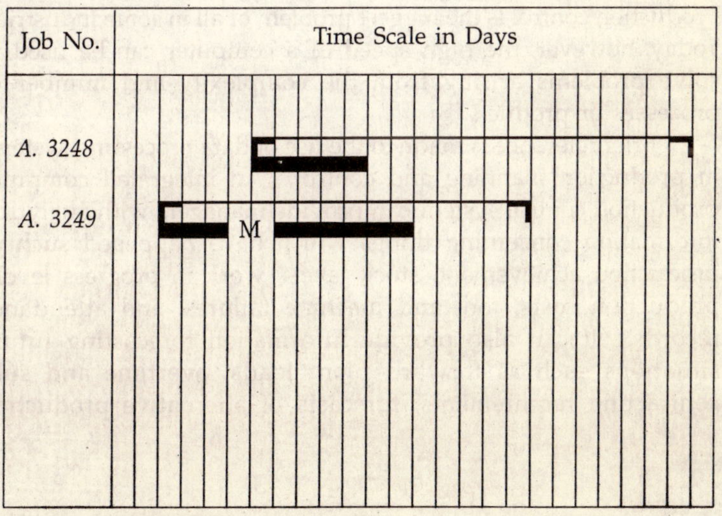

Such a pictorial presentation will immediately show up any failure to maintain the schedule. The chart can be elaborated to show causes of delay. Thus an *M* might indicate shortage of material, an *L* that labour was not available, and so on.

Sometimes it may be necessary to use special forms for progress work. Such forms should be designed to provide the essential controls at a minimum of clerical expense.

One factor demanding much of the progress section's time is the chasing of stock. When production is not up to schedule the chaser is given the job of urging on the missing parts. The weakness of this arrangement is that the corrective effort is begun when the situation is already bad. Follow-up procedure can be simplified if use is made to the exception principle. By flogging only those items behind schedule attention is directed only towards those items in need of it. Among possible courses of action for the handling of items behind schedule there are *(a)* rescheduling; *(b)* completion of a portion of the production on schedule and delaying the balance; *(c)* increasing capacity through the addition of machines, personnel or overtime; *(d)* identification of the job as off schedule so that priority may be granted it. The important thing is to know, at the earliest date, of failures to maintain schedule and to apply corrective measures in sufficient time for them to be effective.

Production Control by Computer

Production control is the biggest problem of all in some industries. Today, however, the high speed of a computer can be used to solve problems arising from the complexity and number of processes or products.

Brief reference is made to the use of data processing systems in production planning and control. An integrated computer production control system can provide managers with analytical information concerning things which have happened such as production achievement, stock levels, work in progress levels, production costs, tool and machine failures, and attendance records. It can also provide information forecasting future situations such as forward plant loads, overtime and subcontracting requirements, forecasts of alternative production policies and plans, and the effects of alternative production methods.

Quality Control Inspection

The function of the inspection department is to ensure that all work leaving the factory is of the required standard. It is generally considered desirable that the department should be quite independent of all other departments, and be responsible to the general manager.

The objects of inspection are :

1. To detect and isolate faulty material or work and so to prevent waste.
2. To prevent further work being done on pieces already spoiled.
3. To protect the firm's reputation by reducing the number of complaints from customers.
4. To detect sources of weakness, troubles or danger in the finished articles and so to check the work of the designers.

Something has been said on the inspection of raw materials before they go into production. It is possible to check some properties of every material that may be used by the factory. The tests may be either chemical or physical, simple and cheap or complex and costly. Chemical tests are generally analytical, although they are not normally complete analyses of the material. It is usually enough to determine the presence of a certain minimum amount of one or two ingredients. Sometimes the exact amount must be known to provide information to the purchasing department if purchases are made on the percentage of certain ingredients present in a particular material.

The physical tests may be purely dimensional or they may be, for example, impact and tensile strength tests. The structure of some materials or partly finished goods may have to be checked by X-rays. These tests must be selected so that any particular property of the material is tested at any one time.

All work produced must be carefully checked at various stages of production and on completion to achieve the objects enumerated above. It is therefore necessary for the technical and planning staffs to agree on the points at which inspection can be most advantageously carried out.

In very high precision work every piece and operation may have to be checked. The usual kinds of inspection of work in progress are :

1. *Roving Inspection* (usually for high precision work) : The inspectors walk round and check the work or samples of the work of various operators.
2. *Fixed Inspection* : The work is brought at intervals for inspectors to check.
3. *Final Inspection* : The amount necessary depends on the thoroughness of the previous inspection. If finished goods are rejected, the production and sometimes the design department must be consulted to see whether radical alterations are required in the design or method of production. In some cases inspection and checking of instruments, for example gauges, may be necessary.

Rejected materials are recorded on a routine document, of which copies are passed to the progress and stores departments, a further copy being retained by the production department concerned and constitutes an authority to draw new supplies.

The effectiveness and results of inspection in productive work are generally summarised in reports on the number and frequency of rejections, such information being useful for considerations affecting production methods, purchasing, and personnel.

Statistical Quality Control

A number of statistical methods has been developed to aid in checking and controlling the quality of manufactured goods. The general aim of these techniques is to balance the cost of inspection against the penalties of allowing faulty materials to escape detection. Thus total cost is minimised.

Quality and Reliability

The importance of product quality and reliability is now widely appreciated. They are two different but closely-interrelated factors contributing to better value for customers. In any market it is *value* which is the prime customer requirement. In the buyer's eyes.

$$\text{Value} = \frac{\text{Quality and Reliability}}{\text{Cost}}$$

Value can be made greater by increasing the numerator and reducing the denominator.

Quality and reliability failures arise primarily out of the design and poor production planning, and are not often due to bad workmanship.

Reliability of product requires *(a)* good design for the purpose; *(b)* testing to reveal potential weaknesses; *(c)* good "quality" manufacture; *(d)* follow-up to take quick advantage of field service experience and to eradicate causes of trouble.

The cost of unreliability is not easy to calculate as it falls most heavily on the user. But the cost to the supplier in supplying free replacements and in placating customers is considerable, whilst the loss of reputation and loss of future markets is, of course, incalculable.

With the enormous scale of production of modern plants, comparatively small improvements in the accuracy of quality control can often achieve considerable savings. The objectives should therefore be :

1. Improvement of quality manufacture which will result in increased productivity and reduced costs.
2. Improved reliability of product in the hands of the user which will have the effect of enhancing its value to him.

2

Pre-Production Factors : Profile of Product Planning

Product Planning is an essential component of the firm's production function. The 90's are seeing the Indian economy opening up, multinationals moving in and Indian companies going global. Let's see the events around us. BPL introduces Frost Free refrigeration systems, Brooke Bond begins marketing ice creams, sauces and juice concentrates.

Oberoi Hotels move into the low cost hotels with the Novotel chain. TATA launches the 'Estate' and 'Sierra' four wheelers, 'Titan' launches 'Timex' watches. Foreign banks expand operations, Indian banks move into other financial services including credit cards, lease financing.

Yes, new products, new sources, new strategies for existing products and newer collaborations are all around us. It is the end deliverable to the consumer which is getting created or given a new form everyday. This is the nucleus of all marketing activity. This is the product or service which a company offers.

In simple terms, a product is a set of tangible and intangible attributes like Design, Features, Performance, Brand name, Packaging and Colour put together in a identifiable form. As defined by Philip Kotler a product is anything that can be offered to a market for attention, acquisition, use or consumption that might satisfy a need.

PRODUCT CLASSIFICATION

Just as it is useful to segment markets for better focus, so also it is necessary to classify products. This can be based on :

- — Their durability and tangibility
- — Consumer buying habits.

Durability and Tangibility

Based on the product's durability and tangibility, it can be classified into :

(i) *Non-durables* : Tangible products, with a limited life span and are normally consumed in one/few uses. For example : Chocolates, salt, soft drinks, soap, lipstick.

(ii) *Durables* : Tangible products with a long life span. Typically being high value items they require greater selling and support effort. For example: Refrigerators, televisions, cameras, microwave oven.

(iii) *Services :* Intangible activities, which may or may not be associated with a physical product. For example : Consultancy, banking, advertising, after sales.

Consumer Shopping Habits

The understanding of shopping habits of a consumer helps a marketer in projecting a product as also in deciding its price and its placement or distribution channel. Take for example a toothpaste, an everyday convenience product easily available from the next door grocer or even a pan wallah. And then there are products like air-conditioners or cars, these are available at select outlets, the price is high and they involve a longer decision process due to comparisons.

Based on such characteristics *i.e.*, on frequency of purchase and availability the following product classifications are derived:

(i) *Convenience Goods* : There are goods purchased routinely or frequently in minimum time and with minimum comparison. The consumer is willing to accept any of several brands and buys what is most accessible. Such products are generally available in mass markets. For example : Tooth paste, soap, newspapers, cigarettes.

(ii) *Shopping Goods* : The purchase frequency for these products is low. They require considerable effort in buying as purchase decision involves comparison of price, quality, style. Availability is limited as compared to convenience goods. Products like furniture, jewellery, household appliances, clothing fit into this category.

(iii) *Speciality Goods* : Their purchase frequency is very low, so value of the product is high. Typically these products have unique characteristics. Consumers have highly strong brand preferences and do not accept substitutes. People are willing to spend time and effort in purchasing the particular brand, which may be available at selected outlets only. For example : Mercedes cars, cross pens, cartier watches.

Now you know what is a product and how are products classified, but how do you manage a product ? What are the essential issues that you need to take care of ? Let us understand the components of a product.

PRODUCT COMPONENTS

The essential components include

— Design and Colour
— Specifications/Features
— Performance Quality
— Packaging
— Brand Name

Let us discuss each of these and also understand how they help in differentiating your product or build an image about it.

Design and Colour : It is the 'look' of the product, which adds to its usefulness and attracts customers. It is being used more and more today to create a distinct product personality and aid in brand identification. Example : The Symphony range of Air-coolers, the All Terrain bicycles and the colour of toys for children

— *Specifications or Features* : These are the contents, raw materials, dimensions, quality and other such tangibles which give it a form. They are a key to creating a differentiation for a product. Example–Television with stereo sound, built-in satellite receiver or video games, diet coke or taste of Pepsi or Thumps Up.

— *Performance Quality* : It is the product's ability to deliver as per and beyond expectations of the target segment. Price also has a bearing on performance expectations. Example : The price, quality and target audience of a Hawkins pressure cooker Vs a local brand.

— *Packaging* : The container/wrapper for a product which today has become a differentiation strategy. It has the ability to sell the product by being 'need' driven, besides being innovative and eye catching. Example : Convenience packs for shampoos, oils, detergents – useful for travel. Re-usuable PET bottles for oils which also gives product visibility.

— *Brand Name* : It is what the product is called. It helps build an image and easy recall. Overtime it can develop a value/ strengths which can be transferred on to other products. Example : TATA, Godrej. It can also have an image distinct from the organisation. Example 'Prestige' Cookers, 'Woodwords' gripe water, 'Kiwi' shoe polish all from the TTK group.

Amongst the above, Branding and Packaging are the two components receiving the attention of today's marketing professional. Let us discuss these in greater detail : A brand is a name, term, symbol or a special design or some combination of these elements, that is designed to identify the goods or services of one seller or a group of sellers.

Selecting an appropriate brand name for a product is an important marketing exercise. To illustrate let us share with you an example.

About 12 years ago, there was a brand of cosmetics launched in India under the brand name 'Kiss and Tell'. But the brand failed to take off because no housewife would be caught going to a retailer and saying "Give me a Kiss and Tell". Sometime later, the company relaunched this range of cosmetics under a new name which is extremely successful today. It is now called 'Tips and Toes'. (A's quoted in an article in Brand Equity, dated July 14, 1993).

This indicates that these days, a large proportion of value in marketing is through the name. As per many marketers, this is the age of "Naam Ka Daam" (Price for a name). However, this does not indicate that a name alone can make or break a product or a company. But one cannot deny, as many a research have shown that a well chosen name can give a product a definite edge over competition. Branding is also a long-term strategy, where by you invest today on building a certain value perception about the name, which later sells for itself.

It may therefore be relevant to discuss some of the characteristics of an effective brand name.

Characteristics of a Good Brand Name

What makes a good brand name ? Which are the brands that you can recall ? Try analysing their characteristics:

— *Short and Crisp* : A brand name should be short, crisp and simple so that the consumer finds it easy to spell, pronounce and remember. This will help in making the brand memorable and will have more recall value. For example well known brand names like LUX, LIRIL, VICKS, HALLS, SONY and many more are short and powerful.

— *Unique* : A unique or distinct name immediately identifies a brand and distinguishes it from others. Such names can be created using fabricated words like Volfarm, Nesfit and Modiluft. Amongst most, unique and distinctive brand names are Kodak and Xerox.

— *Relevance* : A good brand name should be relevant to the product's attributed or the benefits offered by it. The name can convey the essence of a product or service to help in identifying or positioning the brand. For example, names like BAND-AID, GOOD KNIGHT, CEASE-FIRE, FROOTI, RAY-BAN suggest something about the product's characteristics, usage and benefits.

— *Flexible* : A brand name should be broad enough to cover not just the organisation's current business, but also future expansions. It should, therefore be adaptable to new products that may be added to the existing range. For example, names like VICKS, BAJAJ, GODREJ have successfully used the same names for many a product.

Let us now look at the various strategies for branding.

Branding Strategies

Let us discuss the three types of typical names which exist in the brand bazaar:

(i) In the first case, take the products sold by Bajaj—Bajaj Water filters, Bajaj Lighting, Bajaj fans, Bajaj Home Appliances and many more. All products carry the same name—Bajaj. Similarly in the case of Tata—Tata Salt, Tata Tea, Tata Shudh Detergent, Tata Trucks.

(ii) You also have names like Maggi, Rath, Ariel, Hamam, Margo, Surf, Charmis and many more which do not carry the manufacturer's name.

(iii) Then, there are combinations like Mahindra Armada, Maruti Omni, Godrej Stroewell, MRF Nylogrip or Dunlop Spectrawide which have two names – one the manufacturer's or the mother brand's name and the other an independent name.

The above categorisation reveals three different strategies:

— Blanket Family Name as in case one.
— Individual Brand Name as in case two.
— Company Trade Name with Product Name as in case three.

Interestingly, today we see companies using the same names for more than one product. Take the case of Maggi. After the success of its "Two minute noodles', Nestle added Maggi Sauces, Maggi Soups and now Maggi Seasonings to its product fold.

Why do you think a company does this? If you have an established name like TATA or Godrej or Bajaj what would you do? Wouldn't you like to draw on the existing strengths? That's **what** ***Brand Extension*** is all about.

Brand Extension Refers to Using an Existing Brand Name to Launch New or Modified Products

Take the case of Vicks Vaporub which is a mega success today. Based on this success, they introduced Vicks Cough Syrup, Vicks Ginger drops, and Vicks Hot Sip. Or the Clearasil anti-pimple cream success which has been used to launch Clearasil Soap, Clearasil Daily Soap Wash in liquid form. Also Reckitt and Coleman has introduced Dettol Soap, Dettol Plaster, Dettol antiseptic cream, under the same brand name Dettol.

What could be the reason for these companies using the same name for their products?

According to Ashutosh Agarwal, Marketing Manager, Personal Care, Reckitt and Colman "Since the brand Dettol is known for its antiseptic, germ-killing properties, it was only logical to go into a related area such as this". (as quoted in A and M Magazine).

What Ashutosh says is very logical. With a brand extension the following can be achieved :

— Gain instant recognition for the new product by using the 'power' of an existing brand.
— Save time and cost in establishing a new product.
— Gain an edge over competition in established product categories.

But can all brand extensions be successful ? Could 'Nirma' name be used for a sauce, cooking oil ? Could 'Bata' be used for bread ? Can you imagine TTK passing on its 'Prestige' pressure cooker brand name on to its shoe polish (Kiwi brand)?

As a consumer, we have a certain image or perception about a brand. For example T-Series Cassettes for every one carry an image of being a technology item. Therefore, when the 'T-Series' washing powder was launched it was not an overall success since the consumer could not relate to this new extension. Therefore, for a brand extension the following criteria should be kept in mind.

— The new product should be compatible with the original brand and its image, for example: Amul Butter, Cheese, Chocolates and Mi Spray.

— The existing brand should have a 'value perception' which would benefit the extension. It may also give a competitive edge to the new product.

Packaging

You walk into a retail store and find all products packed in black and white newspaper wrappings. Would you be motivated to buy from this store? What perception of product quality would you carry? Would you be willing to pay a premium price for these products? In all likelihood you would feel that these are low quality, low price products and in case of food items you may even feel that they may be unhygienic.

While historically, packaging served the main purpose of protection, today it is truly being used as a competitive strategy for gaining market dominance. With the growing popularity of self service stores and the lack of shelf space, packaging is today required to do the selling job at the point of purchase.

Consider the following strategies:

— In 1993 Thumps up, Citra, Limca, Goldspot and Maaza were made available in 250 ml, takeaway bottles. Do you think they posed a threat to Pepsi? Obviously yes, these takeaway bottles, as claimed by the company, chill faster, occupy less shelf space and add to customer convenience at the same price!

— The innovative tetra packs of 'Frooti', later also used for "Dhara' and Amul Desighee. They guarantee against pilferage, are disposable and have a longer shelf life.

— The sunflower oil, groundnut oil and mustard oils now available in PET bottles, which give product visibility (thus building customer confidence on quality) are re-usable, are low on breakage during handling *vis-a-vis* glass bottles.

All these add to customer convenience, make the product stand out at the retail shelves and help to attract consumers.

What then are the functions that packaging serves today?

Functions of Packaging

(a) Helps in differentiating the product from competitive brands in the retail market.

(b) Helps in easy identification of a brand at the point of purchase.

(c) An attractive packaging may act as a silent salesperson on the retail shelves.

(d) An innovative packaging can add to the image and the value of the product, and the company by using:
   — environment friendly packaging
   — re-usable, non breakable containers
   — transparent containers for product visibility.

(e) Can add to customer convenience.

(f) Protects the product from wastage, spillage, evaporation, spoilage and tampering.

Let us now understand the typical packaging strategies adopted by companies.

(a) Nestle uses its famous Maggi yellow and red colour packaging for all the products in the brand family be it noodles, sauces, soups or the seasonings. This approach is referred to as *Family Packaging*. It is normally used when products are similar or related in use. One would also observe this trend with Vicks and Dettol.

(b) Another type of packaging strategy adopted is *Re-usable Packaging*. For example, Nescafe was earlier available in attractive glass jars, which could be reused to serve water or juices and the BOOST malt chocolate energy drink was available in glass jugs.

(c) The third commonly used strategy is of *Multiple Packaging*. In using this approach several units of a product are packed together with the objective of selling larger quantities or boosting the sale of other products in the family. For example – Catch Salt and Pepper are available as a set. Bombay Dyeing packs its sheets, pillow cases and towels in special gift packs. Maggi noodles are available in packs of three.

Undoubtedly today packaging adds to a product's value by creating the difference between competitive, 'me-too' brands that exist in this crowded market scenario.

Labelling

A Label is that part of the packaging which carries information about the product, the manufacturer and the marketing organisation. For example, it is statutory for medicine labels to carry information on manufacturing date, expiry date, batch no. and contents as well as warning if any.

On cigarettes or tobacco based products, it is necessary for the label to carry a statutory warning.

Other information carried by a label includes the brand name, the manufacturer's name and address, net weight, maximum retail price, contents, usage instructions, price, and manufacturing licence number.

There are also examples of labels being used innovatively to communicate new applications of the product, thereby increasing usage. This is quite prominent in the foods industry. For example Milkmaid tins and Venky's chicken packs carry recipes on the labels.

Product Mix

we have discussed the components that are considered for developing a product. But at any given time, a firm may be marketing some new and some old products and some product ideas may still be on the drawing board.

How does a marketer manage this entire range of products? In this section we will discuss the key Product Management decisions which include an understanding of Product Mix and Product Line.

Consider the range of product offered by Colgate Palmolive India Ltd. They have been known as a toothpaste company for more than half a century. However, besides the range of the well known Colgate Dental Cream, they are also manufacturing and marketing a wide range of products. There are brands like Colgate Dental Cream in 50 gm, 100gm, 150gm, 200gm and 300gm sizes, Colgate Total, Colgate Gel in Blue and Red variants, Colgate Tarter

Control, Colgate White Toothpowder, Tooth Brushes, Halo range of Shampoos, Colgate Palmolive Shaving Creams and foams, Palmolive Extra Care soaps in 3 variants, Scented Castor Hair Oil and Charmis all purpose cream. All these products of Colgate Palmolive constitute the company's Product Mix.

The Product Mix can be structured on dimensions of *length, width and depth.*

Let us take an example from the Colgate Palmolive range to illustrate the concept of Product Mix dimensions.

Dental Care Products	*Soaps*	*Shaving Products*	*Cold Creams*
Dental Cream White	Extra Care — Dry Skin — Normal Skin — Oily Skin	Shaving Cream	Charmis Creams
Tooth Powder		Shaving Foams	Charmis Lotion
Colgate Gel (Red)	Palmolive — Pink — White — Green	Shaving Brushes	
Colgate Gel (Blue)			
Total Tarter Control			
Tooth Brushes			

Fig. 2.1 : Product Mix Dimensions of Colgate Palmolive

From this let us try to describe the length, width and depth of the product mix:

LENGTH — Refers to the total number of items in the product mix.

WIDTH — Refers to the number of Product Lines in the product mix.

DEPTH — Refers to the number of items in each product line.

CONSISTENCY — Refers to how closely related the various

product lines are in end use, production requirements, distribution channels etc.

Managing a Product Mix

What then are the imperatives in managing a Product Mix?

We will share with you what a Product Manager of a Consumer non-durable company has to say.

"A Product Mix should not have too many products such that they become unprofitable or unmanageable by the company. Our company had over 400 products but we found that it was impossible to provide the same inputs in terms of finance, sales promotion, production, and effective advertising support to all these products. Infact, on some of them we were incurring heavy expenses while the returns were very low. So we have now discontinued production and dropped them from our range".

Here we find that a company has adopted the strategy of *'Product Mix Contraction'* whereby low profit generating items are eliminated from the product mix.

Similar strategy was used by Voltas when they discontinued their Volform ketchups, jams, tetrapacks and cookies. It was probably a range which was not so profitable for Voltas.

In contrast to Product Mix Contraction is the *Product Mix Expansion* strategy.

According to Mr. H.K. Press, Vice President Marketing, Godrej Soaps, 'To ensure brand loyalty for Cinthol, it was necessary to add new Cinthol variants like the Cinthol Cologne, and Cinthol Lime. All these product mix extensions are becoming imperative considering that the consumers are widening their brand baskets. They always want something new – new designs, new features, new colours, new pack sizes". (Brand Equity)

Therefore, a firm may chose to expand its present product mix by increasing the number of lines and/or the depth within a line. This may also be done to counter competitive moves like when Hindustan Lever increased its toothpaste variants by adding Close-up Blue and Green and new Pepsodent to counter the Colgate domination of the toothpastes market.

PRODUCT LINE

We have talked earlier of Product Lines being a part of the Product Mix. But let us now try to understand what are Product Lines through the example of Hindustan Levers.

For HLL, Soaps, Shampoos, Toothpastes, Detergent Soaps and Powders constitute different Product Lines. Each line is composed of all sizes and variants within it.

To define it, a *Product Line is* a group of products that are closely related because :

— they function in a similar manner
— are mostly sold to similar customer groups
— are marketed through the same channel
— fall within a given price range.

Now how do marketers manage product lines ? Let us share with you the case of Nestle's Cerelac.

Case Study—Nestlé Cerelac

The baby food market in India is a steadily expanding one. Among the major players in the market are Nestlé, Glaxo, Wockhardt, Dalmia and Amul.

In the initial years, Nestlé had two products with which it catered to the Indian market – Lactogen and Nestum. Nestum is a rice based cereal and sells well in the South and East, the predominantly rice consuming regions of the country. Lactogen is a milk based baby food.

Lactogen was later split into two products : Lactogen - 1 for babies upto 6 months and Lactogen - 2 for babies from 6 months to 1 year. Cerelac a wheat based cereal was then introduced for babies older than 6 months as a weaning food to help move the babies from liquid diet to a fibre based diet.

Cerelac was initially launched in one flavour only, which was Wheat, but other variations were soon introduced namely, Wheat Apple, Wheat Orange, and Wheat Vegetable. This was also necessitated by the competition from Farex which was being marketed by Glaxo. Now Cerelac Soya is also available for the price conscious segment.

Nestlé had also received reports that some customers had

found Lactogen to be quite high priced. To overcome this gap in its product portfolio, Nestlé launches Nestogen-1 and Nestogen-2, two milk based foods. These brands were priced so as to reach the price conscious end of the market. Nestogen-1 was aimed at babies upto 6 months and Nestogen-2 at babies from 6 months to a year.

Today, Nestle has the following product range for the baby food market :

— Cerelac – Wheat, Wheat Apple, Wheat Orange, Wheat Vegetable
— Cerelac Soya
— Nestum
— Lactogen-1, Lactogen-2
— Nestogen-1, Nestogen-2.

What do you think was the necessity of introducing so many brands? Would you have advised Nestlé to follow the course of action which they did? Why? Try to answer these questions, before you read on.

Nestle introduced different flavours of Cerelac to pre-empt the competition from introducing anything new and taking the lead.

A similar strategy was adopted by Amul, by introducing different flavours of cheese spreads.

In managing Product Lines, companies choose to follow different strategies for the following reasons:

— To create entry barriers for competition
— To offer a comprehensive range of products
— To optimise productivity/profits given the product mix
— To keep abreast with changing technology, consumer tastes and preferences.

The question that comes to mind now is that to be able to achieve the end results discussed what route do the companies take ?

Examine for yourself the strategies adopted by P & G-Godrej or HLL, the bigwigs in the TV industry like BPL and Vedeocon or the computer industry giants HCL HP, Modi Olivetti, PCL and many more. You would notice that their strategies revolve around the following typical approaches :

— *Line Stretching* : Add to product line by introducing new items. In can be an upward, downward or two way stretch. Example : HLL adding Surf Ultra and Wheel to their detergents product line, thus streteting it upwards and downwards.

— *Line Filling* : Introduce more sizes, variants of the same item. Example : Amul Cheese Spreads are now available in different flavours.

— *Line Modernisation* : To upgrade the products to keep up with new technology. Example : 8088, 286, 386 and now 486 computers.

— *Line Pruning* : Eliminate or discontinue unprofitable and technologically inferior items from a product line. Example : Voltas had eliminated the Food & Beverages product line which included products like Volfarm Ketchup, Volfruit Juices, Jams and Cookies since it did not generate profits and involved heavy expenditure.

Therefore in adopting any of the above strategies a company has to ensure that the Product Line has an optimal length. If overdone, any strategy can result in cannibalisation of other products or also add to customer confusion. Thus the company needs to differentiate each item in the consumer's mind very distinctly. This distinction can be based on the product itself, its price or its promotion and placement channels.

UNDERSTANDING COMPETITION

We have discussed the role of competition as an environmental factor in the last section. It also emerged that in the present day scenario and the foreseeable future 'competition' will perhaps be the most critical issue requiring a marketing professional attention. Considering its growing role, let's discuss this factor in greater detail.

A snapshot of the existing scenario in the domestic market reveals onslaughts not only from multinationals but also growing competition within the borders. One can see 'the large fish eat small fish' phenomenon happening. At the same time the number of competitors entering any field is growing by the day. A question that may arise at this stage is "Who are my competitors ?" Essentially, there are two concepts of competition :

— Industry
— Market.

Industry Concept of Competition

An industry is constituted by a group of firms that offer the same products. We talk about the Auto Industry, the Sugar Industry, the Pharmaceutical Industry, and so on – where each manufacturer is engaged in the same business. For example in the TV industry, BPL, Onida, Videocon, Philips, Weston and many others are direct competition for each other. Such competitors are also known as 'Product Competitors'.

Market Concept of Competition

Besides looking at companies making the same product (the industry approach), we also look at companies that satisfy the same customer need or serve the same customer group. In the 'industry' approach a manual typewriter manufacturer would normally see his competition as other manual typewriter manufacturers. However, consider the customers need, or the market's point of view, he may really want "writing, typing ability". This need can be satisfied either by a manual typewriter or an electronic typewriter, or even a computer. Also called 'Generic Competitor'– such products are used as alternative satisfiers. Thus Pepsi and Thums Up must also account for Rasna, Rooh Afza, and home made Lime Water as their competition. Undoubtedly, the market concept of competition opens a company's eyes to a broader set of actual and potential competitors and stimulates a more effective market planning in the long-run.

Let's now discuss the kind of information we need as marketing professionals to be able to handle our competition.

To understand this, let us take the case of the Indian Cricket Team. Assume you are the team manager. Now what do you think is the kind of information you need to know about the other team to be able to plan and organise your game better ?

Typically, you would like to know, Who are the team members ? What are their strengths and weaknesses ? What are the usual strategies adopted by the team ? And more such like information.

Yes, the same is quite applicable in a competitive marketing environment. An environment wherein every company needs to monitor its competitors to be able to plan better.

So if Hindustan Motor Ltd. was to collect information about its immediate competitors, they would gather information related to the following :

Who are my competitors?
What is their marketing mix?
What are their marketing objectives?
What are their strengths and weaknesses?
What are their typical reaction patterns?

Who are My Competitors?

What does this question answer? It answers that Hindustan Motors will have to identify their immediate or direct competitors namely, Maruti Udyog, Premier Automobile, TATA Automobiles. Further competition is faced from four wheelers in the Jeep category like Mahindra & Manindra. And then the indirect competition from two wheeler manufacturers.

What is the Marketing Mix of Each Competitor?

Having identified my competition at different levels. I must now study each in detail. This involves understanding their products, pricing, placement channels and promotional strategies. And this has to be done constantly, as it helps in developing plans to pre-empt and counter any competitive strategies. For example Hindustan Motors must monitor the kind of models Maruti is introducing, the variations offered, the pricing strategy and specific promotional activities like loan schemes etc.

What are Their Marketing Objectives?

This tells me exactly where my competition is headed and how they plan to get there. Such knowledge helps me define winning strategies for my product. For example I must know what is the relative importance they place on market shares *vs* market growth vs cashflow and profitability. As a two wheeler manufacturer if I know that my largest competitor Bajaj is working towards largest market shares, then I may plan a niche for myself as Kinetic Honda did.

What are Their Strengths and Weaknesses?

This needs to be answered in terms of :

(a) The resources of each competitor like Finances, Technology, Managerial capability, Infrastructure, Skilled Manpower. For example, Godrej would perceive a threat from BPL Ltd. because of its production technology and financial capability, besides the Japanese collaboration. At the same time the fact that Kelvinator had poor labour relations and faced a lock out problem would reduce the threat from Kelvinator for some time.

(b) The share that the competitor enjoys in different markets? As a national level player in the television market, I must be worried about BPL, Videocon, Onida and the likes with major market shares and not Konark. The low presence of a leader in certain markets might allow me a more open field to target.

(c) The image of the competitor with respect to its products, corporate activities if any. For example – HLL's Surf faces stiff competition from Ariel of P & G Godrej. Since both have a similar premium image as compared to the image of Key, T-Series and Nirma.

What are their Reaction Patterns?

A competitor's objectives and strengths weaknesses help in predicting its likely moves and reactions to a company's Marketing Mix strategies. Besides this, every organisation has a certain pattern in its method of conducting business. These typical reaction patterns assist in anticipating competitor's moves. Typically companies exhibit the following reaction patterns:

(a) *'Sleepy'*: The kind who do not react quickly or strongly

to a given competitor move *e.g.* Doordarshan not reacting quickly or strongly to STAR TV and thus suffering a loss in viewership.

(b) *'Selective'* : Reacts to only certain kinds of moves and not to others. It might make a counter move to price cuts by a competitor but may not fight against heavy promotion campaigns.

(c) *'Unpredictable'*: They do not exhibit any fixed behaviour. In this case, there is little you can do to anticipate reactions based on past trends. Such unpredictability is mostly associated with small businesses.

(d) *'Aggressive'* : When a competitor reacts swiftly and strongly to any assault in its terrain. This pattern reminds us of the famous Pepsi *Vs* Coke wars which are now being duplicated in India. Amongst the Indian stable, we see Hindustan Lever reacting very strongly to any move in its arena, earlier by Nirma and now by Procter & Gamble Godrej.

Therefore to sum up, a constant and vigilant effort needs to be maintained by an organisation on its competitors, their strategies and infrastructure to be able to take pre-emptive action and thus counter any move that may lead to losses either in terms of image, market shares, growth rates or profitability.

PRICE DETERMINANTS

In the previous section we have discussed the various components of product development and also the different strategies adopted by companies to manage the individual product line and also the complete product mix.

Now, that a product has been developed do you think it is ready to be offered to the end consumer for use or consumption?

We will give the consumer a product but what are we getting in return?

Profits yes, but how, till we do not fix a price for the product?

In this section we will discuss the 2nd 'P' of the Marketing Mix - Price. What it is? How do the companies fix a price? What are the various pricing strategies that companies adopt? These are some of the questions that we will attempt to answer in this section.

Through most of history price has operated as the major determinant of buyer choice. Price still remains one of the most important elements determining a company's profits and market share. In fact, price is the only element of the marketing mix that produces revenues for a company unlike other elements which produce costs.

If we take a look at the products in the market we find that all the products or services have a value attached to them.

— Godrej Two door Frost-Free Refrigerator is price at Rs. 14,975/-.
— Onida's KY series TVs are in the price range of Rs. 21,500 to Rs. 23,500.
— 'Revive' Instant Starch is available in a price range of Rs. 3.75 for 50 gm sachet to Rs. 27.50 for a 400 gm jar.

Price is the Sum of Money that is Needed to Acquire a Product and its Accompanying Services.

IMPORTANCE OF PRICE

Pricing is today, undoubtly, key activity for any business enterprise to flourish in a free-market economy. A product's price influences salaries, rent, interest and profits, besides the price paid for the factors of production like land, labour, raw material or equipment and *vice-versa*.

As an allocator of scarce resources, price determines what will be produced and who will get the goods that are produced.

Consider the competitive environment, and it is price which determines the demand, market share, revenues and profits. At the same time there are factors which limit the importance of pricing. In certain cases, differentiated features or a brand may be more important to be a consumer than the price. In fact today companies use branding to reduce the impact of price on demand.

In the final analysis price has a definite relationship to quality. Consumers rely heavily on price as an indicator of product quality, especially when they are taking a purchase decision with incomplete information. Thus higher the price, the better the quality is perceived to be. And marketers are exploiting this perception to their best advantage. However, this in no manner implies that quality can be compromised while maintaining price.

Now let us see what are the factors that companies consider to set a Price.

KEY FACTORS FOR PRICE DETERMINATION

We will illustrate this with examples.

P & G Godrej's Managing Director, David Thomas talks of the pricing of the Camay Soaps at only Rs. 8.50 for a 75 gm bar. He says, "to meet the company's objectives of gathering volumes, the product had to be priced low and at par with other popular soaps in the Indian market.

After the A.M. P.M. mouth wash, Elder Pharmaceuticals, has launched the A.M. P.M. tooth brushes, priced at Rs. 12. The price according to Satish R. Senior Product Manager is justified since,"the toothbrush bristles are imported Tynese ones from Dupont, USA. The brush is made from the latest engineering plastic which is also expensive."

Amongst the factors which determine pricing are :

- Identifying the Corporate Objective towards Price and Profits
- Estimating all costs on products, promotion and placement
- Analysing competitor's price and offer
- Determining the consumer demand for a product
- Government laws and regulations.

Let us discuss each factor individually and study its impact on pricing.

Identifying Corporate Objectives towards Price and Profits

The company has to decide what it wants to accomplish with the particular product. If the company has targeted a product at a certain segment and has also decided on its positioning platform then the pricing strategy would be fairly straight - forward. Bata India launched its 'Hush Puppies' range of shoes in Delhi and Calcutta in October, 1993. The shoes are priced between Rs. 1,649 to Rs.1,799 since they are positioned as an exclusive range of footwear for the successful, westernised, well travelled, urban professional or senior executive in upper income bracket. Therefore as per Vinesh Singh, Brand Manager, "the objective is to create an aura of exclusivity around the shoe, which will come with the price tag." (A&M).

Further the company may want to increase its profits through pricing. As we discussed, the company's objectives may be to achieve maximum volumes therefore larger profits at a lower price.

Estimating Costs on Product, Promotion and Placement

(a) Product Costs

What are these Product Costs? The total unit cost of a product is made up of several types of costs. These costs react differently to changes in the quantity produced. We will take into account two types of costs which are :

— *Fixed Costs* : These costs do not vary with the level of production or sales revenue.
— *Variable Costs* : These costs vary with the level of production or the number of units produced.

For example each Liril Shower Gel involves costs of packaging material, raw material or ingredients etc. Therefore companies will fix a price that will at least cover the total production costs at a given level of production. In other words a company may charge a price by which it is only achieving a 'Break-Even' or a no loss-no profit price, or it may add a 'Mark-up' amount or an additional amount as its desired profits to the total production cost.

(b) Promotion Costs

Many companies include the cost of advertising and cost of extra incentives in the form of Sales Promotion Schemes in calculating its profits or returns. In products like consumer non-durables this may be essential as advertising costs are significant and it is more or loss the medium of selling. However, in case of industrial products this may not hold good.

(c) Placement Costs

The channels selected will influence a product's pricing. Companies try to include the margins extended to middlemen in its basic price. Also the pricing may differ from middlemen to middlemen. For example price for a distributor would be different from the price for a retailer. In case of companies which sell through their own field force, the dealer margins are saved, however the cost of selling has to be accounted for while taking a pricing decision.

Analysing Competitor's Price and Offers

Competitor's pricing and possible price reactions help companies to establish their own price. It is necessary to understand what are the competitor's charging for a product and what they offer for that price. This information will help in building value into our own prices. If a company's offer is similar to a competitor's it may have to price its product close to it, if it is inferior, then the company may have to price itself lower and if its offer is superior to that of competitor's it may charge a higher price. For example BPL's 4 door refrigerator offers more features than competitors therefore commands the highest price as well.

Determining Consumer Demand for a Product

Each price that a company might charge will lead to a different level of demand. In normal cases higher the price charged lower the demand for it. But if we look at speciality products, like 'Drakkar Noir' after—Wospace shaves, if premium priced they may sell more units than if low priced. However, if too high a price is charged the level of demand may be lower. Also if the price is much lower than expected, consumers may be suspicious of the quality of the product and consequently the demand will once again drop.

Therefore price is largely influenced by the target segment's ability to pay which is endorsed by the demand created for a product at a given price.

Government Laws and Regulations

The government laws and regulations of the country influence the basic price of a product. For example the excise duty charged may differ from product to product. The excise paid on cigarettes is far higher than on most other products. On cosmetics also the excise duty is very heavy. Further the local tax and the central sales tax structures also determine the basic price.

Now given all these factors the company is ready to select the final price.

Questions that arise at this point are :

Should the company charge a high price which would serve as a psychological indicator of good quality and image?
Should the price be kept low to generate higher sales?
Should the price be at par with competitive products?
Should the company only price its products for a short term return with the objective to merely survive ?
Should the price be such that it captures masses?
Should it be initially high and consequently lowered?

All these questions form the basis of the following Pricing Strategies adopted by marketers :

Market Penetration

In using this strategy, companies set low initial prices to capture mass markets. This is done to encourage rapid adoption of the product, which can help capture significant market shares.

At the same time profit margins may be low and it takes longer to recover costs. In India Videocon has used this strategy to their advantage in the fields of consumer durables.

Market Skimming

In this case the primary focus is to recover major investments in a short time span.

A company would typically estimate the highest price its initial target segment would be willing to pay and price accordingly. Each time sales slow down, the price is dropped to attract the next lower level of customers. In doing so product variations, like economy models, may be introduced or savings due to lower costs, may be passed on.

This strategy is followed for 'new-to-the-market products which face minimal competition. We saw BPL India using it effectively for their range of Frost-Free refrigerators.

There are two major advantages in using this strategy :

— Price lowering is easier than price increase hence mistakes can get taken care of
— High prices help keep demands within limits of production capacity.

Competitive Pricing

This is often used to position the product in a highly competitive environment. The strategy therefore considers prices offered by competitors.

If the company's product/service is similar to a major competitior, then the company will have to price its product close to the competitor or lose sales. In case the product offers unique benefits then a higher price may be justified.

Survival Pricing

A short-term strategy implemented when companies are in dire straits due to overcapacity, competition or changing customer needs.

The primary focus is to keep the company going and profits take a back seat.

Psychological Pricing

Here pricing is intended to appeal to the buyer's emotion rather than logic.

(a) Odd-Even Pricing

This theory presumes that customers will perceive a product priced at Rs. 99.95 as approximately Rs .90 rather than Rs. 100.

For example the BATA pricing of shoes.

(b) Premium Pricing

For expensive luxury items, a high price is part of the image that buyers seek. The demand for a Rolls Royce (a luxury automobile) will not increase dramatically if the price is cut by $1000. However, the demand may fall as the buyers may perceive lesser status with the product. This is applicable to products like perfumes, sports cars, fine China, Aged whiskies. The new Lakme 'Orchid' range of cosmetics are premium priced with this purpose.
Let us now evaluate a case.

Case Study : Burroughs Wellcome

The Burroughs Wellcome Company (BW) is a pharmaceutical manufacturer whose parent company is located in England, in 1986 the company introduced into the US market, a drug – Azidothymidine (AZT) – that is effective in controlling advances of the AIDS virus in human beings. AZT also slows down the onset of AIDS in people who have been infected with the virus, but who do not yet show any symptoms of the disease.

In mid - 1989 AZT was priced at about $8000 for a year's supply per patient, thus making it one of the most expensive drugs ever sold. The gross margin on AZT was 70 to 80 per cent – obviously high, but still in line with what other firms get for major new drugs. Later in 1989 the price was reduced to about $6400 for a year's supply because of two factors. One was the strong protests from AIDS activists, and the other was the anticipated market growth stemming from the increasing acceptance of AZT as a treatment for AIDS.

Critics of BW's pricing strategy included not only people with AIDS, but also some medical people involved in AIDS treatment and research. These activists contended that BW was profiteering shamelessly and that the high price was both unethical and immoral.

BW, on the other hand pointed out that the company needed to recover the high costs associated with its research, development, and production of AZT. BW also noted that it is quite usual and necessary for drug companies to use profits from successful products (1) to support R & D work for future products and (2) to recoup R&D costs from past products that failed either in the laboratory or in the market. What pricing strategy do you think BW should employ for AZT ? Would your answer be any different if AZT were a cure for cancer ? For the common cold?

(*Source* : Fundamentals of Marketing : Stanton)

In this case it was obviously market skimming approach. But was it appropriate? What needs to be understood is that pricing today is evolving to become 'market-driven'. The strategy must account for consumer needs and the environment or it is bound to fail. After all the consumers will only respond if the 'price is right'!

3

Fundamentals of Productivity and Work Study

Objective of Industry

The objective of a manufacturing or service organisation is to provide as many goods and services as possible with minimum consumption of real resources.

More goods and services can be produced, broadly speaking by:

- *(i)* increase in the resources deployed for production of goods and services;
- *(ii)* effective utilisation of these resources; and
- *(iii)* development of improved resources, processes, etc., through research and development.

Alternative *(i)* has number of limitations. Firstly, in developing countries the capital and skilled labour are always scarce; secondly, deployment of increased resources does not necessarily lead to cost reduction.

Alternative *(ii)* has limited scope for increasing output as compared to alternative *(i)*, but efficient utilisation of existing resources will always lead to cost reduction. A combination of both the alternatives, supported by research and development, is necessary for rapid economic development.

The resources used in any industry are materials, manpower, land and building, plant and equipment. Alternative *(ii)* seeks efficient and effective utilisation of these resources.

Productivity, Employment and Standards of Living

Efficient utilisation of resources means cost reduction, and hence more savings. These savings must be equitably distributed among all sections of the society. Part of these savings invested in the industry would lead to economic growth and more employment. Part of the savings distributed among workers, consumers, and investors lead to higher purchasing power, and lower prices. Efficient utilisation of the resources, therefore, leads simultaneously to the availability of more goods and services, and higher purchasing power for consumption of these. Both these put together means higher standards of living. In fact, this approach generates a chain reaction which, if allowed to continue, brings about higher and higher standards of living and more and more employment.

Definition and Scope of Productivity

Any production process involves input of resources and output of goods and services. In other words it means a ratio of output/input. Productivity stands for "change for better" in this ratio. Rise in productivity can be obtained by :

(i) reduction in waste of resources;
(ii) increase in value of product;
(iii) marginal increase in input of resources, and proportionally high output in the value of product.

Yet there is another way of looking at productivity. Fig. 3.1 illustrates the production consumption cycle. This cycle shows the customer buying goods and services. The money so obtained goes back to the suplier. He uses a major part this money to provide materials, manpower, machinery, etc., which are fed into the factory for producing goods and services required by the customer. The objective of productivity is to improve the efficiency

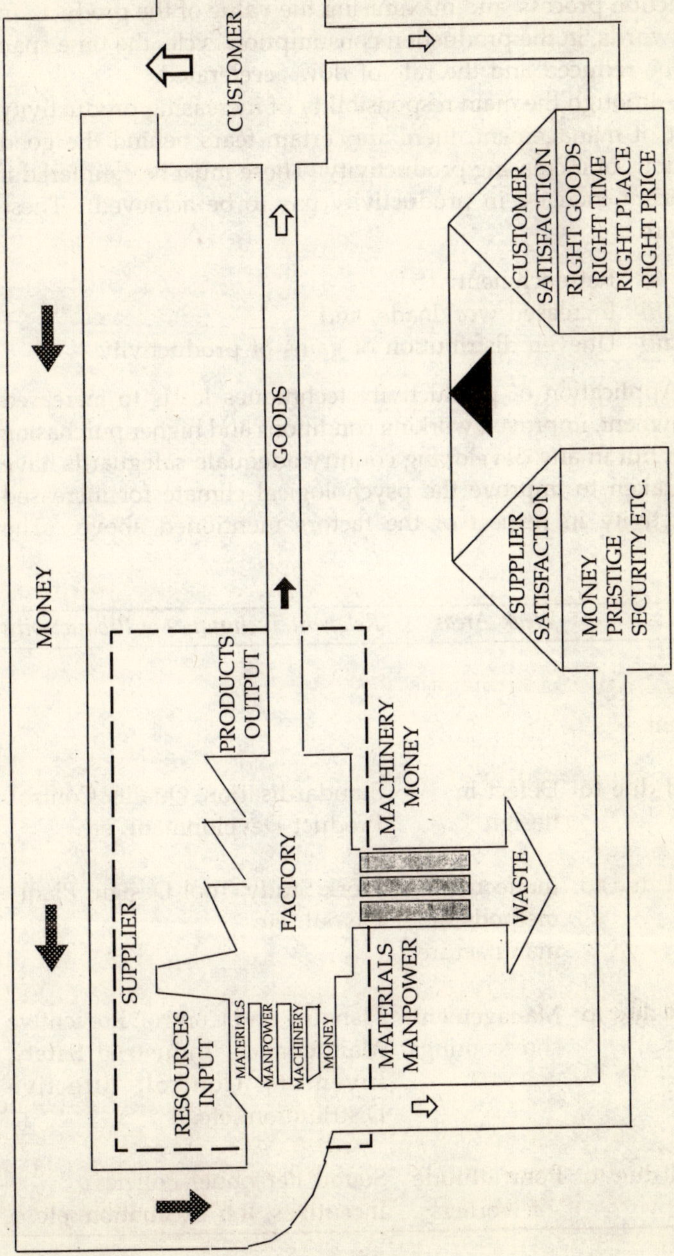

Fig. 3.1 : Production-Consumption Cycle and Stabilising Balance

of the production consumption cycle minimising waste in the production process, and maximising the value of the product. In other words, in the production consumption cycle, the time span must be reduced and the rate of flow accelerated.

Although the main responsibility of increasing productivity is that of management, there are certain fears behind the good intentions of increasing productivity. These must be countered if significant increase in productivity has to be achieved. These fears are :

(i) Retrenchment;
(ii) Increased workloads; and
(iii) Uneven distribution of gains of productivity.

Application of productivity techniques leads to increased employment, improved working conditions and higher purchasing power, but in any developing country adequate safeguards have to be taken to improve the psychological climate for increased productivity in respect of the factors mentioned above. The

	Weak Areas	*Relevant Techniques of Productivity*
Basic work Content ↓		
added due to ↓	Defect in design	Standardisation, Quality Control, Product Development, etc.
added due to ↓	Ineffective methods of manufacture	Work Study, Tool Design, Plant Layout, etc.
added due to ↓	Management shortcomings	Planning and Control, Preventive Maintenance, Industrial Safety, Inventory Control, Effective Distribution, etc.
added due to	Poor attitude of workers	Sound Personnel Policies, Incentives, Job Evaluation, etc.

working class has to be assured that productivity efforts will not lead to retrenchment or excessive work load, but at the same time it should be made clear to the working class that it has to give a fair day's work. Confidence will also have to be instilled in them that the gains of productivity will be equitably shared with them.

At an enterprise level, there are many weak areas which impede productivity. It is these weak areas which increase time span and decelerate flow in production consumption cycle. The common weak areas and relevant techniques of productivity to counteract the effect of weak areas are detailed on page 54.

A detailed analysis of weak areas would reveal that in 9 out of 10 cases, management is responsible for eliminating these. It is, of course, true because it is the management who must plan, direct, coordinate, control, and above all, motivate.

WORK STUDY

Work Study is a term used to embrace the techniques of Method Study and Work Measurement which are employed to ensure the best possible use of all resources in carrying out a specified activity.

Work Study provides a basic discipline of looking at things. It develops a questioning attitude of not accepting things for granted. Work Study succeeds when everyone in the organisation is filled with an attitude of avoiding waste of any type in any form, and not to accept anything without questioning it. Work Study is the most penetrating tool of investigation. It lays bare the weakness of an organisation and, therefore, one requires the skill of a surgeon in handling Work Study because no one in the organisation will like to be told of his weakness. Further, Work Study provides the basis on which scientific planning and control methods as well as sound financial incentive schemes can operate. Everyone concerned with the industry benefits from Work Study:

- *(i)* *Management* benefits through increased efficiency, and therefore increased profits.
- *(ii)* *Worker* is assured of a fair return for a fair day's work. He is protected from unfair demands. The work is made easier and more productive.
- *(iii)* *Trade Union* is provided with a reliable data for measuring a fair day's work for a fair day's pay and

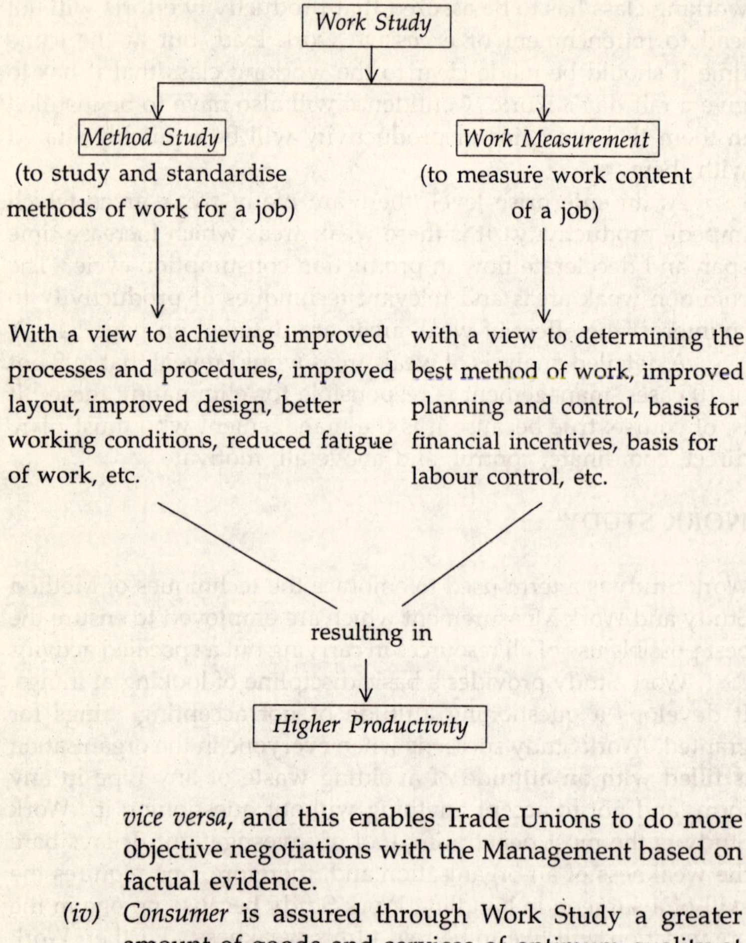

vice versa, and this enables Trade Unions to do more objective negotiations with the Management based on factual evidence.

(iv) *Consumer* is assured through Work Study a greater amount of goods and services of optimum quality at lower prices.

Human Factor in Work Study

Work Study is primarily concerned with operation rather than with technical process. As operation involves human beings, whether as Managers, Technicians, or Workers, the human element in Work Study must be recognised. It is, therefore, imperative that good relations must be established before Work Study is applied.

If the application of Work Study in any enterprise is to succeed it must have the understanding and the backing of the Management at all levels, starting from the top.

The Work Study man should enjoy the confidence of supervisors if he has to obtain good results from his work; indeed their hostility may prevent him from doing any effective work at all. The whole purpose of Work Study, and the procedure involved should be carefully explained to the Supervisors before the Work Study man starts work in the shop.

The worker's attitude towards Work Study greatly governs its success in any industry. If the workers have confidence in the sincerity and integrity of the Management, almost any sound technique will be accepted and can be made to work. In Work Study, properly applied, tends to improve industrial relations. There are, however, some important factors which may cause workers to resist the introduction of Work Study. These factors are mainly resistance to any change, retrenchment and increased workload. If the worker is assured and given guarantee against retrenchment and increased workload, his cooperation and participation in the success of Work Study can easily be obtained. But workload should be properly assigned to workers, *i.e.*, it means fair day's work.

METHOD STUDY

Introduction

Method Study may be defined as a systematic and scientific evaluation of existing or proposed plans and performance of any work system, and the evolution of improvements through the analytical process of Critical Examination. The contributions that can be expected of Method Study are :

Better design of plant, buildings and equipment,
Improved layout of factories and offices,
Effective materials handling,
Better working conditions and environment,
Higher standards of safety, and health,
Greater job satisfaction,

Improved flow of work and reduced time spán,
Waste reduction, and
Standardisation and rationalisation.

The initiation of a Method Study project may be promoted by any one of the following considerations—Human, Economic, Technical, and Reaction.

Human : If the working conditions are bad, if there is excessive fatigue involved in the processes, if the effort put in is too much, if the safety standards are low, if conditions of health are below par, and if morale is low then a Method Study may be instituted.

Economic : Where the cost of operation is high, where the dividends are not commensurate with the investment, where the utilisation of resources is not of optimum level, where results achieved are unsatisfactory—then again a Method Study can be initiated.

Technical : From the technical point of view, Method Study would lead to optimum throughput, reduction in scrap, improved flow of work, and standardisation and rationalisation.

Reaction : The resistance to change must be reckoned with.

Basic Steps

The six basic steps in Method Study are :

SELECT	the work ιo be studied.
RECORD	all relevant facts by direct observation.
EXAMINE	these facts critically.
DEVELOP	the most economical, effective, and practical method.
INSTAL	that method as standard practice.
MAINTAIN	that standard practice by regular checks.

These steps are like a staircase and have to be followed one after another systematically.

Selection : The selection of subjects for Method Study is the responsibility of management. Once a problem has been highlighted, it is the responsibility of the practitioner to establish the feasibility, desirability, and scope of the study and formulate the subject and aim of the study for approval of the management.

He also recommends, for consideration by management, the relative order of priorities for various studies.

The higher the level of the problem, the more sustaining and profitable the results of the study are. Studies beamed at the aim, tasks and organisation of the establishment yield richer dividends than studies confined to one man and his job, or to a small process. Method Study is most efficacious when it starts from the Board Room.

Method Study can be carried out not only on existing activities, but on proposed plans as well. The results of a study done within the limitations of the existing work systems, many facets of which are unalterable, are often not as spectacular as studies which evaluate proposed plans and physical mean of achievements. Method Study achieves startling returns only when applied at the design and the pre-production stages.

Recording of Facts : In order to give a factual picture of activities occurring in the existing system, or as they are envisaged to happen in a proposed system, certain specialised recording techniques are used. A large variety of these techniques, including some highly sophisticated photographic processes, is available to suit different types of activities.

To render the recording concise, and to focus attention on important activities, certain special charting symbols are used. These symbols help to reduce the recording to a more or less shorthand form, and, at the same time, preserve the salient aspects in their proper perspective of importance.

Critical Examination : Critical examination challenges all the facts of an activity, its purpose, the resources used, the method employed, the place where it is carried out, movement involved, environmental conditions, the sequencing of activities, the persons concerned with the operations, etc. In the old pattern of Motion Study, the existing task was studied in order to effect improvements. In the present form of modern Method Study, the very necessity for the existence of the task is challenged. Only when the necessity for the achievement is established beyond all doubt and only then, does Method Study go on to analyse the other aspects.

Many activities originate due to causes and circumstances prevailing at some period in the past. Since there is a general lack of review-consciousness, the universal tendency is to carry on with the old methods even when they are no longer necessary. When a procedure is instituted, or a specific activity sponsored, it is based on a current reason. It is not necessary that what is current today must be the prevailing circumstance tomorrow. There is, therefore, an urgent need for constant review of all the facets of existing activities. The challenging of the very purpose of an activity, during the critical examination, meets this vital need.

The primary aim of critical examination is to eliminate the achievement itself. When it is not possible, and only then, do the secondary aims come into play. These are :

To modify the achievements,
To simplify the method of achievement, and
To combine or change the sequence, the place and the people.

The techniques of critical examination are analytical, and are adapted to make use of the latest statistical and technical methods of analysis. For this purpose, a standard format of a critical examination sheet is used.

Development : 'Development' is a crucial stage of Method Study. Critical examination throws up a number of alternatives, and these are woven into composite demand processes at the development stage. Development is not a separate process but carried out on completion of the critical examination. In order to be truly effectives development must be integrated into each phase of critical examination. The procedure helps in arriving at wholesome alternatives which can be evaluated and tested for their relative merits and advantages. After detailed examination of the merits of the several alternatives, the best ones are recommended to management, in an order of preference.

Implementation : After the recommendation made as a result of the study is received by management , the plan is implemented. 'Implementation' has two aspects : 'Installation', and 'Maintenance'. At the 'Installation' stage, the developed good is subjected to tests and confirmed by pilot plant projects where necessary. On complete assurance that the developed method is workable, the method is installed. Due to the prevailing habit of discarding any new system or method, it is necessary to 'maintain' that method by constant checks. This will ensure that the new method is discarded, and minor adjustments and deviations are made out of practical considerations.

Method Study and Work Measurement are not two independent techniques of Work Study which can be used in isolation. Work Measurement is needed to make a comparative analysis of 'existing' and 'proposed' methods which are developed through Method Study. Again, Work Measurement, aimed at planning, manning, and alternatives, cannot be carried out unless it is preceded by a proper Method Study. Thus the two techniques are inter-related in any work situation.

SELECTION PROCEDURE

Introduction

Among the basic steps of Method Study, 'Selection' presents the greatest problem at the initial stages of any project. The first few days of any project demand exacting analysis in order to clarify and crystallise areas for detailed investigation. Though selection of the problem is the prerogative of management, the basis on which a judicious selection is made is the specialised knowledge of the Work Study practitioner. Even if management selects the problem, it enunciates the same in broad terms. The exact areas for detailed investigation have to be outlined by the Work Study practitioner.

In a minor assignment, like the study of a specific process, selection is a comparatively easy task. In major assignments, however, where the problem is large in magnitude, and wide in scope, a preliminary or diagnostic survey may be called for in order to highlight the potential spheres for study in depth.

Diagnostic Approach

In major assignments of larger magnitude and wider scope, the diagnostic approach is useful in the selection of specific areas for investigation.

The steps involved in the diagnostic approach are:

(i) Breakdown of the capital structure;
(ii) Arrangement in terms of succession of cost;

(iii) Making spot check;
(iv) Rearrangement in succession in order of feasibility of cost reduction and value added; and
(v) Drawing of action programme.

Even where a specified resource is to be investigated, the diagnostic approach is useful in order to select areas of priority for detailed investigation. For instance, the total cost of materials can be broken down into different heads—effective materials consumed, value of product, process waste, handling waste, inventory of raw materials and finished products, in-process inventory, etc. Listing of various cost heads in order of succession and feasibility point of view, enables the Work Study practitioner to select areas for studies in depth.

Considerations in Selection

While selecting the subject for study, the following considerations should be borne in mind:

(i) Where a large problem throws up a number of subjects which are independent of each other, it is better to have small individual studies instituted on each subject.
(ii) Where a problem brings to light two or more subjects which are inter-related, independent studies on each might be carried out in the preliminary stages, but they should later be continuously integrated by coordinating the recording of the different teams working on each subject. The critical examination has to be composite, and carried out by the teams as a whole.
(iii) The scope and magnitude of the problem would determine the number of subjects to be studied. The aim is to ensure that each subject is capable of comprehensive analysis.
(iv) Short studies which can yield appreciable dividends quickly are to be preferred to long-term studies whose benefits may be difficult to foresee.
(v) Work Study effort costs money. The value of the anticipated results must be commensurate with the efforts put in thus proving that 'Work Study begins at home'.
(vi) Studies that would lead to better working conditions,

improved environment, or increased earnings for the workers must be given due precedence over others.

(vii) Where resistance to change or reaction is likely to be great, the subject should not be proceeded with until acceptance has been gained . A specific improvement, imposed against the will of the staff, can never be as effective a modest improvement implemented through the cooperation of the staff.

Every subject for study must have a clearly defined aim, so that the focus of the study is guided towards the prescribed goal. Although the aim of the study is to effect improvements, the specific objectives intended to be achieved must be clear wherever possible. In many cases, the question is 'what improvements can be effected?' In such cases, an investigation is needed to bring the problem into sharper focus so that the relevant channels of improvement can be distinctly recognised.

After selecting the subject and the aim of the study, the next step is to obtain the details of the constraints, if any, that may influence the study. Constraints are limitations imposed by the management on the physical conduct of the staff on the implementation of the study.

RECORDING TECHNIQUES

Introduction

After the selection of the subject for study, Recording is a preparatory step towards the Critical Examination of all the governing factors influencing the situation, and the devolopment of a new system. In order to undertake critical examination, one must have facts, the whole range of facts, and nothing but facts. Recording Techniques enable these facts to be reduced to written form.

Recording comprises two elements: Obtaining all the information needed by direct and reliable means; and sifting and committing to writing all the data that have a bearing on the study. The collection of data may be by :

(i) direct observation,

(ii) interview, and
(iii) examination of documents and records.

To the extent practicable, facts should be collected by direct observations. Where it is not possible, the interview method may be resorted to. The defect in this system is that bias and subjective judgement tend to creep in. This has to be taken into account. Facts obtained by direct observation or by interview have to be supported by the examination of documents and records, and relevant data extracted.

Reducing the observations to writing is essential because the normal human memory cannot be trusted with the task of storing up all the information collected, and reproducing it at the appropriate time. Recording techniques in Method Study use graphic forms of representation which reduce the facts to something akin to shorthand without detracting from the value of the information contained. For this purpose, certain special symbols are employed.

Recording of Facts

The facts pertaining to a work system may be conveniently grouped under the following categories:

(i) Background,
(ii) System procedure or process,
(iii) Physical means of implementation, and
(iv) Movements and transportation.

The background information includes features like the history of the organisation, current aims, functions and tasks, future trends, availability of capital and other resources and industrial climate.

Facts relating to processes and procedures would bring out the details of the current practices and the activities involved in each sphere of the task under study. Major facets of a process would be highlighted in sequential order without getting involved in minor details concerning the method of performance of an activity. This would facilitate a survey after which the activities that warrant study would be selected.

When selected activities are to be studied in detail, the facts concerning the physical means of executing the activities would have to be recorded in a comprehensive manner. Since these recordings would be providing the necessary data for critical examination, they have to be charted with a great deal of attention to details.

Movement is a necessary evil in a work system. It adds to the cost of an achievement, but not to its value. Where a problem is predominantly movement-oriented, information regarding transportation and flow of work should be collected and recorded separately.

Techniques

For recording background data, the following aids may be utilised: graphs, tables, schematic models, pie charts, ideographs, histograms, frequency polygons, and ogives. In process recording, the charts frequently used are Outline Process Chart, Flow Process Chart (Man), Flow Process Chart (Material), and Multiple Activity Chart.

An Outline Process Chart depicts the principal activities in a task. It does not include details of movements, delays and storages. The aim is to present a bird's-eye view of the whole task. A Flow Process Chart lists out the complete details of activities performed by a man or on a material. It would contain information on the movements, delays and storages involved.

Methods and physical means of execution can be recorded in a number of ways. The technique used would depend on the complexity of the method, and the degree of details required. Generally, a Flow Process Chart would be adequate to describe the performance in fair detail. Where a more detailed description of the work done by an individual is required, a Two-Handed Process Chart would be necessary. In the recording of a man-machine system, a Multiple Activity Chart is more useful.

The most commonly used technique for recording the nature, details and characteristics of movements is the Flow Diagram. Here, a plan of the working area is made to scale. The location of the various points where the events occur are plotted, and the path and direction of various movements involved are drawn. When far too many movements are involved, the complexity of a large number of lines drawn on the Flow Diagram may defeat the very purpose of recording. The confusion that may be caused by this can, however, be avoided by depicting the movements with the aid of pins and strings, the pins marking the various locations, and the strings tracing the movements. This recording is called the String Diagram.

When the problem under study is predominantly one of layout and transport control, it would be necessary to record the details of the movements in three dimensions. Models and Templates would be ideal for this purpose. The String Diagram, like the Flow Diagram, can also be three-dimensional.

Charting Symbols

Symbols used in recording are designed not only to reduce the effort involved in longhand writing, but also to segregate the

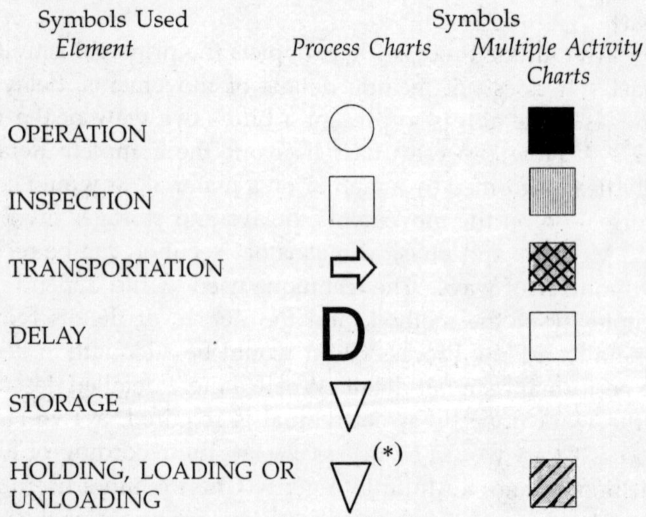

(*) The Symbol for Storage is used in Two-handed Process Charts to depict a hand being used as a Grip or Vice.

Fig. 3.2

effective part of the activity from the ineffective. There are, in all, five distinct elements of activities: Operation, Inspection, Transportation, Delay, and Storage (See Figure 3.2).

An operation is that part of an activity which causes a distinct change in the physical or chemical characteristics or properties of any material. An operation would bring about an 'addition', 'subtraction', or a 'change of state/shape or quality'.

If the standard of quality or quantity of anything is verified to a pre-determined specification, an Inspection is said to be carried out. Where a person or an object is displaced from one point to another, a transport or movement is said to have taken place. Whenever the furtherance of an activity is hampered due to any reason, thereby arresting its progress temporarily, a delay is said to have set in. Storage denotes an item in authorised retention. It is virtually a delay, since it is awaiting further disposal. The essential difference between a storage and a delay is that the former is deliberate and under authorised custody.

For the sake of clarity, a brief notation is given at the right side of a symbol to bring out the nature of the activity. Where time or distance traversed has a bearing, it is indicated on the left side of the symbol. For constructing a chart, all the symbols are placed in the chronological order of their occurrence, and connected through by a single line. A chart may be drawn horizontally or vertically as given in Figure 3.3.

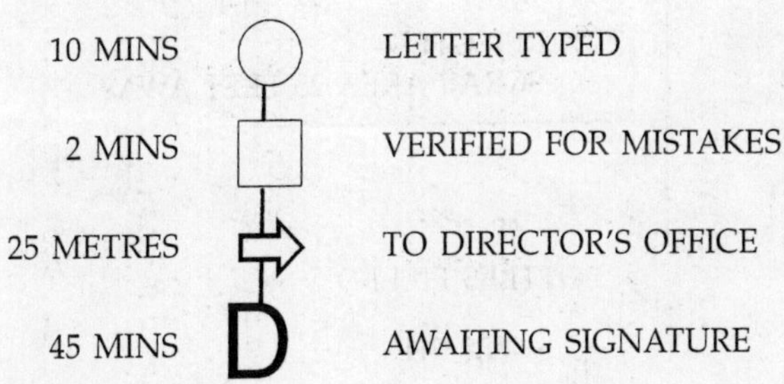

Fig. 3.3

Charting Conventions

The following are some of the important conventions observed in charting:

(i) A chart should depict the activity of only one task.
(ii) It must be consistent. If material is charted then operator's work should not be mixed with it.
(iii) There should be consistency in the scale of recording in a chart.
(iv) There are three distinct contents of the chart:
  (a) introductory information, *viz.*, name of the chart, the task under study, present or proposed method, beginning and ending of chart, the date of charting,
  (b) body of the chart, and
  (c) summary, giving the number of occurrence, time and distance involved for each activity.
(v) In the body of the chart, all symbols pertaining to one type of activity are numbered in sequence.
(vi) Materials or components discarded or rejected are indicated in Figure 3.4.

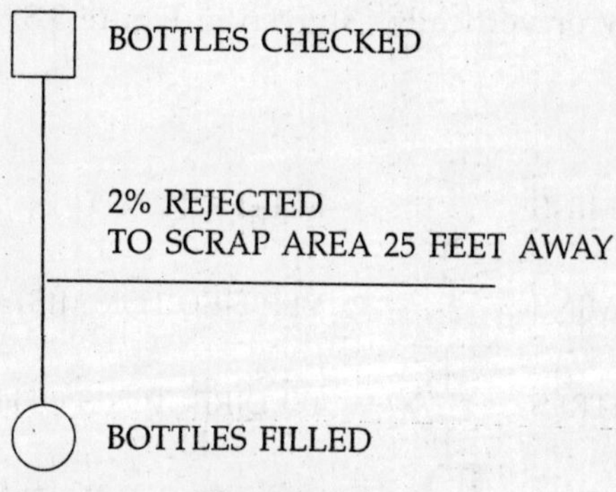

Fig. 3.4

(vii) Where a component is rejected and has to be reprocessed, it is shown in Figure 3.5.

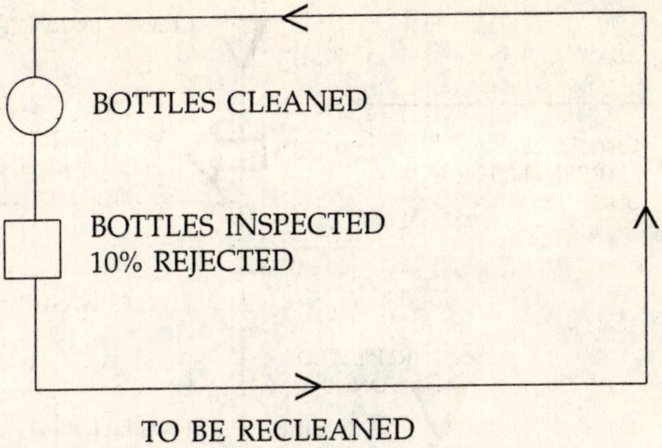

Fig. 3.5

(viii) Sometimes an activity or a series of activities have to be repeated. This is shown in Figure 3.6.

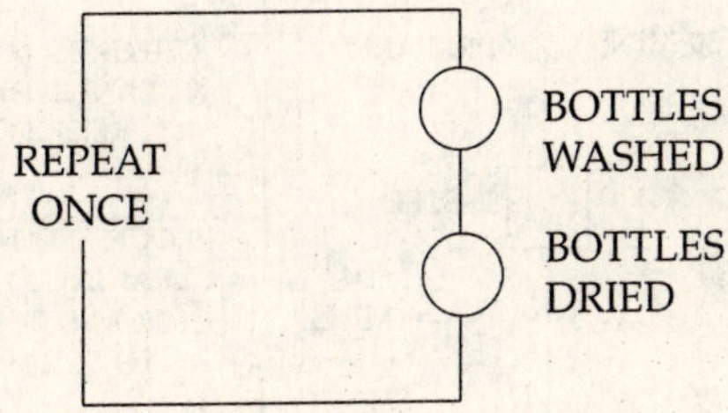

Fig. 3.6

(ix) During the process, any change of state should be clearly brought out as shown in Figure 3.7.

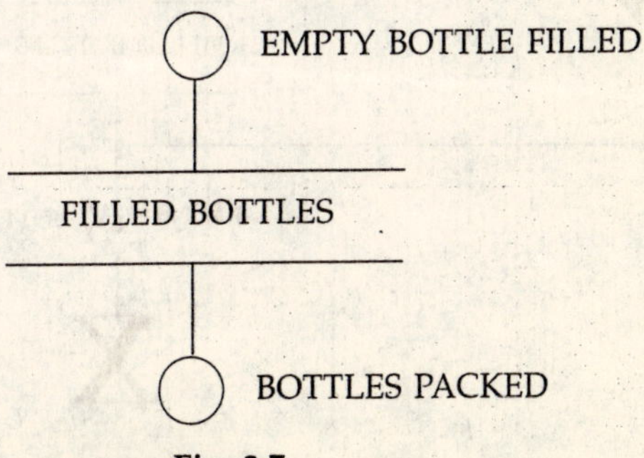

Fig. 3.7

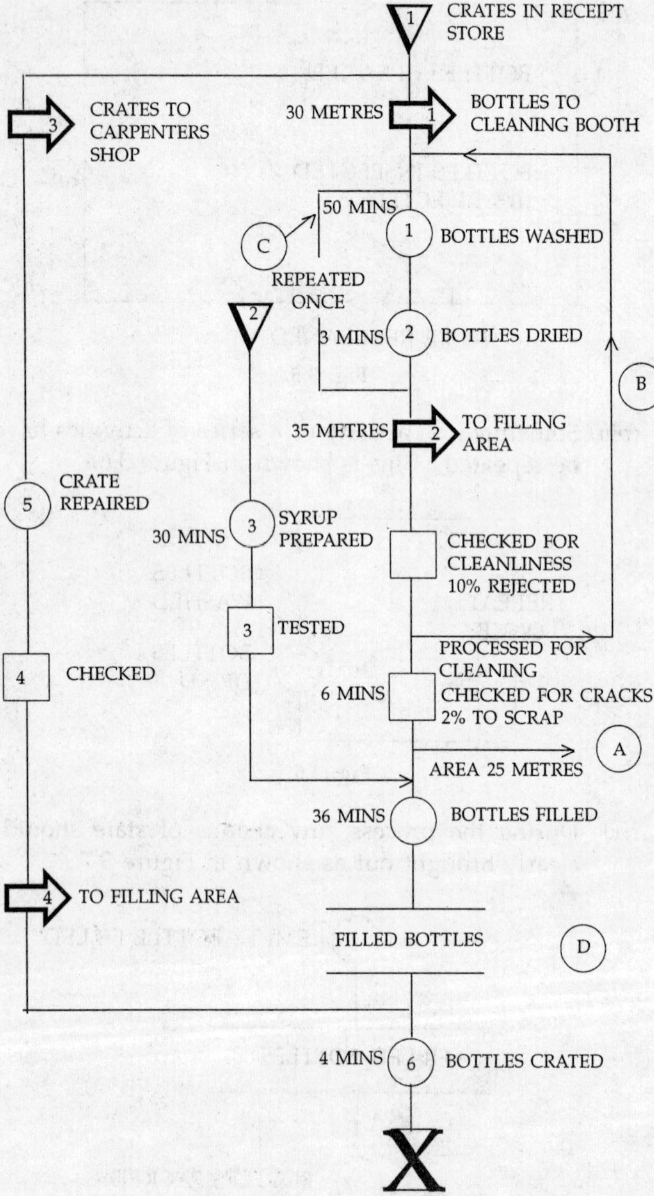
CRATES IN RECEIPT STORE
CRATES TO CARPENTERS SHOP
30 METRES
BOTTLES TO CLEANING BOOTH
50 MINS
C
REPEATED ONCE
BOTTLES WASHED
3 MINS
BOTTLES DRIED
B
35 METRES
TO FILLING AREA
CRATE REPAIRED
30 MINS
SYRUP PREPARED
CHECKED FOR CLEANLINESS 10% REJECTED
TESTED
PROCESSED FOR CLEANING
CHECKED
6 MINS
CHECKED FOR CRACKS 2% TO SCRAP
A
AREA 25 METRES
36 MINS
BOTTLES FILLED
TO FILLING AREA
FILLED BOTTLES
D
4 MINS
BOTTLES CRATED

Fig. 3.8

(x) Figure 3.8 represents the complete picurte. A shows the rejection as scrap, 'B' shows the rejection for re-processing, 'C' denotes the repetition of activities, and 'D' a change of state.

RECORDING OF PROCESSES

Outline Process Chart

The Outline Process Chart (OPC) is the foremost technique of recording process. It records the main activities of the process through the symbols, 'Operation' and 'Inspection'. The OPC is the basis for:

(i) presenting a bird's-eye view of the entire process;
(ii) selecting key operations for critical examination;
(iii) determining the requirements for detailed recording; and
(iv) establishing logical sequence of activities in processes like assembly.

The major conventions used in drawing an OPC, where different processes work simulatneously, are given below:

(i) The sequence in which the events are performed is represented by an arrangement of process chart symbols on VERTICAL FLOW LINES.
(ii) Materials, either purchased or on which work is performed during the process, is shown by HORIZONTAL MATERIAL LINES.
(iii) For pleasing appearance, the component which has the greatest degree of operations is charted on the extreme right hand side of the chart. If the chart is to be used as a basis for laying out a progressive material line, the parts having the greatest bulk to which the smaller one are assembled would be chosen.
(iv) Brief description of the material recorded directly above the horizontal material line.
(v) The name and identifying number of the parts is recorded in capital letters directly above the material description.

Outline Process Chart

PRESENT METHOD

TASK	:	RESTRICTED REPAIRS TO BICYCLE
CHART BEGINS	:	DAMAGED BICYCLE RECEIVED IN THE WORKSHOP
CHART ENDS	:	BICYCLE READY FOR COLLECTION
CHARTED BY	:	PGY
DATE	:	SEPT. 1, 1970

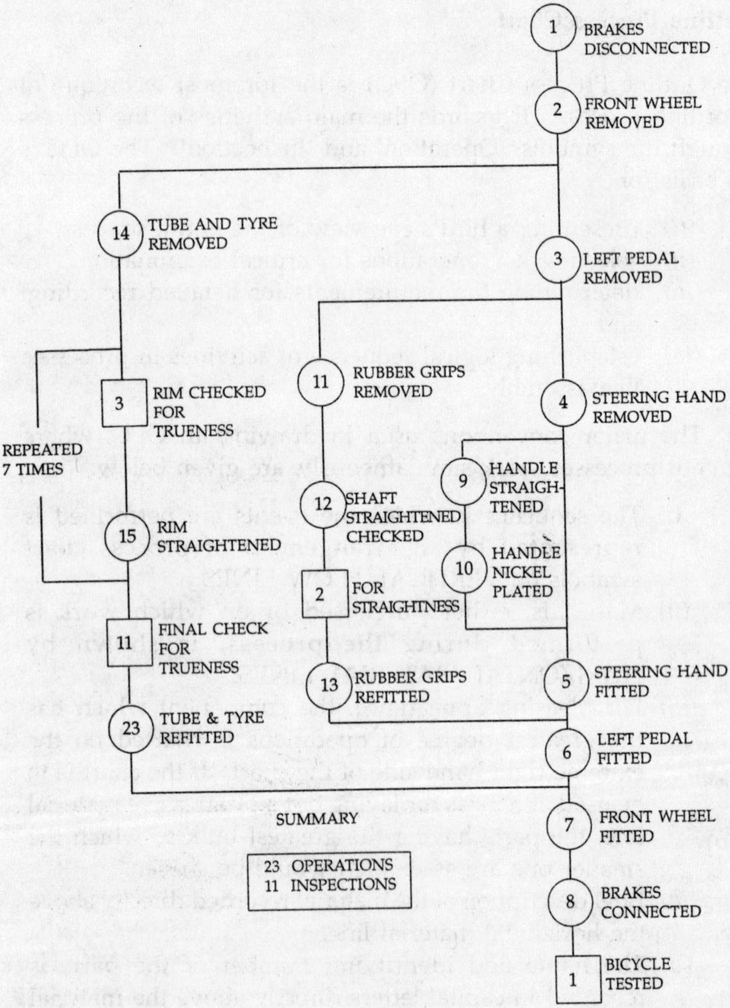

Fig. 3.9

(vi) Vertical flow line is drawn from the right hand end of the material line, and at approximately (¼") below the intersection the first symbol is recorded.

(vii) To the right of the symbol a brief description of the event is recorded.

(viii) To the left of the symbol the time required to perform the event is recorded.

(ix) Other pertinent information which is considered to add to the value of the chart is recorded, in brackets, below the description of the event.

(x) Operations and inspections are numbered in separate series, and each operation or inspection is numbered in serial order according to its sequence.

(xi) Identification information at the top of the chart should include:

- *(a)* Name of the Chart (Operation Process Chart),
- *(b)* Subject charted,
- *(c)* Present/Proposed Method,
- *(d)* Drawing number or any other identification number of product,
- *(e)* Location,
- *(f)* Chart Span—
  - *(i)* Point in the process at which chart begins
  - *(ii)* Point in the process at which chart ends
- *(g)* Charted by,
- *(h)* Approved by.

(xii) For dismantling ,the materials is represented as flowing from the process by a horizontal material line drawn to the right from the vertical flow line approximately ¼" below the symbol for the disassembly operation.

A simple illustration of constructing an OPC for restricted repairs to a bicycle is given in the Figure 3.9.

Flow Process Chart (Material)

After an OPC has been reviewed, the need for further recording in regard to key operations will be known. Additional data can be recorded by means of a Flow Process Chart (Material)—FPC (M). Figure 3.10 depicts all the elements of a task. It sets out the

Flow Process Chart (Battery)

PRESENT METHOD

TASK	:	RECHARGING OF AUTOMOBILE BATTERIES
CHART BEGINS	:	DISCHARGED BATTERIES DELIVERED BY CUSTOMER
CHART ENDS	:	CHARGED BATTERIES COLLECTED BY CUSTOMER
CHARTED BY	:	MSX
DATE	:	SEPT. 2, 1970

SUMMARY

ELEMENT	*NUMBER*	*TIME (MINS)*	*DISTANCE METRES*
○	10	960+	—
□	17	+	—
⇨	4		88M+
D	2	485	—
▽	2	1680	—

Fig. 3.10

sequence of flow of a product or document, recording all the events affecting these.

When charting FPC (M), it should not be confused with the work of the operator. Before charting one should be very clear of the unit being charted. The description against each activity should be brief and given in passive voice. Approximate time against each operation and inspection and distance against each transport should be indicated. The time against delays and storage is generally given per occasion. In addition, the accepted conventions should be followed in drawing FPC (M).

A simple illustration of constructing FPC (M) for recharging of automobile batteries is given in Figure 3.11.

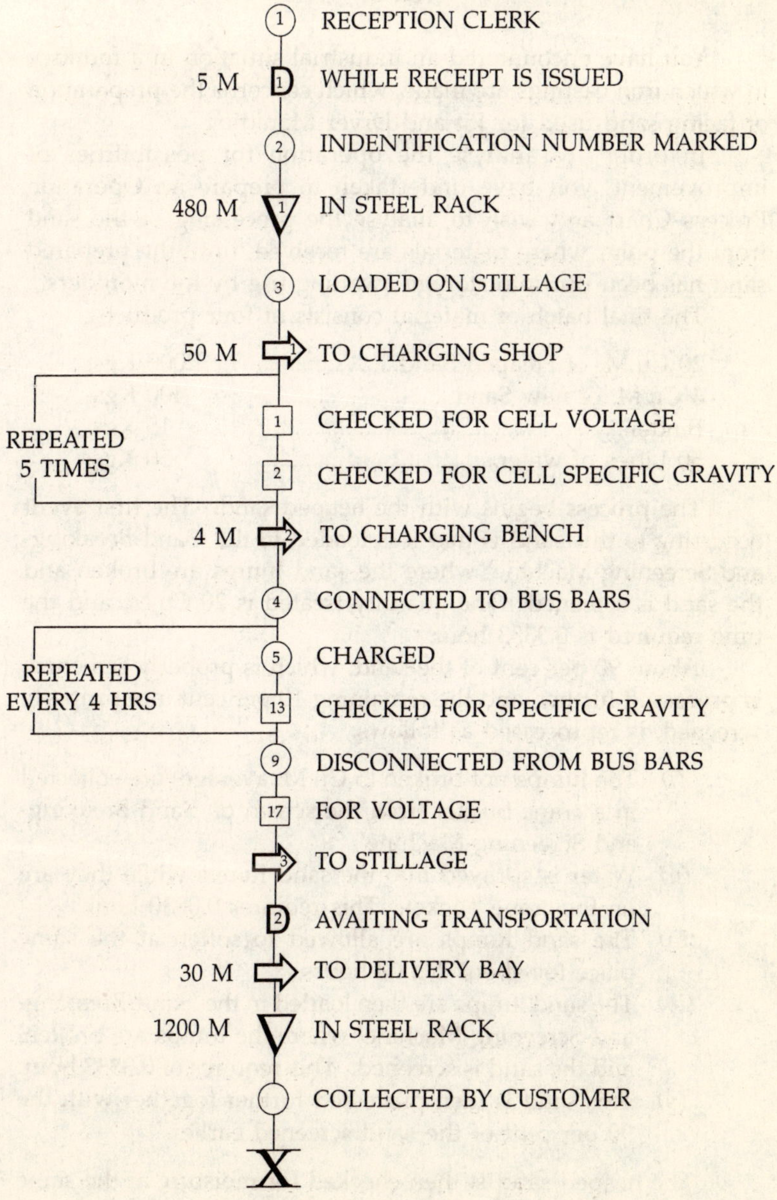
RECEPTION CLERK
5 M
WHILE RECEIPT IS ISSUED
INDENTIFICATION NUMBER MARKED
480 M
IN STEEL RACK
LOADED ON STILLAGE
50 M
TO CHARGING SHOP
CHECKED FOR CELL VOLTAGE
REPEATED
5 TIMES
CHECKED FOR CELL SPECIFIC GRAVITY
4 M
TO CHARGING BENCH
CONNECTED TO BUS BARS
CHARGED
REPEATED
EVERY 4 HRS
CHECKED FOR SPECIFIC GRAVITY
DISCONNECTED FROM BUS BARS
FOR VOLTAGE
TO STILLAGE
AVAITING TRANSPORTATION
30 M
TO DELIVERY BAY
1200 M
IN STEEL RACK
COLLECTED BY CUSTOMER

Fig. 3.11

EXERCISE
(OPC)

You have encountered an industrial situation in a foundry in which iron castings are made, which concerns the preparation of facing sand used for Pit and Dryer Moulding.

In order to analyse the operation for possibilities of improvement, you have undertaken to prepare an Operation Process Chart and wish to analyse the processing of the sand from the point where materials are received, until the prepared sand has been put into storage awaiting use by the moulders.

The final batch of material consists of four products:

20 Cu.M. of Heaped Sand....................	2000 Kgs.
4 Cu.M. of new Sand............................	400 Kgs.
Binder..	15 Kgs.
50 Litres of water..................................	50 Kgs.

The process begins with the heaped sand. The first event occurring to this sand is that it is loaded in the 'Sand-Breaking-and-Screening-Machine' where the sand lumps are broken and the sand is screened. The quantity treated is 20 Cu.M. and the time required is 0.3333 hour.

About 90 per cent of the sand, which is properly screened, is processed further, and the remaining 10 per cent, not properly screened, is reprocessed as follows:

(i) The lumps not broken (5 Cu.M. average) are collected in a crane bucket from the screen of 'Sand-Breaking-and-Screening-Machine'.

(ii) Water is sprayed into the sand lumps while they are on the crane bucket. This requires 0.0830 hour.

(iii) The sand lumps are allowed to soften at the same place for about 2.0000 hours.

(iv) The sand lumps are then loaded in the 'Sand-Breaking-and-Screening-Machine' where the lumps are broken, and the sand is screened. This requires of 0.3333 hour.

(v) This sand is then processed further together with the 90 per cent of the sand screened earlier.

The heaped sand is then checked for moisture at the same time that it is being loaded into the Simpson Mixer (Mixing

Machine). One batch of 20 Cu.M. is handled, and a time of 0.0830 hour is required.

Four Cu.M. of new sand is then placed in the mixing machine. This requires 0.0380 hour.

The third ingredient, the binder, is also placed in the mixing machine. The quantity loaded is 15 Kgs., and the time required is 0.0050 hour.

The fourth ingredient, 30 litres of water is added while the batch is being mixed.

One batch (24 Cu.M., 2400 Kgs.) of facing sand is then mixed in the Simpson Mixer, the required time being 0.0835 hour.

After the mixing, the sand is dumped on the floor, and the moisture content is checked simultaneously. The required time is 0.0500 hour.

Problem

Prepare a chart of this process, showing the operations, and inspections occurring in the processing of the facing sand.

EXERCISE
(FPC (M)—I)

Your have uncountered an industrial situation in a mill in which the operations are performed as described below. The layout of the work area is as shown in Figure 3.12.

Seven men are employed for bagging a powdery material in sacks, stitching the sack and delivering them for storage through a chute. The assignments of men are as follows:

Three men do 'bagging' operation; allowing the material to flow automatically from three vertical spouts into three ordinary sacks fastened around the spouts. The baggers need not pay attention to the sacks during the filling operation. After the sack is filled the bagger engages the spout shutter, releases the sack and sets it aside. He fastens a fresh sack (which he had brought earlier from the empty sack stock) on to the spout and opens the spout shutter allowing powdery material to flow into the bag. He then hauls the filled-in sack, on a two-wheel cart to a scale where he weighs the bag to an established weight adding or

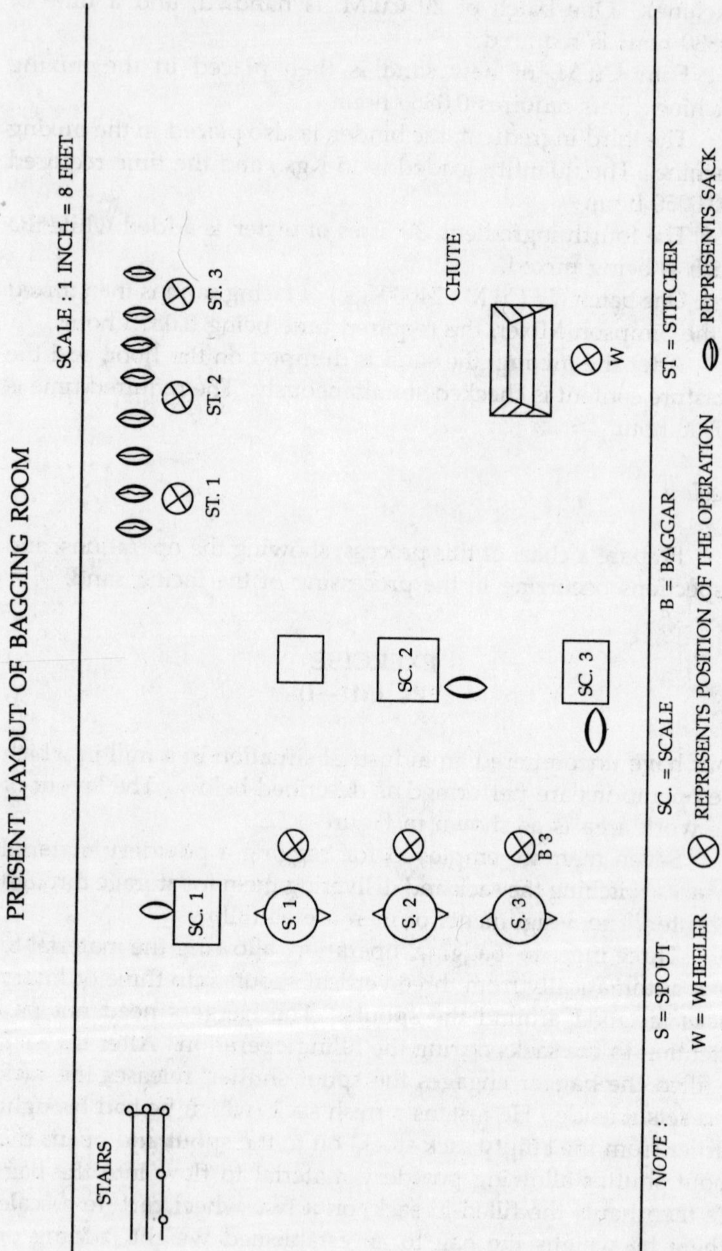
PRESENT LAYOUT OF BAGGING ROOM
SCALE : 1 INCH = 8 FEET
STAIRS
SC. 1
S. 1
S. 2
S. 3
B 3
SC. 2
SC. 3
ST. 1
ST. 2
ST. 3
CHUTE
W
NOTE : S = SPOUT SC. = SCALE B = BAGGAR ST = STITCHER
W = WHEELER
REPRESENTS POSITION OF THE OPERATION
REPRESENTS SACK

Fig. 3.12 :

removing material as required. After weighing he reloads the sack on the two-wheel cart, hauls it to the 'stitchers', unloads it there, returns back to the spout with empty cart, releases the cart, and fetches an empty sack.

The three stitchers work on the sacks brought by the baggers putting 10 stitches in each sack, manually. The seventh man, the 'wheeler', wheels the stitched sacks to the chute, for movement by gravity to a lower floor for further handling.

The elemental times you have secured by Time Study are :

		Minutes
1.	Walking from spout to empty sack pile, or *vice-versa*, an average distance of 4M. @ 0.015 mins./metre	=0.06
2.	Pick up empty sack from sack pile	=0.05
3.	Putting empty sack on floor	=0.05
4.	Pick up empty sack from floor, fasten it on spout and open the spout shutter	=0.80
5.	Filling time per sack	=1.50
6.	Close spout shutter, release filled sack and set it aside	=0.25
7.	Load one sack on a two-wheel cart	=0.10
8.	Unload one sack from a two-wheel cart	=0.10
9.	Wheel one filled-in sack on a two-wheel cart from spout to scale, an average distance of 3M. @ 0.018 mins/metre	=0.06
10.	Weigh the sack	=0.25
11.	Wheel one filled in sack, on two-wheel cart from scale to stitchers, an average distance of 8 metres @ 0.016 mins./metre	=0.15
12.	Return with empty cart—from stitchers to spout and release cart. An average distance of 8 metres @ 0.016 mins/foot	=0.13
13.	Stitch, on an average, 10 stitches per bag	=0.40
14.	Wheel one stitched sack on two-wheel cart from stitchers to chute, an average distance of 8 metres @ 0.018 mins./metre	=0.15

or

return to stitchers with empty cart.

Problem

1. Prepare a Material Flow Process Chart of a sack according to the present method.

EXERCISE
(FPC (M)—II)

Cast iron waterpipes for a Cooling Tower are 7 ft. long with 2" bore, and ¼" wall thickness and weigh about 40 lb. each. They have to be tested for leaks under pressure, and checked for straightness to ensure they can be assembled without difficulty. Rejects are approximately 10 per cent for straightness, and ½ per cent for leaking. A team of two men is occupied on a full time basis on this job.

Present Method (See Flow Diagram)

Tubes are kept in a stack pile. A bundle of 50 tubes is slinged to a crane, brought 120 ft. from stack pile to test building and dumped near the door. The two men together carry the tubes, two at a stack near the test bench. The pressure testing cycle is in Figure 3.13

B clamps the tube between rubber pads for pressure testing. **A** closes the drain valve and opens the water inlet valve. **B** waits until water runs out of the vent, then closes the vent, and watches the pressure gauge. When the test pressure is reached, **B** signals **A** to close the water inlet valve, and watches the gauge for 1 minute to see that the pressure does not drop below the specified limit. **B** signals **A** who opens the drain valve and walks to get the next tube, while **B** opens the vent, unclamps the tube and carries it to the straightness test rails if found good and to reject pile if found defective.

The straightness testing is done when 10 tubes have accumulated on the test rails, and is carried out by the two operatives working together.

A rolls each tube on the rails to test its straightness, and **B** places it on a stack on the floor if found good, and on reject pile if found defective.

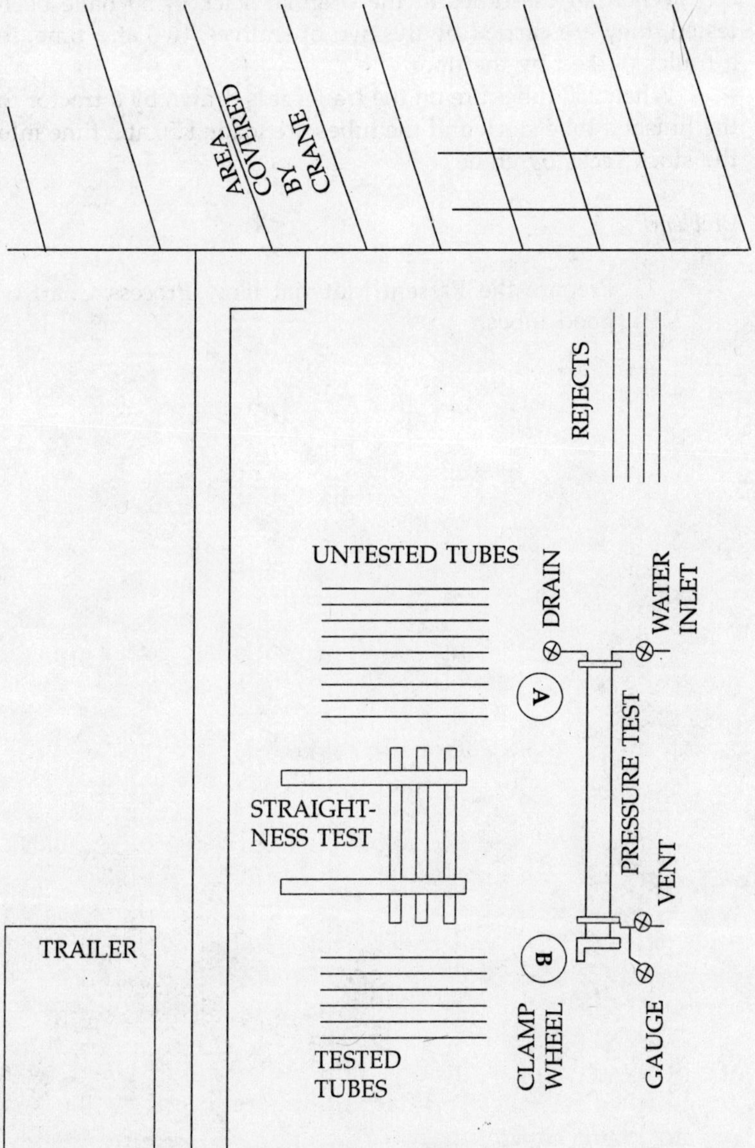

Fig. 3.13 : Flow Diagram

When all the tubes in the original stack of 50 have been tested, they are carried by the two operatives, two at a time, to a trailer parked by the door.

When 250 tubes are on the trailer it is drawn by a tractor to the finished tube stock and the tubes are loaded 50 at a time into the stock racks by crane.

Problem

1. Prepare the Present Material Flow Process Chart of good tubes.

4

Mathematical Dimensions of Inventory Control

I

POLICIES IN DYNAMIC INVENTORY PROBLEM

We consider a discrete-time inventory model with one indivisible commodity. The model is of the type investigated by Veinott (1966), Johnson (1968), and Tijms (1972). In each period the initial stock is observed. It may be increased to any amount by placing an order which is delivered immediately. The demand is met out of the stock on hand after ordering. The stock which passes to the next period is reduced by the demand. Any unfilled demand in a period is completely backlogged. The stock on hand may take on any integral value, where a negative value indicates the existence of a backlog. We shall assume that the demands are independent random variables with the same probability distribution having a finite and positive expected value.

If the order is positive, a positive setup cost, which does not depend on the amount ordered, is incurred. There is no purchase cost. All costs of storage and shortage will be considered together in the form of a function L expressing the expectation of those costs depending on the stock on hand after ordering. The total expected cost is defined as the undiscounted sum of costs over a finite number of considered periods.

We define policies of (multi-S)-type as a generalisation (different from that due to (Porteus 1971) of policies of (s, S)-type. Some properties of these policies, analogously for (multi-S)-type and (s, S)-type, are given by Theorems 1 and 2. The next Theorems 3 and 4 relate to the existence of optimal policies for the model investigated.

1. Policies of (multi-S)-type

In each period our decision is whether to increase the stock or not. If the initial stock i is observed then by our decision, the stock on hand after ordering will be $f(i) \geq i$.

The set of integers we shall denote by I. Any function f defined on I assuming integers as its values and satisfying is called an ordering decision function.

$$f(i) \geq i \qquad \text{for} \qquad i \in I$$

An ordering decision function f is of (s, S)-type if and only if there exist two integers $s \leq S$ such that

$$f(i) = \begin{cases} S & \text{for } i < s \\ i & \text{for } i \geq s \end{cases}$$

We shall write too (s, S) (i) *i.e.* f (s, S).

An ordering decision function f is of (multi-S)-type if there exist n+1 integers $S^0 \leq S^1 < ... < S^n$ such that

$$f(i) = \begin{cases} S^1 & \text{for } i < S^0 \\ i \text{ or } S^r & \text{for } S^{r-1} \leq i < S^r \text{ and } r = 1, \dots, n \\ i & \text{for } i \geq S^n. \end{cases}$$

By $A(S^0, S^1, ..., S^n)$ we shall denote the set of all such functions. We see that if n=1 and $S^0 \neq S^1$ then the policy (S^0, S^1) of (s, S)-type satisfying $(S^0, S^1) \in A(S^0, S^1)$ but there are policies not of (s, S)-type in the set $A(S^0, S^1)$ too.

Any t-tuple ordering decision function $(f_1, ..., f_t)$ is called a t-period ordering policy. We assume that in the first period the ordering amount is determined by the function f_t, in the second period by f_{t-1}, and so on, therefore in period t by f_1. If all of the decision functions are (multi-S)-type [(s, S)-type] then the policy is (multi-S)-type [(s, S)-type].

2. Total Expected Cost of an Optimal Policy

For a given triple (ϕ, K, L) where ϕ is a probability distribution

$\phi(n) \geq 0$, $\sum_{n=0}^{\infty} \phi(n) = 1$ and $\phi(0) \neq 1$, $K > 0$ is a setup cost and L is expectation of storage and shortage costs, we shall study finite-period planning problems. The total expected cost of a t-period policy $(\pi_1, ..., \pi_t)$ under assumption that the stock on hand at the beginning of the first period is i, may be calculated by an interactive method as follow :

$$C_1(i;\pi_1) = C[i, \pi_1(i)]$$

and for t >1

$$C_t(i;\pi_1, ..., \pi_t) = C[i, \pi_t(i)] + \sum_{n=0}^{\infty} \phi(n)\, C_{t-1}[\pi_t(i) - n; \pi_1, ..., \pi_{t-1}]$$

where for a $\geq$i

$$C(i,a) = K\delta(a-i) + L(a)$$

with $\delta(0) = 0$ and $\delta(j) = 1$ for $j > 0$.

Let us define by induction on t two sequences of functions $V_t(.)$ and $L_t(.)$, all of them from integers to reals :

$$V_0(i) = 0 \qquad \text{for any integer } i \in I$$

$$L_t(i) = L(i) + \sum_{n=0}^{\infty} \phi(n) V_{t-1}(i-n)$$

$$V_t(i) = \inf_{a \geq i} K\delta(a-i) + L_t(a) \qquad \text{for } i \in I.$$

The quantity $V_t(i)$ expresses the total expected cost of the optimal policy in the t-period planning problem with the initial stock i. The quantity $L_t(i)$ expresses the total expected cost when i is the initial stock achieved by the following policy : In the first period no order is placed, in the subsequent periods an optimal (t–1)-period policy is used.

We see that

$$V_t(i) = \min \{L_t(i), K + \inf_{j \geq i} L_t(j)\} \tag{0}$$

Assumption 1 : There exist integers m<M and a real number $\lambda > 0$ such that

(i) $$L(i) > \inf_{j \in I} L(j) + K \qquad \text{for } i \leq m$$

and

(ii) $$L(i) \geq \inf_{j \in I} L(j) + K + \lambda \qquad \text{for } i \geq M.$$

This assumption is nearly Johnson's assumption (Johnson 1968) :

$$\frac{\lim}{(i) \to \infty} L(i) > \inf_{i \in I} L(i) + K,$$

and is weaker than Veinott s assumption (Veinott 1966) :

$$\lim_{(i) \to \infty} L(i) = +\infty.$$

Key Lemma : If the function L satisfies Assumption 1 and $\overline{S} = \max\left\{S \middle| L(S) = \inf_{i \in I} L(i)\right\}$ then for any t = 1, 2, ... there exist an integer M_t and a real number $\lambda_t > 0$ such that

(a) $$L_t(i) = L(i) + \sum_{n=0}^{\infty} \phi(n)\, V_{t-1}(i-n) \qquad \text{for } i \in I,$$

(b) $$V_t(i) \geq V_t(S) + K + \lambda_t \qquad \text{for } i \geq M_t,$$

(c) for $i \leq \overline{S}$

$$V_t(i) - V_{t-1}(i) \leq \left[L_t(m) - L_1(m)\right] - \left[V_{t-1}(m) - V_1(m)\right],$$

(d) for $i \leq \overline{S}$

$$L_{t+1}(i) - L_t(i) \leq \left[L_{t+1}(m) - L_1(m)\right] - \left[V_t(m) - V_1(m)\right],$$

(e) for $i \geq M_t$

$$L_t(i) \geq \inf_{j \in I} L_t(j) + K + \lambda_t,$$

(f) for $i \leq m$

$$L_t(i) > \inf_{j \in I} L_t(j) + K,$$

(g) there exists $S_t \in I$ such that for $i \leq m$

$$V_t(i) = K + \inf_{j \in I} L_t(j) = K + L_t(S_t) =$$

$$= K + \inf_{j \in I} V_t(j) = K + V_t(S_t).$$

Proof : We first prove that (a), (b), (c) and (f) are satisfied for t=1. Further we can prove the following implications : (b) $\Rightarrow$ (e); (e) and (f) $\Rightarrow$ (g); (g) for t $\Rightarrow$ (a) for t+1; (a) for t and t+1 and (c) for t $\Rightarrow$ (d) for t; (d), (g) for t and (a) for t+1 $\Rightarrow$ (f) for t+1; (b) for t and (a) for t+1 $\Rightarrow$ (b) for t+1; (a), (d), (b) for t and (a) for t+1 $\Rightarrow$ (c) for t+1. This proof is given by Bylka (1979).

Corollary of Key Lemma : For each t = 1, 2, ... there exists a sequence of integers (S^0, S^1, ..., S^n, ...) (infinite or finite) such that $S^0 \le S^1 < S^2 < \ldots < S^n < \ldots$ and the following four conditions are satisfied:

(P_t) $\begin{cases} \text{(i) If there exist } j_1 < j_2 \le j_3 \text{ such that} \\ \quad L_t(j_1) > L_t(j_2) + K \text{ and } L_t(j_3) = \min\limits_{i \ge j_1} L_t(i) \\ \quad \text{then there is } k \ge 1 \text{ such that} \\ \qquad \min\limits_{i \ge j_1} L_t(i) = L_t(S^K) \\ \quad \text{and if } k > 1 \text{ then } S^{k-1} < j_1 < S^k, \\ \text{(ii) } L_t(i) \ge L_t(S^1) + K \qquad \text{for } i < S^0 \\ \text{(iii) } L_t(s^0) \le L_t(S^1) + K, \\ \text{(iv) for any } S^0 \le S^k < S^{k+1} \text{ there exist integers } i_1 \\ \quad \text{and } i_2 \text{ such that } S^k < i_1 < i_2 \le S^{k+1} \text{ and} \\ \quad L_t(i_1) > L_t(i_2) + K. \end{cases}$

Remark : The sequence is finite if and only if there is an integer i_1 such that $L_t(i) \le L_t(j) + K$ for each $i_1 \le i < j$ or

$$\inf_{j \ge i_1} L_t(j) < L_t(i) \text{ for each } i = i_1 + 1,\ i_1 + 2,\ \ldots .$$

Veinott (1966) formulates conditions (P_1) for two integers $s \le S$, with equalities in (ii) and (iii) because of continuity of L.

3. Existence Theorems

It can be easily derived from the definitions and the Corollary of Key Lemma.

Theorem 1: Let Assumption 1 be fulfilled; then for each t = 1, 2.... and a sequence $S^0 \le S^1 < ... < S^n$ the following three conditions are equivalent :

(i) the sequence $(S^0, S^1, ..., S^n)$ satisfies (P_t) and $L_t(i) \le L_t(j) + K$ for $S^n \le i < j$,

(ii) there exists an optimal t-period policy $(\pi_1, ..., \pi_t)$ such that $\pi_t \in A(S^0, S^1, ..., S^n)$,

(iii)

$$V_t(i) = \begin{cases} L_t(s^1) + K & \text{for } i < S^0 \\ \min\{L_t(i), L_t(S^k) + K\} & \text{for } S^{k-1} \le i < S^k \\ & \text{and } k = 1, ..., n \\ L_t(i) & \text{for } i \ge S^n \end{cases}$$

For policies of (s, S)-type we have :

Theorem 2 : Let Assumption 1 be fulfilled; then for each t=1, 2, ...and a pair $S^0 \le S^1$ the following three conditions are equivalent:

(i) the sequence (S^0, S^1) satisfies (P_t) and $L_t(i) \le L_t(j) + K$ for $S^0 \le i < j$;

(ii) there exists an optimal t-period policy $(\pi_1, ..., \pi_t)$ such that $\pi_t = (S^0, S^1)$.

(iii) $$V_t(i) = \begin{cases} L_t(S^1) + K & \text{for } i < S^0 \\ L_t(i) & \text{for } i \ge S^0. \end{cases}$$

To establish the existence of an optimal policy of (multi-S)-type some additional assumptions for L are needed.

Assumption 2 : There exist integers $M_0 < M^0$ such that

(i) $L(i) \le L(j)$ for $M_0 \le i < j$

(ii) $L(i) > L(M_0) + K$ for $i \ge M^0$

Theorem 3 : Let the function R satisfy both Assumption 1 and 2. If a sequence $S^0 \le S^1 < S^2 < ...$ satisfies conditions (P_t) then it is a finite sequence $S^0 \le S^1 < ... < S^n$ and there exists an optimal t-period policy $(\pi_1, ..., \pi_t)$ such that $\pi_t \in A(S^0, S^1, ..., S^n)$ and

(i) $m < S^0 \le S^n \le M^0$

and

(ii) $S^{n-1} \le M_0$

Proof : Let $t \in I$. By Assumption 1 there exists a sequence $(S^0, S^1, ...)$ satisfying (P_t). Because assumption 2 then for each $M_0 \le i < j$

$$L_t(j) - L_t(i) = L(j) - L(i) + \sum_{n=0}^{\infty} \phi(n)\left[V_{t-1}(j-n) - V_{t-1}(i-n)\right] \ge$$

$$\ge L(j) - L(i) - K \ge -K.$$

We see that the set $\{t / S^t > M_0\}$ has at most one element. This sequence is finite sequence $(S^0\ S^1, ..., S^n)$ and (ii) is satisfied.

for $i > M^0$

$$L_t(i) - L_t(M_0) \ge L(i) - L(M_0) - K > 0$$

which means that for any $i \le M^0$

$$\inf_{j \ge i} L_t(j) = \min_{i < j \le M^0} L_t(j) \tag{1}$$

and $S^n \le M^0$.

By (i) of (P_t) and Assumption 2

$$L_t(i) \le L_t(j) + K \quad \text{for } S^n \le i < j. \tag{2}$$

Condition (i) follows from Eq. (1) and (f) of the Key Lemma. Equation (2) implies (i) of Theorem 1. This completes the proof.

By Corollary of Key Lemma and Theorem 3 we have *Main Conclusion.* If Assumption 1 and Assumption 2 are fulfilled, then for each t = 1, 2, ... there exists an optimal policy of (multi-S)-type.

Assumption 3 : There exist integers $\underline{S} \le \overline{S}$ such that

(i) $L(i) \ge L(j)$ for $i \le j \le \overline{S}$,

(ii) $L(i) \le L(j)$ for $\underline{S} \le i \le j$,

(iii) $L(i) > L(\overline{S})$ for $i < \underline{S}$ or $i > \overline{S}$.

In other words, it is assumed that there exists an integer S such that function L is non-increasing for $i \le S$ and is non-

decreasing for $i \geq S$.
If Assumption 1 then assumption 3 implies Assumption 2.

Assumption 3 is Veinott's assumption of unimodality of –L. Veinott proves the existence of finite period optimal policy of (s, S)-type. As in Veinott s Theorem 1 in (Veinott 1966) we have:

Theorem 4 : Let function L satisfy both Assumption 1 and 3. If a sequence $S^0 \leq S^1 < ...$ satisfies conditions (P_t) then is a pair $S^0 \leq S^1$ and there exists an optimal t-period policy $(\pi_1, ..., \pi_t)$ such that $\pi_t = (S^0, S^1)$ and

(i) $\quad m < S^0 \leq S^1 \leq M$

and

(ii) $\quad S^1 \geq \underline{S}$.

Proof : If M and $\underline{S}$ satisfy (ii) of Assumption 1 and (ii) of Assumption 3 respectively then the pair M_0, M^0 where $M_0 = \underline{S}$ and $M^0 = M$ satisfies Assumption 2. From Theorem 3 follows that for any t =1, 2, ... and $(S^0, S^1, ..., S^n)$ satisfying (P_t) we have

$$S^{n-1} \leq \underline{S}.$$

We shall show by indication that for T = 1, 2, ...

$$L_T(i) - L_T(j) \geq L(i) - L(j) \geq 0 \text{ for } i \leq j \leq \bar{S}. \tag{4}$$

For T=1 this is (i) of Assumption 3. Let us suppose that Eq. (4) is satisfied for $T \geq 1$. It follows from Eqs. (0) and (4) for T that

$$V_T(i) \geq V_T(j) \quad \text{for } i \leq j \leq \bar{S}. \tag{5}$$

Conditions (a) of Key Lemma and Eq. (5) imply that Eq. (4) is satisfied from T+1.

By Eq. (4) and (iii) of Assumption 3, $S^1 \geq \underline{S}$ which together with Eq. (3) imply n=1.

Let $S^0 \leq i \leq S^1$ and $i < j$. It follows from (i) and (iii) of (P_t) and Eq. (4) that

$$-K < L_t(S^1) - Lt(S^0) = \left[L_t(i) - L_t(S^0)\right] + \left[L_t(j) - L_t(i)\right] +$$

$$\left[L_t(S^1) - L_t(j)\right] \leq L_t(j) - L_t(i).$$

Therefore (S^0, S^1) satisfies condition (i) of Theorem 2. The proof is now complete.

II

INVENTORY PLANNING USING ROLLING PRODUCTION SCHEDULING

Although algorithms exist for finding optimal solutions to multiperiod production scheduling problems, the solution found is rarely implemented in its entirety. Typically, the solution s first period decision is implemented, the model is updated to recognize the acquisition of new or improved information, and a new (and possibly different) solution is found to the updated problem. The process then repeats itself. This method of solving a multiperiod problem, implementing the first period decision, updating, and resolving creates what is called a *rolling schedule.*

Past research had dealt extensively with the optimisation of finite horizon models, but little attention has been paid to the effectiveness of such solutions when implemented on a rolling basis. Progress has been made in this direction by Baker (1977) using simulation techniques with a dynamic lot-sizing model. In this research we further pursue the answer to the question which Baker (1977, p. 20) posed: "How good are model-optimal decisions for the actual system, when implemented on a rolling basis?"

Baker found that choosing a proper forecast window length for each problem was important to achieving an efficient rolling schedule. The result of interest is that Baker found that the longest possible forecast horizon was not necessarily the best. He encountered large fluctuations in rolling schedules' effectiveness which depended upon the length of the forecast horizon. In an attempt to smooth these fluctuations, we experimented with forecasting demand beyond the forecast horizon. The results were not always as expected. Some results confirmed Baker's conclusion that less information is better than more, while others pointed toward a conclusion that "the more information, the better."

Baker's Experiments

The multiperiod planning model used in Baker's experiments, and ours as well, is the Dynamic Lot Size model. Briefly, it is :

$$\text{Minimize} \sum_{t=1}^{N}\left[k\delta(Q_t)+hI_t\right] \quad \text{subject to : } I_{t-1}+Q_t-I_t=d_t$$

$$Q_t \geq 0,\ I_t \geq 0$$

Where : h = unit holding cost $\quad k$ = production setup cost

Q_t = production lot size $\quad d_t$ = demand which must be met

I_t = ending inventory level $\quad N$ = horizon length or forecast window

$$\delta(x) = \begin{cases} 0 \text{ for } x = 0 \\ 1 \text{ for } x > 0 \end{cases}$$

The Wagner-Whitin (1958) algorithm is used to find the optimal values of Q_t for this model.

Baker's measure of the effectiveness of rolling schedules is the ratio of the cost of the rolling schedule to the cost of the theoretically optimal schedule for the same problem, C_r/C_0. The C_0 value is the cost of the Wagner-Whitin optimal policy for a 48-period problem. The C_r value is the cost of a rolling schedule constructed by solving a series of N-period problems, each time saving the first period solution, until a vector of 48 decisions has been formed. To make the comparison with the optimal cost equitable, costs associated with production for periods beyond the 48-period interval are ignored in calculating the cost of the rolling schedule.

Three factors are varied in Baker's experiments. The forecast window, N, is the number of future periods for which demand is known deterministically. In Baker, N is the number of periods of data used by the Wagner-Whitin algorithm; it takes on values of 2, 4, 6, 8, 10, 12, 14, and 24. The second factor varied is the length of the natural cycle, T, which is defined as $T=\sqrt{2k/dh}$; it is the time between successive orders or production setups in an Economic Order Quantity system where demand is constant at d units per period. Baker uses values of 2, 4, 6, 8, 10, and 12 for T. Finally, he tests four demand patterns: uniform, trend, seasonal, and trend-seasonal.

Analysis of Baker's Results

Baker (1977) concludes that there is "no simple answer" to the question of how well model-optimal decisions perform on a rolling basis. He does however find that, in many cases, *less information is better than more* when solving the multiperiod problems to create the rolling schedules. This is especially true for the uniform demand pattern. Table 4.1 (from Baker, 1977, p. 22) contains results for uniform demand with a range of 75. The tabled values are the average C_r/C_0 ratios.based on 50 problems. Notice what we refer to as the *diagonal effect*—the ratios found along the diagonal where N=T are consistently smaller than the other ratios in their respective rows. The apparent conclusion is that the planning forecast horizon should never be longer than the natural cycle. This conclusion is counterintuitive because it argues in favour of ignoring potentially valuable information.

Table 4.1
Values of C_r/C_0 from Baker : Uniform Demand (Range = 75)

T \ *N*	2	4	6	8	10	12
2	1.002	1.002	1.002	1.002	1.002	1.002
4	1.29	1.004	1.05	1.004	1.03	1.01
6	1.74	1.10	1.004	1.05	1.04	1.01
8	2.21	1.27	1.04	1.003	1.03	1.06
10	2.70	1.48	1.14	1.03	1.007	1.02
12	3.09	1.70	1.27	1.09	1.03	1.003

As demand becomes more variable, and in particular when seasonality is added, Baker finds this diagonal effect to be less marked. Nevertheless, he still finds that the choice of an inappropriate forecast window can significantly damage the effectiveness of the rolling schedule. Furthermore, the appropriate window is again not necessarily the longest possible.

Although it is not used in this research, the Period Order Quantity (POQ) lot-sizing technique (Gorham, 1968) offers some useful insights into the diagonal effect. Assume initially that demand is constant. The optimal production schedule in the case of constant demand requires that a setup occur every T periods, or once every natural cycle as it is defined in the POQ context.

In the case of N < T, the Wagner-Whitin algorithm processes only N periods of information at each decision point. Clearly, the algorithm will not find the optimal trade-off duration, T, because it does not have enough information. Instead it will set up once every N periods, thus producing for the longest cycle it possibly can. This results in a cycle shorter than the optimal cycle and a cost larger than the optimal cost. In the case of N = T, one expects the algorithm to be able to make approximately the same tradeoffs as a POQ analysis and have a setup every T periods.

The case of N > T is more difficult to analyze. Here the algorithm has more than one full natural cycle of information on future demand; and in making the tradeoff between setup costs and carrying costs, will often choose to produce lot sizes different than those dictated by a POQ analysis. For example, consider a problem in which k = 1600, h = 1, and demand is given by

Period	1	2	3	4	5	6	7	8
Demand	192	187	195	219	205	180	205	186

The mean demand is 200, which results in a natural cycle of 4. The Wagner-Whitin algorithm yields these optimal values for production in period 1, x^*_1, as a function of N :

N	1	2	3	4	5	6	7	8
x^*_1	192	379	574	793	998	574	574	793

On the average, one would like to produce approximately once every fourth period—the POQ result—which means that $x^*_1 = 793$ is probably a good selection. For N =1, 2, and 3, not enough data is supplied to the algorithm. This leads to a low, and therefore poor, value of x^*_1 as previously discussed.

For N = 5, the algorithm is in the peculiar position of having "not enough" data, but at the same time "too much". There is not enough data in that the Wagner-Whitin algorithm operates on the implicit assumption that demand beyond the horizon equals zero. However, in a rolling scheduling context it is clear that demand after period 5 will not be zero. It is just not yet known. There is too much data in the sense that given this mode of operation of the algorithm and given its implicit assumption, we would have been better off to have had data for only 4 periods.

For N = 6, the same analysis holds except in this case the algorithm adjusts by producing too little in period 1 rather than too much. The tradeoff between setup costs and holding costs for the 6-period problem is such that two setups are scheduled and small amounts produced at each. Finally, at N = 8, an integer multiple of the natural cycle, things are back "in phase" again, and x^*_1 = 793, just as it did for N = 4.

This case is a particularly interesting one. One would expect that giving the Wagner-Whitin algorithm m × T (m integer) periods of demand data would result in decisions close to those made in the optimal schedule, and indeed this result is observed. In examining Baker's results, we notice that the ratios improve at points where N is an integral multiple of T. Unexpectedly, however, the best horizon choice in many of these cases is still the natural cycle, T. Thus, for N > T, when N is "out of phase" with T, there is a likelihood of choosing an incorrect lot size for the first period.

Overall, one can conclude on the basis of such analysis that the ratio values on the diagonal where N = T will be low. Indeed for cases of uniform and trend demand, Baker finds this to be true. However, as demand becomes more variable, as in the case of seasonal demand, one expects these conclusions to be less valid as inventory is no longer drawn down uniformly.

Extending the Horizon

The awkward situation of simultaneously having "too much" and "not enough" data is a result of what is called the horizon effect in which the optimal first period lot-size is highly sensitive to the horizon length, N. McClain and Thomas (1977) demonstrated the significance of the horizon effect in rolling scheduling problems. Research to date has concentrated on overcoming this difficulty by specifying a terminal inventory level (a single number) as a constraint on the dynamic programming procedure. However, such research has also demonstrated that cost of the solution obtained is extremely sensitive to the terminal inventory condition imposed upon the problem.

Our approach is to eliminate the horizon effect by extending the horizon. Thus, instead of relying on known demand data for future periods beyond N, we forecast that demand and use the

Wagner-Whitin algorithm on a combination of known future demand (through period N) and forecast future demand (beyond N). In this way, we use the data of the problem to implicitly determine terminal conditions. Instead of solving a fixed-horizon problem with a specified terminal inventory level, we extend the horizon of the problem, one period at a time, until a stopping rule condition is met. Each extension creates a new problem to which the Wagner-Whitin procedure is applied.

Experimental Setup

Our experiments were structured as Baker's except for the use of forecasting to extend the horizon. For each combination of the 8 values of the forecast horizon, N, (2, 4, 6, 8, 10, 12, 14, 24), with the six values of the natural cycle, T, (2, 4, 6, 8, 10, 12), we solved 20 randomly generated problems and calculated an average C_r/C_0 ratio. We conducted tests using uniform demand patterns with ranges of 75 and 400. Demand forecasts were made using a five-period moving average method.

The Wagner-Whitin algorithm is a nearly ideal methodology to use with horizon extension because it is a forward dynamic programming technique. Thus, each extended problem is easily solved using the results of the solutions of all previous problems. Our procedure was to add periods to the problem, one-at-a-time, and to forecast demand for each of these periods, one-at-a-time, each time solving a new problem. Our stopping rule was to extend the problem 5T periods past the horizon as suggested by Lundin and Morton (1975) unless the process could be stopped earlier. We know from the Wagner and Whitin (1958) horizon theorem that once a setup occurs in the final period of Wagner-Whitin problem, a setup will occur in that period for all longer (extended) problems. When this happens, the decisions in all prior periods will be fixed and will not change as more periods are added to the problem. Therefore when such an occurrence takes place after the first period, we can discontinue the extensions.

Results

Tables 4.2 and 4.3 contain values of C_r/C_0 for each type of demand tested for rolling schedules created without forecasting demand beyond the N periods for which data were available. These results are essentially the same as Baker's and are presented primarily for comparison with results achieved when forecasting was used. Two observations are worth noting. First, the diagonal effect described earlier is particularly strong for the uniform demand pattern with range = 75 (Table 4.2), but it is virtually non-existent for the other more variable demand pattern (Table 4.3). This would seem to indicate that as demand becomes more variable, more information is better than less in solving the multiperiod problems. Secondly, values for ratios below the diagonal (where N < T) are consistently very large.

Table 4.2

Values of C_r/C_0 without Forecasting : Uniform Demand (Range = 75)

T \ *N*	*2*	*4*	*6*	*8*	*10*	*12*	*14*	*24*
2	1.001	1.001	1.001	1.001	1.001	1.001	1.001	1.002
4	1.29	1.004	1.05	1.004	1.02	1.008	1.01	1.01
6	1.73	1.09	1.004	1.05	1.04	1.01	1.02	1.01
8	2.21	1.27	1.05	1.003	1.03	1.06	1.02	1.02
10	2.69	1.48	1.14	1.03	1.006	1.02	1.06	1.04
12	3.18	1.70	1.26	1.09	1.03	1.003	1.05	1.04

Table 4.3

Values of C_r/C_0 without Forecasting : Uniform Demand (Range = 400)

T \ *N*	*2*	*4*	*6*	*8*	*10*	*12*	*14*	*24*
2	1.11	1.009	1.003	1.002	1.002	1.002	1.002	1.002
4	1.42	1.10	1.06	1.02	1.01	1.006	1.007	1.008
6	1.87	1.18	1.08	1.09	1.04	1.02	1.01	1.007
8	2.34	1.35	1.11	1.06	1.08	1.05	1.03	1.01
10	2.82	1.55	1.20	1.08	1.05	1.07	1.07	1.03
12	3.31	1.77	1.32	1.13	1.07	1.05	1.09	1.03

For the same demand patterns, we next created rolling schedules using forecasting to extend the number of periods used in the Wagner-Whitin algorithm. For these rolling schedules, the values C_r/C_0 are given in Tables 4.4 and 4.5. These tables contain some surprising results as well as some which were expected. First, values of C_r/C_0 below the diagonal decreased dramatically as expected. It is for these situations where N < T that extending problem horizons via forecasting will be most valuable. Second, for a given T, the minimum C_r/C_0 is most often found for N = 24, the largest value of N employed. Furthermore, this rightward movement of the row minima in these tables is much more pronounced for demand with high variability (Table 4.5). In general, the minimum C_r/C_0 ratios are no longer found on the diagonal. All minima have moved to the right, and most to the last column. Thus in general it can be said that more information is better than less when forecasting is used to extend the horizon.

Table 4.4

Values of C_r/C_0 with Forecasting : Uniform Demand (Range = 75)

T \ *N*	2	4	6	8	10	12	14	24
2	1.11	1.04	1.03	1.02	1.01	1.01	1.008	1.003
4	1.19	1.08	1.02	1.01	1.01	1.01	1.01	1.01
6	1.11	1.12	1.04	1.02	1.02	1.01	1.007	1.01
8	1.08	1.10	1.12	1.04	1.02	1.02	1.04	1.01
10	1.10	1.06	1.10	1.11	1.03	1.01	1.01	1.01
12	1.09	1.09	1.11	1.11	1.10	1.03	1.03	1.03

Table 4.5

Values of C_r/C_0 with Forecasting : Uniform Demand (Range = 400)

T \ *N*	2	4	6	8	10	12	14	24
2	1.15	1.01	1.002	1.002	1.002	1.002	1.002	1.002
4	1.29	1.20	1.02	1.01	1.007	1.007	1.008	1.008
6	1.21	1.18	1.08	1.03	1.01	1.01	1.01	1.007
8	1.17	1.17	1.14	1.08	1.04	1.01	1.01	1.01
10	1.15	1.14	1.13	1.10	1.05	1.04	1.02	1.02
12	1.12	1.14	1.12	1.15	1.12	1.08	1.05	1.02

A third result is that the values of C_r/C_0 in Tables 4.4 and 4.5 exhibit far less fluctuation with changes in N (for a given T) than their counterparts, Tables 4.2 and 4.3. Smoothing these fluctuations was one of the objectives of this research, as this will protect the scheduler against the vagaries of having selected a "bad" value of N. Thus it appears that forecasting makes the choice of N less crucial.

Conclusions

There are some tentative conclusions that can be drawn from our results. First it appears that if N = T and thus the interval over which demand is known deterministically exactly equals the natural cycle, extending the horizon via forecasting is not a food idea. Extending the horizon using forecasting has been shown to be most valuable for cases where N < T. For cases in which N > T, we must be more specific in interpreting our results. When N = mT (m integer), we say that N and T are "in phase" and in general extending the horizon is less valuable than when N and T are out of phase. A relatively clear-cut and important result is that horizon extension via forecasting provides better and better (relative to not extending the horizon) rolling schedules as the variance of demand increases.

III

CONTINUOUS REVIEW INVENTORY MODELS WITH STOCHASTIC LEAD-TIME

1. The General Model (M)

The objective of this section is to present some results on continuous review inventory models with stochastic lead-time under varying assumptions concerning the demand process and the lead-time distribution. It will be convenient to formulate a general model, referred to as (M), of which the models discussed in Sections 2-4 will be special cases. In Section 5 a different type of model will be considered (with (s, S)-policies). This section concludes with some comparisons. Now we turn to the description of the general model. To do so, we specify *(i)* the demand process, *(ii)* the ordering process and *(iii)* the cost structure.

The Demand Process

Consider a probability space (Ω, J, P) and random variables

$$X_n = \Omega \to \overline{M}, \quad {}^{*)}$$

$$T_n = \Omega \to R_+, \quad {}^{**)}$$

such that $T_0 = 0$, $T_n \leqq T_{n+1}$ for $n = 1, 2, \ldots$ with $T_n \to \infty$ a.s., where T_n denotes the instant of the n-th demand and X_n its size; the interarrival time between successive demands is $Y_n = T_n - T_{n-1}$, the process $\{X_n, Y_n\}$ satisfies the Markov property, i.e.,

$$\begin{aligned} P(X_{n+1} = j, Y_{n+1} \leqq t | X_0 = j_0, X_i = j_i, Y_i = t_i, i = 1, \ldots, n) \\ = P(X_{n+1} = j, Y_{n+1} \leqq t | X_n = j_n), \end{aligned} \tag{1}$$

for all $j, j_i \in \overline{M}$, $t, t_1 \geqq 0$.

Note that (1) encompasses models allowing for Markovian dependency between sizes of successive demands as well as between demand size and interarrival time, and will be specialized later on.

The Ordering Process

Only (S-1, S)—policies will be considered. The lead-time of a reorder is the sum of the waiting time in a reorder queue and the service time (the service mechanism can be thought of as a repair center). Simplifying assumptions will have to be made to characterise the lead-time distribution.

---

* $\overline{M} = \{1, 2, \ldots, M\}$, $M < \infty$

** Nonnegative reals.

The Cost Structure

The cost structure is linear and consists of

- — an ordering cost of the form $C_0 + c_0 x$, when x items are ordered,
- — a unit inventory carrying cost rate of c_1,
- — a unit backorder cost rate of c_2.

The objective is to find a critical number minimising the expected average cost.

2. A Model with Semi-Markovian Demand, (S-1, S) Ordering Policy and Exponential Service Mechanism with Fifo-Service (K-1)

This is a model described in Koevoets (6). How this model, referred to as (K-1), is a specialisation of (M) is clear from this section's title.

The service time distribution has meant $1/\beta$. As to the cost structure note that the ordering costs are determined by the demand process and not dependent of S. So we evaluate the expected inventory carrying costs, C_1 (S), and the backorder costs, C_2(S).

If now, Z(t) denotes the on-hand inventory and N(t) the number of units in the reorder process, we have

$$Z(t) = S - N(t). \tag{2}$$

Observe that

$$C_1(S) = c_1 \sum_{k=0}^{S} k \lim_{t\to\infty} P[Z(t) = k],$$

$$C_2(S) = c_2 \sum_{k=-\infty}^{0} k \lim_{t\to\infty} P[Z(t) = k],$$

or, in view of (2) and denoting $P_k = \lim_{t\to\infty} P[N(t) = k]$ (the limit exists under "plausible" assumptions, see below)

$$C_1(S) = c_1 \sum_{k=0}^{S} (s - k) p_k, \tag{3}$$

$$C_2(S) = c_2 \sum_{k=s} (k-S)p_k . \quad (4)$$

To obtain expressions for the P_k's, the results of Cinlar (1) were adapted for bulk arrivals in Koevoets (6). The underlying idea is to consider a demand, say the n-th of size j with interarrival time Y_n, as j single demands were j – 1 single demands have an interarrival time of zero and 1 with an interarrival time Y_n. This simply means that $\overline{M}$ can be artificially written as

$$\underline{\overline{M}} = \{1_1, 2_1, 2_2, ..., M_1, M_2, ..., M_M\}.$$

The results of Cinlar can be applied to $\underline{\overline{M}}$. There is, however, a technical detail : even if the imbedded Markov chain $\{X_n\}$ defined over $\overline{M}$ is aperiodic, the imbedded Markov chain over $\underline{\overline{M}}$ may be periodic in which case the limiting results of Koevoets do not apply directly. Nevertheless, Koevoets showed that

$$P_0 = 1-(\beta\mu)^{-1} \text{ (clearly assuming } \beta\mu > 1)$$
$$P_k = (\beta\mu)^{-1} \lim_{n\to\infty} P(N_n = K-1) \text{ for } K \geq 1, \quad (5)$$

where μ is the steady state expected value of the "extended" interarrival time and where N_n denotes the number of items in the reorder queue at the time of the n-th arrival in the extended process. Actually, (5) only holds under some further technical assumptions. The limiting probability of N_n, can be expressed in terms of the steady-state probabiliting vector of the extended chain, denoted by α, and the matrices Γ and T whose elements are rather complicated. The elements of Γ are the (distinct) roots, say q_i (s, w), of an equation of the form det $[zI - wA(s+\beta - \beta z)] = 0$ evaluated in s = 0, w = 1 where A(.) is the matrix of Laplace transforms of the semi-Markov matrix associated with the extended demand process. The elements of T are obtained from the reduced adjoint matrix of $g_i(s,w)\ I - w\ A(s+\beta - \beta g_i(s,w))$ again evaluated at s =0, w= 1. The technical details are contained in Cinlar [1, p. 372], and the expression takes on the following form:

$$\lim_{n\to\infty} P(N_n = k-1) = \alpha T^{-1}(I-\Gamma)\Gamma^k T\underline{1} \quad (6)$$

From (3)—(6), every (S – 1), S) ordering policy can be evaluated—at least from a theoretical point of view. Needless to say that for realistically sized models the computational burden becomes overwhelming.

3. (K-1) with a Compound Poisson Demand Process (K-2)

Here we specialise (K-1), by nothing that the interarrival times in a compound Possion process are independent, identically exponentially distributed (with parameter λ), and that the demand sizes are also i.i.d. random variables with

$$\text{Prob}\,(x_n = j) = f_j \qquad j \in \overline{M}.$$

It can be shown (recall (5) and (6) that :

(i) $\alpha = (\alpha_{i_k}) = (\frac{f_i}{\delta})$

with $\delta = E\,[X_n]$,

(ii) $\mu = (\lambda\delta)^{-1}$,

see Koevoets [6].

In view of (6), one is still left with the computation of T and T which is still not a trivial task but manageable for reasonable sized problems. If $\overline{M} = \{1, 2\}$ a complete analytical solution can be obtained (see also Gross, and Harris [4]). In fact, it is relatively straight forward to show that (6) reduces to

$$\lim_{n\to\infty} P(N_n = k) = \frac{[1-(z_1+z_2)+z_1 z_2][z_1^{k+1} - z_2^{k+1} + f_2(z_1^{k-} - z_2^{k})]}{(1+f_2)(z_1 - z_2)} \tag{7}$$

where z_1 and z_2 are the roots

$$-\frac{\beta}{\lambda} z^2 + z + f_2 = 0.$$

of course, (7) can be computed recursively, and finding an optimal (s – 1, s)—policy is straightforward.

4. (K-1) with Exponential Interarrival Time with Dependence on Preceding Demand-Size; $\overline{M} = \{1, 2\}$ (K—3)

Here it is assumed that

$$P(Y_n \leqq t | X_{n-1} = 1) = 1 - e^{-\lambda_1 t},$$

$$P(Y_n = t | X_{n-2} = 2) = 1 - e^{-\lambda_2 t}$$

It can be shown that

$$\mu = \frac{1}{\delta}(\frac{f_1}{\lambda_1} + \frac{f_2}{\lambda_2},$$

and that (6) is of the form given in (7) with z_1 and z_2 as the roots of

$$\beta^2 z^3 - \beta(\beta + \lambda_1 + \lambda_2)z^2 + \lambda_1(\lambda_2 + \beta f_1)z + f_2\lambda_2(\beta + \lambda_1) = 0$$

satisfying $|z_i| < 1$, see Koevoets [6].

5. A Model with Compound Poisson Demand Process, (s, S)—Ordering Policy, no Reorder Queue and General Service Distribution (D-K)

The development of this section are, although related, distinct from the assumption that (S-1, S) policies are used. This has the immediate implication that we can no more concentrate on the properties of the demand process alone. Since the results of this section are widely known, .see, e.g., Dirickx-Koevoets [3] and Gross-Harris [5], a brief review will suffice. We discuss the D-K model.

No reorder queue is assumed and the lead-time distribution is simply a "well-defined" distribution, say G(t), which is assumed to be independent of the other size (this is consistent with the absence of queues).

A restrictive assumption is needed to obtain workable results, namely :

Assumption : No orders can overlap, *i.e.*, if an order is outstanding the next order can only be placed after the arrival of the outstanding order. The overall cost rate is now

$$C(s, S) = C_0 (s, S) + C_1 (s, S) + C_2 (s, S),$$

since ordering costs can no more be neglected and overall costs are dependent on two critical numbers.

It can be shown that (involving results from Markov renewal theory) that

$$C_0(s, S) = \frac{C_0 + c_0\left(S - \sum_{j \leq s} j \frac{\pi_j}{\sum_{j \leq s} \pi}\right) \sum_{j \leq s} \pi_j}{\sum_{j=s+1}^{S} \pi_j (m_j - m') + m'},$$

$$C_1(s, S) = c_1 \sum_{j=0}^{S} jP_j^*,$$

$$C_2(s, S) = c_2 \sum_{j=-\infty}^{0} jP_j^*,$$

where

$$m_j = \begin{cases} \int_0^\infty t\, dG(t) \quad (= m') & j \leq s, \\ \frac{1}{\lambda} & j = s+1, \\ \frac{1}{\lambda}(1 + \sum_{k=1}^{j-s-1} \sum_{n=1}^{k} f_k^{(n)} & j > s+1 \end{cases}$$

$f_k^{(n)}$ denotes the n-fold convolution of the demand-size distribution); the π_j's are the steady state probabilities associated with the Markov chain $\{Z_n\}$ – Z_n denotes the inventory level at the time of arrival of the n-th order, and can be computed very easily (see Dirickx-Koevoets [3], Lemma 2); furthermore

$$P_j^* = \lim_{t \to \infty} P[Z(t) = j / Z(0) = i],$$

which, again, can be computed rather easily (see D-K [3], Theorem 1 and Lemma. 5).

If, for instance, $G(t) = 1 - e^{-\mu t}$, results simplify considerably.

6. Some Comparisons

Models of the type considered in Sections 1-4 (S-1, S) and of the type of Section 5 (s, S) deal with different types of methodologies. "(S-1, S)-models" can deal with complex reordering mechaisms and heavily rely on queueing theory whereas the complexities of "(s, S)-models" can be handled rather satisfactorily by using results from Markov renewal theory. For comparisons with other existing models we can refer to Dirickx-Koevoets [3] and Koevoets [6].

IV

A SPARE PARTS INVENTORY PROBLEM WITH SEASONAL FLUCTUATIONS

The purpose of this Section is to give a case study of a practical study of a practical inventory problem. This problem arose in a large agricultural company situated in Nãdudvar, East Hungary. This company is responsible to supply about 300 smaller agricultural cooperatives and companies with machines and spare parts for agricultural machines produced by the John Deere Company. The demand processes have heavy seasonal fluctuations, which makes standard methods hard to apply.

The contact between Nãdudvar and John Deere Co. has the following main characteristics. Orders can be placed every week. The lead time, *i.e.* the time between placing and receiving an order may be three weeks or three months. The first kind of orders may make up 20% of the total annual order.

The equipments arriving in Hungary are stored in a special store until they are sold. All machines and spare parts in this special store are the property of John Deere Co. Their prices are paid only when they are actually sold to some of the smaller companies. The consequence of this agreement was that Nãdudvar was not motivated to keep the inventory level low. Therefore some additional constraints on the maximum inventory level were introduced by John Deere Co. These constraints work well if the demand process is uniform, but they are unsuitable when heavy seasonal fluctuations are present.

Therefore we propose a new strategy. The requirements on the new strategy are :

— taking into account seasonal fluctuations,
— low inventory level,
— easy implementation.

As for the second demand, the inventory level is evaluated by John Deere in the following way : if the ratio (annual turnover): (average inventory level) is at least 4, then the inventory level is acceptably low.

In the new strategy we shall place orders monthly.

Let us describe our strategy. For a specific article let

$x(t)$ demand of t-th month
$S(t)$ inventory state after placing an order at the beginning of month t
$\xi(t)$ physical inventory at the end of month t.

The inventory state S(t) is the sum of the physical inventory plus the orders that has been placed up to time t. The lead time is three months S t is realised as physical inventory by the beginning of month t+3. Therefore we have

$$\xi(t+3) = S(t) - x(t) - x(t+1) - x(t+2) - x(t+3). \tag{1}$$

The optimal choice for S(t) would be such that $\xi(t+3)$ becomes 0. As at time t future demands are not known, we propose the strategy

$$S(t) = \hat{x}(t) + \hat{x}(t+1) + \hat{x}(t+2) + \hat{x}(t+3) \tag{2}$$

where $\hat{x}(t)$ denotes a suitable predicated value of x(t). If S(t) is greater than $\xi(t-1)$, then $S(t) = \xi(t-1)$, *i.e.* no order is placed.

There are not sufficient data to perform a refined statistical analysis of the past. Therefore, the predicted values are given by experts with great experience.

The computations for this strategy are very simple, and the strategy is computationally feasible-even for those 1000 articles, which make out 40 per cent of the annual capital turnover.

The simulation results have shown that the new strategy ensures a good supply with low inventory costs and it will be used in a one year experimental period.

V

RELIABILITY TYPE INVENTORY MODELS WITH ORDERING TIME LIMIT

Introduction

Most inventory models are concerned with the analysis of systems in which some kinds of costs arise, and are subject to control. But in practice the determination of shortage cost is very difficult. That is why in the early 1960's Hungarian scientists began to construct the so-called reliability type models. The inventory problem in this kind of model is to control the reliability of the system characterised by the probability that no excess demands arise in the time interval T :

$$\alpha(z,a) := P\,(\sup_{t\in T}\,(\beta_t - \delta_t(z) - a) \leqq 0), \tag{1}$$

where β_t is the cumulative demand and $\delta_t(z)$ the total delivery of stock up to the time t.

In the models studied by Prékopa (1973) and Prékopa/Kelle (1978) only the initial stock level a is the decision variable and the delivery process $(\delta_t)_{t\in T}$ is a non-controllable stochastic process. Our goal is to extend the decision rules. We proceed from the ordering time limit condition found in the management of the G.D.R. economy which is analysed by Klemm (1980), and ask for a static ordering rule, ensuring with a prescribed probability that during the time T no shortage occurs. We consider three special models.

Using Model I we show that even under very strong conditions on the demand process the criterion given by Eq. (1) generates considerable numerical inconvenience. In the two other models we take an easier criterion based on

$$\alpha_i(z,a) := P(\sup_{t\in T_i}\,(\beta_t - \delta_t(z) - a) \leqq 0),\ i = 1, \ldots, n, \tag{2}$$

obtained from Eq. (1) by decomposing T.

Model II describes a simple system with a deterministic delivery process and a stochastic demand process which may be a good adaptation to different constructions of the production plan.

Model III consists of a special stochastic delivery process and a Poisson process as a demand process.

The Delivery Process

In an inventory system with ordering time limit the replenishment action is initiated at time $t_0 = 0$. At this time the decision-maker has to order n quantities $z_1, ..., z_n$. The quantity z_i arrives after the passage of a deterministic or stochastic leadtime of $t_i - t_0 \geqq 1 > 0$ time units, *i.e.* at time t_i the order quantity $z_i \geqq 0$ is available. The quantity z_0 is ordered before t_0 and arrives in the period $(t_0, t_0 + 1)$.

Thus, the delivery process of an ordering time limit model is realised in the simple form

$$\delta_t(z) = \sum_{k=0}^{i} z_k =: v_i \text{ for } t \in T_i = \begin{cases} (1, t_1), i = 0 \\ (t_i, t_{i+1}), \ i = 1, ..., n \end{cases} \tag{3}$$

with $t_0 < t_1 < t_2 < \ ... \ < t_{n+1}$.

The Reliabilities

First of all, the demand process $(B_t)_{t \geq 0}$ may be a stochastic process with left-continuous and monotonically non-decreasing sample paths and $B_0 = 0$. If we choose a decomposition of $T = (1, t_{n+1})$ and a delivery process according to Section 2, using the inventory process

$$\eta_t(z, a) := a + \delta_t(z) - \beta_t,$$

we obtain for the reliability in view of Eq. (1)

$$\begin{aligned} \alpha\ (z, a) &= P\ [\inf_{t \in T} \eta_t(z, a) \geqq 0] \\ &= P\ [\min_{i=1, ..., n+1} \eta_{t_i - 0}(z, a) \geqq 0] \\ &= P\ [\max\ (U_1, ..., U_{n+1}) \leqq a] =: q(a/z), \end{aligned} \tag{4}$$

$$\text{where } U_k = \sum_{i=1}^{k} X_i, \ k = 1, ..., n+1 \tag{5a}$$

with

$$X_{i+1} = \begin{cases} \beta_{t_1} - z_0, \ i = 0 \\ \beta_{t_{i+1}} - \beta_{t_i} - z_i, \ i = 1, \ldots, n \end{cases} \tag{5b}$$

For the reduced reliabilities we have in view of Eq. (2)

$$\begin{aligned} \alpha_i(z,a) &= P\,[\inf_{t \in T_i} \eta_t(z,a) \geqq 0] \\ &= P\,[\eta_{t_{i+1}-0}(z,a) \geqq 0] \\ &= P\,(\beta_{t_{i+1}} \leqq a + v_i) =: p_i(a + v_i), \end{aligned} \tag{6}$$

where $p_0, p_1, \ldots, p_n$ are monotonically non-decreasing functions.

Optimisation

In the reliability type inventory models constructed by A. Prékopa an co-workers for the safety-stock level a an optimisation problem is to be solved, which we specialise to

$$\begin{aligned} &a = \min ! \\ &q(a/z) \geqq 1 - \epsilon, \end{aligned} \tag{7}$$

where q given by Eqs. (4), (5) is a monotonically non-decreasing function of a and $z \in R_+^{n+1}$ is fixed.

In the ordering time limit models the level a and the quantity z_o shall not be controlled. But for the order quantities $z_1, \ldots, z_n$ we have to solve the optimisation problem

$$\begin{aligned} &\sum_{i=0}^{n} z_i = \min ! \\ &\alpha_1(z,a) \geqq 1 - \varepsilon, \ z_i \geqq 0, \ i = 1, \ldots, n. \end{aligned} \tag{8}$$

Using Eqs. (3) and (6) we obtain an equivalent problem

$$\begin{aligned} &v_n = \min ! \\ &P_i(a + v_i) \geqq 1 - \varepsilon, \ v_{i+1} \geqq v_i \geqq 0, \ i = 1, \ldots, n \end{aligned} \tag{9}$$

and the iterative solution

$$z'_1 = \inf\ [z_i = 0 / p_i(a + z'_0 + \ldots + z'_{i-1} + z_i) \geqq 1 - \varepsilon] \tag{10}$$

$i = 1, ..., n$, where $z'_0 = z_0$ and a are prescribed.

Model I

We Consider an inventory system under the following assumptions:

(i) The demands $B_0, B_1, ..., B_n$ in periods $T'_0, T_1, ..., T_n$ for a single product are independent random variables with probability density functions $f_0, f_1, ..., f_n$.

(ii) Excess demand is backlogged. – $T'_0 = [t_0, t_1]$.

(iii) A delivery process according to Section 2 and with fixed order quantities is given.

(iv) The safety-stock level satisfying the optimization problem (7) is to be determined.

This model leads for the reliability q given by Eq. (4) with

$$X_{i+1} = B_i - z_i, \qquad i = 0, 1, ..., n \tag{11}$$

to the expression

$$q(a/z) = \int_{R(a)} \cdots \int \prod_{i=1}^{n+1} f_{i-1}(x_i + z_{i-1})\, dx_i,$$

where the region of integration

$$R(a) = (x_1, ..., x_{n+1}) / \sum_{k=1}^{i} x_k \leq a, \ i = 1, ..., n+1$$

may be transformed to R_+^{n+1} according to

$$y_1 = a - x_1,\ y_i = y_{i-1} - x_i,\ i = 2, ..., n+1.$$

As the transformed multiple integral we obtain

$$q(a/z) = \int_0^\infty f_0(a + z_0 - y_1)\, G_n(y_1, z)\, dy_1, \tag{12}$$

where the function

$$G_n(y_1, z) = \int_0^\infty \cdots \int_0^\infty \prod_{i=1}^{n} f_{iL}(y_i - y_{i+1} + z_i)\, dy_{i+1} \tag{13}$$

can generally be calculated only approximately by a quadrature formula or by Monte-Carlo methods.

An Example

In this Section we determine the optimal safety-stock level of Model I for a very special case.

We consider a decomposition of T consisting of only two parts. Let the demands B_0, B_1 obey a normal probability law with parameters

$$m_k = E(B_k),\ \sigma_k^2 = \text{var}(B_k),\ k = 0,1.$$

We use the symbol to denote the probability density function of the standard normal law, i.e.

$$\varphi(x) = (2\pi)^{-\frac{1}{2}} \exp\left(-\frac{1}{2}x^2\right),$$

and Φ denotes the corresponding distribution function. Then we have

$$G_1(y_1, z) = \int_0^\infty f_1(y_1 - y_2 + z_1)\, dy_2 = \Phi\left(\frac{y_1 + z_1 - m_1}{\sigma_1}\right).$$

Consequently, the reliability is given by

$$q(a/z) = \frac{1}{\sigma_0}\int_0^\infty \varphi\left(\frac{a + z_0 - y_1 - m_0}{\sigma_0}\right)\Phi\left(\frac{y_1 + z_1 - m_1}{\sigma_1}\right) dy_1,$$

and may be obtained as a simple expression in the case

$$z_0 = m_0,\ z_1 = m_1,\ \sigma_0 = \sigma_1 = 1$$

using the table of integrals given by Khadzhi (1971) :

$$q(a/z^0) = \frac{1}{2}\left[\Phi(a) + \Phi^2\left(\frac{a}{\sqrt{2}}\right)\right],$$

where the decision z^0 is of the form $z^0 = (m_0, m_1)$. Therefore, the optimal safety-stock level a′ is the unique solution of the reliability equation

$$\Phi(a) + \Phi^2\left(\frac{a}{\sqrt{2}}\right) = 2(1-\varepsilon). \qquad (14)$$

Model II

The inventory system of this section modifies that of Section 5 by passing from the reliability given by Eq. (1) to the reliabilities of

Eq. (2). Thus, in the Model II only the assumptions *(iii)*, *(iv)* of Model I will be changed, and T_0 will be substituted for T'_0.

(iii) A delivery process according to Section 2 with prescribed z_0 and initial stock a is given.

(iv) A decision $z' = (z'_1, \ldots, z'_n)$ solving the optimisation problem (9) is to be chosen.

Because of the assumed independence of the demands and Eq. (6) we determine the function p_i as a convolution of the density functions $f_0, f_1, \ldots, f_i$ by the recurrence formula

$$p_i(x) = \int_{-\infty}^{\infty} p_{i-1}(x-u) f_i(u)\, du$$

with $p_0' = f_0$. By $k_i(s)$ we denote the corresponding lowest quantile of order s, i.e.

$$k_i(s) = \inf(x / p_i(x) = s). \tag{15}$$

Then, in view of Eq. (9) we set

$$a + v_i^* = k_i(1-\varepsilon), \quad i = 1, \ldots, n.$$

If the sequence (p_i) is monotonically nonincreasing, i.e.,

$$p_1(x) \geqq p_2(x) \geqq \ldots \geqq p_n(x), \quad x \in R, \tag{16}$$

and holds $k_1(1-\varepsilon) = a + z_0$

then we have the optimal order quantities

$$z'_1 = k_1(1-\varepsilon) - a - z_0, \tag{17}$$

$$z'_i = k_i(1-\varepsilon) - k_{i-1}(1-\varepsilon), \; i = 2, \ldots, n.$$

In the normal case

$$p_i(x) = \Phi\left(\frac{x - \tilde{m}_i}{\tilde{\sigma}_i}\right), \quad \tilde{m}_i = \sum_{j=0}^{i} m_j, \quad \sigma_i^2 = \sum_{j=0}^{i} \sigma_j^2$$

it follows immediately that

$$k_i(s) = \tilde{m}_i + \tilde{\sigma}_i\, k(s), \tag{18}$$

where k(s) fulfil the equation

$$\Phi\,[k(s)] = s,$$

and the Eq. (17) under $z_0 = m_0$ may be reduced to

$$z'_1 = m_1 - a + \tilde{\sigma}_1\, k(1-\varepsilon) \quad (19)$$

$$z'_i = m_i + (\sigma_i - \sigma_{i-1})\, k(1-\varepsilon),\; i = 2, \ldots, n.$$

If Eq. (16) is not satisfied, we obtain from Eq. (10) for the optimal order quantities

$$z'_i = \begin{cases} 0, \text{ for } a + z'_0 + \ldots + z'_{i-1} \geq \tilde{m}_i + \tilde{\sigma}_i\, k(1-\varepsilon) \\ \tilde{m}_i + \tilde{\sigma}_i\, k(1-\varepsilon) - (a + z'_0 + \ldots + z'_{i-1}), \text{ else.} \end{cases} \quad (20)$$

The reader who is interested in numerical examples and economical interpretations of Model II is referred to Girlich (1980) and Klemm (1980).

Model III

In our last Section we consider an inventory system where the inventory is replenished at random delivery.

We shall proceed from the following assumptions :

(i) The demand process is a Poisson process $[N(t)]_{t\geq 0}$ with parameter λ.

(ii) Excess demand is backlogged.

(iii) A delivery process according to Section 2 is given, where the delivery time t_i is uniformly distributed between r_i and $r_{i+1} = r_i + \frac{1}{n}$, i=1, ..., n, and r_1=1.

(iv) A decision $z' = (z'_1, \ldots, z'_n)$ solving the optimisation problem (9) is to be chosen, where z_0 and a are prescribed.

In order to find the optimal order quantities, we have to determine the p_i using the formula of total probability

$$p_i(v) = \int_{t_0}^{\infty} P[N(t_{i+1} - 0) \leq v / t_{i+1} = t]\, d\, P(t_{i+1} \leq t).$$

For $v = m \in N$ we obtain

$$p_i(m) = \int_{t_{i+1}}^{I_{i+2}} \exp(-\lambda t) \sum_{j=o}^{m} \frac{(\lambda t)^j}{j!} n\, dt$$

$$= \frac{n}{\lambda} \exp[-\lambda(1+\frac{i}{n})] \sum_{j=0}^{m} [h\{j/\lambda(1+\frac{i}{n})\} - e^{-\frac{\lambda}{n}} h\{j/\lambda(1+\frac{i+1}{n})\}]$$

where $h(j/y) := \sum_{k=0}^{j} \frac{y^k}{k!}$. (21)

If we successively compute $p_i(m)$ for m = 0, 1, 2, ... we arrive at a number n_i with the property

$$P_i(n_i - 1) < 1 - \varepsilon,\ P_i(n_i) \geqq 1 - \varepsilon. \quad (22)$$

These numbers $n_1, n_2, \ldots, n_n$ determine the optimal order quantities in view of Eq. (10) and $z'_0 = z_0$ to

$$z'_i = \begin{cases} 0, \text{ for } a + z'_0 + \ldots + z'_{i-1} \geqq n_i \\ n_i - (a + z'_0 + \ldots + z'_{i-1}), \text{ else.} \end{cases} \quad (23)$$

Finally, we give a numerical example [cf. Küenle (1980)]

$$\lambda = 2,\ n = 4,\ 1 = \frac{1}{4},\ \varepsilon = 0, 1 \quad (24)$$

m\i	*1*	*2*	*3*	*4*
0	0,290	0,175	0,106	0,065
1	0,645	0,479	0,344	0,241
2	0,867	0,743	0,610	0,482
3	0,960	0,898	0,809	0,698
4		0,966	0,921	0,863
5				0,950
n_i	3	4	4	5

For a + Z_0 = 3, it follows from (23) $z'_1 = z'_3 = 0$, $z'_2 = z'_4 = 1$.

VI

A SIMPLE METHOD OF DETERMINING NEARLY OPTIMUM ORDER QUANTITIES FOR A MULTI-PRODUCT SINGLE-SUPPLIER SYSTEM

In this Section a simple method has been presented for determining nearly optimum order quantities for products which are jointly procured from a single supplier. The orders are placed upon the supplier at equal intervals (T), and, each product is replenished at equal intervals which is restricted to be an integer multiple of T.

An example has been solved to illustrate the method.

Introduction

The problem of determining economic order quantities for a multi-product single supplier system is akin to the problem of determining economic packaging frequency for an unpackaged product which is packaged into a number of packaging sizes immediately after manufacture. In the published literature it has been invariably assumed that the cost of placing a purchase order consists of two components : one which is independent of the number of products on order and the other which depends on the products being ordered in a particular order. Hence, reduction in cost can be achieved by ordering products jointly. In the published papers, it was assumed that orders are placed on the supplier at equal time intervals, see Goyal (1973, 1974, 1979), Nocturne (1973), Shu (1971) and Silver (1976). Andres *et al.* (1976) pointed out that when there are more than two products it may not be always optimal to place orders at equal time intervals, furthermore, it may not even be optimal to order each product at equal time intervals. However, in this section it is being assumed that orders are placed at equal time intervals on the supplier in order to have a simpler operating policy for the buyer as well as for the supplier.

Silver (1976) suggested a heuristic method of determining economic packaging frequencies of jointly replenished items. His method was, however, improved upon by Goyal *et al.* (1979). In this section a further improvement in Silver's heuristic method is being incorporated.

An example has been solved and the suggested method has been compared with other heuristic methods.

The Mathematical Models

The following assumptions are being made :

1. Lead time for procuring supplies is zero.
2. Stock outs are not permitted.
3. Time horizon is infinite.
4. Minimisation of cost is taken as the criterion of optimality.
5. The purchase orders are placed at equal time intervals.
6. Demand for each product is constant over time.
7. Each product is ordered at equal time intervals.

The following notations are being used in this section:

n = number of items
s = that part of cost of placing a purchase order which is independent of the number of items on order
T = time interval between successive purchase orders (in years), for the i th item
d_i = demand per year
h_i = stock holding cost per item per year
S_i = that part of the cost of placing a purchase order which must be incurred whenever the item is ordered
D_i = the order quantity.

Let the i th product be ordered in every K_i the purchase order (Note that K_i is restricted to have only integer values), then the total annual variable cost, $V(T, K_i)$ is given by

$$V(T.K_i) = (S + \sum_{i=1}^{n} S_i / K_i)/T + \frac{T}{2} \sum_{i=1}^{n} Q_i H_i K_i \qquad (1)$$

At a given value of T, the variable cost for the i th item can be minimised by obtaining $K_i = K_i(T)$ from the following condition:

$$K_i(T).[K_i(T) - I] \leq \frac{2S_i}{Q_i h_i T^2} \leq K_i(T).[K_i(T) + 1] \qquad (2)$$

(See Goyal (1974) for the derivation of such a condition).

For a given set of $K_i(T)$ values the minimum annual variable cost is given by :

$$V^*[K_i(T)] = [2\{S + \sum_{i=1}^{n} S_i / K_i(T)\} \{\sum_{i=1}^{n} Q_i h_i K_i(T)\}]^{\frac{1}{2}} \qquad (3)$$

The economic order quantity for the i th product is given by:

$$D_i^*(T) = Q_i [2\{S+\sum_{i=1}^{n} S_i / K_i(T)\} / \sum_{i=1}^{n} Q_i h_i K_i(T)]^{\frac{1}{2}} \qquad (4)$$

Silver (1976) suggested that in order to determine K_i values by (2), first identify the item for which the ratio $2S_i/Q_ih_i$ is least (he called it as item 1) and then determine $K_i(T)$ value for each product by (2) after substituting $[2(S+S_i)/Q_ih_i]$ for T^2.

Goyal *et al.*, suggested that the $K_i(T)$ value for each product be obtained after substituting least value of $[2(S + S_i)/Q_ih_i]$ for T^2 in (2).

Their suggested approach resulted in equally good or better results as compared to Silver's method for the 40 examples examined by them.

In this section the following approach is being suggested for determining T^2 value for substitution in the condition given by (2) for determining $K_i(T)$.

Step 1. Determine $\text{Min}_i \dfrac{[2(S + S_i)]}{Q_i h_i} = T_0^2$.

Step 2. Arrange products in ascending order of $2S_i/Q_ih_i$ ratio.

Step 3. Determine the m th product which satisfies the condition

$$\frac{2S_m}{Q_m h_m} \le T_0^2 \le \frac{2S_{m+1}}{Q_m h_m}$$

Step 4. Determine T^2 as follows :

$$T^2 = \frac{2(S+\sum_{i=1}^{m} S_i)}{\sum_{i=1}^{m} Q_i h_i}$$

The value of T^2 as obtained in step (4) is then substituted in the condition given by (2) and hence $K_i(T)$ values for each product is obtained. The minimum annual cost and the order quantity for each product can be obtained on applying (3) and (4) respectively.

An Example

The data for the example is given in Table 4.6.

Table 4.6
Data for the Example

Item No.	S_i	$Q_i h_i$
1	8	20000
2	13	30000
3	10	18000
4	9	15000
5	8	10000
6	10	4800
7	8	2000
8	8	1500
9	9	1125
10	8	560

S = 45 per order

Determination of K_i values by Silver's Method *Method—1*

$$T^2 = \frac{2(S+S_i)}{Q_i h_i} = \frac{2(45+8)}{20000} = 0.0053$$

(On applying the decision rule (2) the $K_i(T)$ value are obtained as 1, 1, 1, 1, 1, 1, 1, 1, 2, 2 and 2 for i = 1, 2, ---10. The annual cost of this policy equals 2560.47.

Determination of K_i values by Goyal and Belton's Method *Method—2*

$T^2 = \text{Min}\,[2(S + S_i)/Q_i h_i] = 0.003866$ on applying the decision rule (2) the $K_i(T)$ values are obtained as 1, 1, 1, 1, 1, 1, 2, 2, 2 and 3. The annual cost of this policy equals 2534.51.

Determination of K_i values by the method given in this section

Mehtod–3

$$\text{As} \quad \frac{2S_5}{Q_5 h_5} \leq 0.003866 \leq \frac{2S_6}{Q_6 h_6}$$

$$\text{so} \quad T^2 = \frac{2(S + \sum_{i=1}^{5} S_i)}{\sum_{i=1}^{5} Q_i h_i} = 0.002$$

The following $K_i(T)$ values are obtained on applying the decision rule given by (2) : 1, 1, 1, 1, 1, 2, 2, 2, 3 and 4 for i = 1, 2, ---, 10. The annual cost of this policy equals 2528.72. The order quantities can be obtained on applying (4).

The Table 4.7 gives the summary of results obtained for a sample of 40 test problems :

Table 4.7

Summary of the Results of 40 Test Problems

Number of Problems		*Number of examples where optimal solution was achieved by method*			*Number of examples having penalty cost less than 0.05% by method*			*Average 7 Cost penalty by method*		
		1	*2*	*3*	*1*	*2*	*3*	*1*	*2*	*3*
4	10	4	4	8	6	6	9	0.27	0.27	0.10
5	10	2	3	5	4	5	9	0.80	0.50	0.12
10	10	1	2	4	2	3	8	1.30	0.75	0.20
20	10	0	0	2	0	1	6	2.00	0.91	0.31

Concluding Remarks

The method suggested in this section is capable of achieving nearly optimal order quantities for items procured from a single supplier as is shown by Table 4.7.

VII

AN IMPROVED PROCEDURE FOR DETERMINING INVENTORY HOLDING COSTS

Introduction

The following summarizes some results from analytical models and from simulation experiments reported in two previous sections [Grubbström, 1980; Grubbström, Thorstenson, 1980]. Apart from this is provided a new analysis of the simulation results.

The objective of the method set forth has been to provide evidence that usual accounting principles tend to give an under -estimation of the capital costs associated with inventories and work-in-progress and to point at ways in which traditional accounting procedures might be improved.

The ultimate consequence of decisions in a manufacturing firm are to be found in the form of payments between the firm and its environment. Decisions that have no effect on the monetary stream at some point in time are of no economic importance. In practice, analyses of payment streams (cash flows) are usually carried out for the few infrequent decisions associated with substantial payment consequence, i.e. major investments of different kinds etc. It is argued, however, that payment consequences of the many small everyday production decision also should be analyzed along similar lines. Payments are characterized by their amount, their temporal allocation and sometimes by additional stochastic properties.

It can be shown [Williams, Nassar, 1966] that the only consistent measure evaluating a payment stream, if certain basic axioms are to be satisfied, is the *net present value (NPV)* or some positive montonic transformation of this value. Any such transformation would be equally useful from the point of view of making correct decisions, since the ranking of alternatives will be preserved.

However, one simple transformation translating the net present value into a constant continuous stream of payments, the *annuity stream (AS)*, has the advantage that this stream usually can be given a direct concrete economic interpretation.

If given a series of payments a_0, a_1, ..., occurring at the times t_0, t_1, ..., the *NPV* of this series is defined as :

$$NPV = \sum_{i=0}^{\infty} a_i \, e^{-\rho t_i} \tag{1}$$

where ρ is the continuous interest rate. The annuity stream providing the same *NPV* is obtained as :

$$AS = \rho NPV = \rho \sum_{i=0}^{\infty} a_i \, e^{-\rho t_i} \tag{2}$$

which for a series of constant payments at constant intervals becomes :

$$AS = \frac{\rho a}{1 - e^{-\rho T}} = a\left(\frac{1}{T} + \frac{\rho}{2} + \frac{\rho^2 T}{12} - \frac{\rho^4 T^3}{720} \ldots\right) \tag{3}$$

where a is the amount of each payment and T the time interval between each pair of consecutive payments. The right-hand member being a Maclaurin expansion of the middle member, provides an economic interpretation; the first term being the payment averaged out over the time interval (such as an average depreciation), the second an interest on the average capital associated with this payment, the third an interest on interest, etc. For example, with an interest rate of $\rho = 20$ per cent per annum and an interval of $T = 10$ years, the first and second terms each will give a contribution of *10* per cent (of a), the third a positive contribution of *3.3* per cent and the fourth a negative contribution of *–0.22* per cent. The first two terms would then provide an error of *13.5* per cent (too low) and the first three terms an error of *0.9* per cent (too high).

In the case of production situations in which capital is tied up in inventory and work-in-progress, the first term would correspond to an average profit and the second to a first approximation of the inventory holding costs.

Analytical Models and Hypotheses

The basic idea in the foregoing section to evaluate payment streams associated with production decisions was applied in

[Grubbström, 1980] to some simple analytical models of inventory theory.

In Figure 4.1 two elementary cases are shown. In *(a)* we have the standard situation with a periodical discrete replenishment and constant demand and in *(b)* its mirror image with a constant production rate and demand taking place in periodic batches.

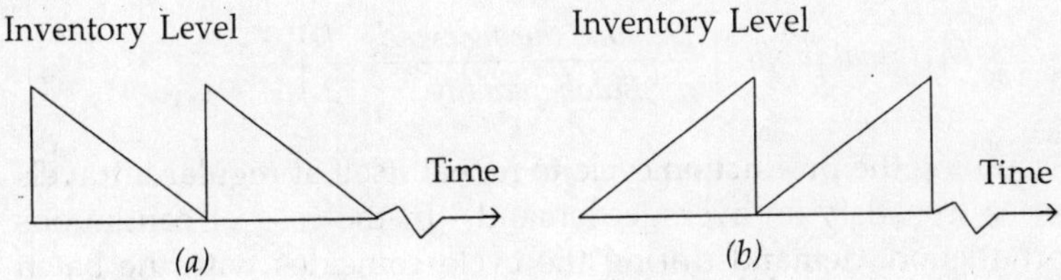

Fig. 4.1 : Two Elementary Inventory Models

Applying the *AS*-principle to these two cases shows that inventories in case *(a)* should be evaluated at unit production (purchase) cost and in *(b)* at unit sales price. Although the *(b)*-section shows an unrealistic case, the example does point out that the correct evaluation depends on characteristics of the production process.

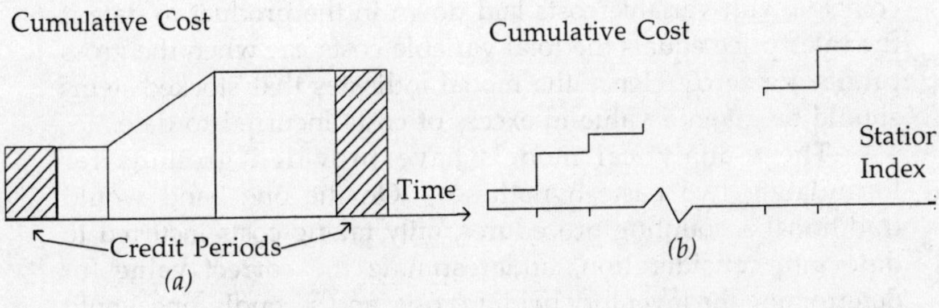

Fig. 4.2 : Batch and Line Production Models

Two other analytical models are depicted in Figure 4.2, the first being a batch production model *(a)* and the second a line production model *(b)*. In the batch case, material is purchased in the beginning of the cycle, after being in inventory for sometime it is manufactured during which it increases its value, and finally it is stocked and sold. Also there is one credit period provided by the supplier and one provided to the customer. The figure shows the cumulative cost to date.

If the *AS*-principle is applied to the batch case, it may be shown that the inventories on the average should be evaluated above average cost by an amount of :

$$\text{Marginal profit.}\left(\frac{\text{Demand during cycle}}{\text{Batch quantity}}-\frac{1}{2}\right) \tag{4}$$

assuming the production cycle to repeat itself at regular intravels so as to satisfy an average demand. In the case of continuous production, demand during the cycle coincides with the batch quantity which implies that in such a case the inventories should be assessed at a level of half of the marginal profits above their average cost. In the normal case we would have a cycle longer than the interval satisfied by the batch (in any case longer than half of this interval) which means that inventories certainly should be ascribed values above average production cost.

In the *(b)*-section of Figure 4.2 is shown the case of values being added to the product at different stations in a production line. Applying the *AS*-prinçiple shows that inventories at a particular station should be evaluated at sales price less remaining variable costs to be incurred at later stations. This value will coincide with variable costs laid down in the product to date if the sales price equals the total variable costs, *i.e.* when the gross profits are zero. Hence the model indicates that stocked items should be given a value in excess of costs incurred to date.

These analytical models have provided grounds for formulating two basic hypotheses. On the one hand would traditional accounting procedures, only taking costs incurred to date into consideration, underestimate the correct value for determining the inventory holding costs, and secondly, one would anticipate that the differential which should be added to costs laid down would increase with the profit margin of the product. In order to test these two hypotheses some simulation experiments were carried out [Grubbström, Thorstenson, 1980].

Simulation Models

In order to further investigate the impact of considering payments when evaluating inventory holding costs we carried out a simulation study thereby regarding stochastic elements underlying the payment consequences. The cases studied include two different production system structures as shown in Figure 4.3 where circles denote production stations and triangles denote intermediate buffer stocks and inventories—for finished goods. Structure *(a)* is a pure production line in which raw material is at first purchased and then machined at three consecutive work stations after which finished products are stocked into a final inventory in order to satisfy demand. The second structure *(b)* consists of two parallel sub-lines in which raw material is purchased and the components machined at one work station in each sub-line. The two sub-lines then merge at a third work station, *e.g.* a point of assembly, whereupon the finished products are stocked in an inventory from which they finally are sold.

For each of these two structures the simulations have been run with respect to two different kinds of models, namely on the one hand a queueing model using Erlang-distributed interarrival and service times, and on the other hand a model based on the physical flows between the stocks and inventories.

The calculation of economic consequences for the four cases thus created has been carried out both in accordance with standard

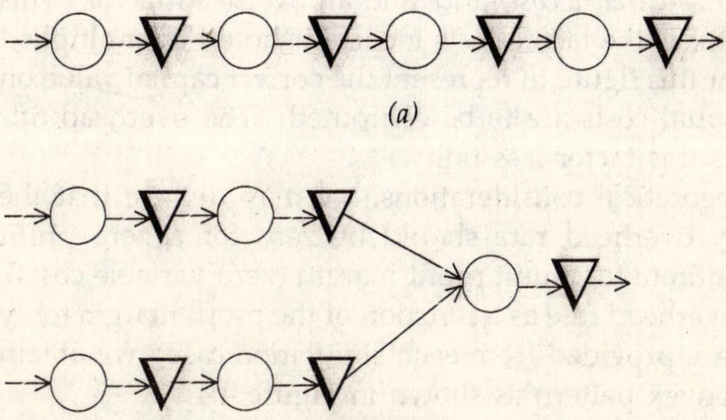

Fig. 4.3 : Two Basic Production Structures

accounting procedures, first using the value added (at variable cost) as a base for evaluating inventory holding costs, and secondly, by considering the payments that occur at different points in time. The ultimate objective of these computations has been to test the basic hypotheses stated above; on the one hand that standard procedures underestimate the true inventory holding costs, and on the other that this underestimation increases with the profit margin.

A number of variations have been included in the cost structures and in the stochastic properties of the different models. The economic parameters introduced consist of unit purchasing costs and unit production costs, a given interest rate and a unit revenue parameter. No credits have been allowed.

Results of Simulations

As reported in [Grubbström, Thorstenson, 1980] the first of our basic hypotheses was given an overwhelming support in all cases simulated. This was shown using a *t*-parameter test and a Wilcoxon test, both of which provided high levels of significance in favour of the presumption that traditional practices produce too low holding costs.

In this report, as mentioned earlier, we shall look further into the simulation results with regard to our second basic hypothesis. Our interest in this respect is to determine characteristics of the relationship between the profit margin, defined as *(price-variable cost)/price* and an overhead factor. This overhead factor is the factor costs incurred should be multiplied by in order for this figure to represent the correct capital value on which the capital costs are to be computed. The overhead *rate* used below is this factor less unity.

From theoretical considerations, we may deduce that the compensatory overhead rate should be zero for a zero profit margin and infinite for a unit profit margin (zero variable costs). Plotting the overhead rate as a function of the profit margin (only three points are provided from each simulation case), we obtain the typical convex pattern as shown in Figure 4.4

Based on analytical considerations the following mathematical relationship is hypothesized :

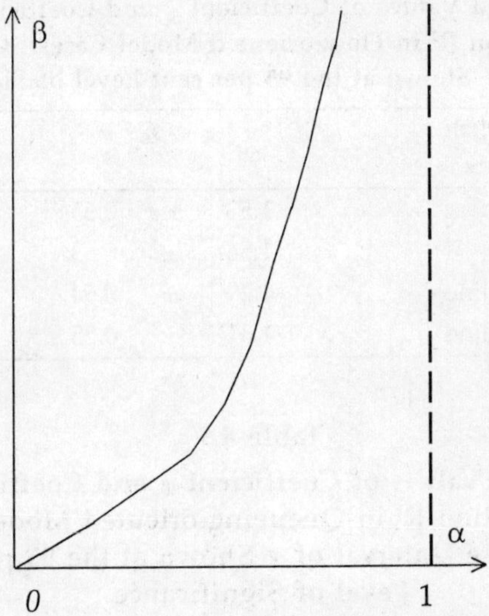

Fig. 4.4 : Typical Overhead Rate as Function of Marginal Profit

$$\beta = \ell \frac{\alpha}{1-\alpha} \tag{5}$$

where α is the profit margin, β the overhead rate and ℓ a constant depending on other circumstances than the profit margin. It is clear that $\alpha = 0$ yields $\beta = 0$ and that $\alpha \to 1$ requires $\beta \to \infty$ which therefore satisfies our theoretical requirements. The proportional relation between $\alpha(1-\alpha)^{-1}$ and β may then easily be tested by regression analysis from which the constant will be estimated and a coefficient of determination computed.

Applying this procedure to each of the simulation results from the four cases of flow-oriented models (line production and two sub-line cases, each with two different ranges of stochastic disturbances) and from the twelve cases of queueing-oriented models (line production and two sub-line cases, each with two different mean service rates and three different values of the Erlang parameter determining the shape of the service time distribution) gave the results summarized in Tables 4.8 and 4.9.

Table 4.8

Estimated Values of Coefficient ℓ and Coefficient of Determination R^2 in Flow-oriented Model Cases. Confidence Interval of ℓ Shown at the 95 per cent Level of Significance

Case	*Production structure*	ℓ			R^2
1	Line	1.53	±	0.63	0.995
2	Line	1.56	±	0.63	0.996
3	Two sub-line	1.29	±	0.54	0.995
4	Two sub-line	1.31	±	0.55	0.995

Table 4.9

Estimated Values of Coefficient ℓ and Coefficient of Determination R^2 in Queueing-oriented Model Cases. Confidence Interval of ℓ Shown at the 95 per cent Level of Significance

Case	*Production structure*	ℓ			R^2
1	Line	5.33	±	0.96	0.999
2	Line	4.34	±	0.75	0.999
3	Line	4.26	±	0.67	0.999
4	Line	5.16	±	1.04	0.999
5	Line	4.94	±	0.93	0.999
6	Line	4.43	±	0.73	0.999
7	Two sub-line	5.01	±	0.70	0.999
8	Two sub-line	3.77	±	0.50	0.999
9	Two sub-line	3.80	±	0.43	0.999
10	Two sub-line	4.76	±	0.79	0.999
11	Two sub-line	4.47	±	0.65	0.999
12	Two sub-line	3.89	±	0.46	0.999

From studying the results shown in these two tables we can immediately draw the conclusion that on the one hand, the mathematical approach given by (5) provides an almost perfect relationship for explaining the dependence of the overhead rate β on the profit margin α (in no case does the coefficient of determination fall below 99.5 per cent), and on the other that the two different kinds of models (flow-oriented versus queueing-oriented) produce significantly different estimated values of the coefficient ℓ, whereas this value varies only slightly between the different stochastic parameter values within each of these two sets of cases ($1.29 \leqq \ell \leqq 1.56$ in flow-oriented cases; $3.77 \leqq \ell \leqq 5.33$ in queueing-oriented cases).

An intuitive explanation of the difference in ℓ =values is the following. In the flow-oriented cases total holding costs represent a greater share of total costs than in the queueing-oriented cases. This is due to structural discrepancies between the two models. The higher ratio of holding costs over total cost implies that a lower overhead rate β should be applied in order to arrive at a correct capital value, *i.e.* a correct capital cost for a given profit margin. Therefore , the values of ℓ, which depend on other circumstances than the profit margin, such as the characteristics of the particular model that is being used, should be of a higher magnitude in the queueing-oriented cases.

Future Research

The results reported here and in the two previous sections referred to indicate that evaluation of payment consequences from production systems may have a significant impact on the determination of capital costs of work-in-progress and inventory. Since the interest of industry in many ways focuses on these costs future research within this area would be highly momentous.

In the first place a wider spectrum of cases should be given care attention both by using an analytical approach and by using simulation approaches as the cases studied have been limited with respect to configuration as well as complexity.

In the second place further sophistication should be brought into the models, thereby enabling the possibility of drawing conclusions from more realistic settings. This could be achieved by means of simulation utilizing existing production simulation models such as the on described in [Andersson, Jönsson, 1979] in which production control in a job-shop is based on material requirements planning.

Finally, an important line of research would be to develop practical accounting procedures based on the ideas presented here that could be applied in industry. Essentially these procedures would have to be simple, compatible with traditional accounting and easy to implement.

VIII

RELIABILITY TYPE INVENTORY MODELS FOR RANDOM DELIVERY PROCESS

Inventory models are formulated in which the order given for the supply of a period arrives until the end of the period but not at one occasion—as supposed usually—but in random time points of the period in random amounts. We give the initial stock level that ensures a continuous material supply in the whole period on a given probability level. Such models have been constructed by some Hungarian authors. We give generalisations of these models which we need for special applications.

A Practical Inventory Problem and its Model

First we give a general model formulation of an inventory control problem. The factory considered has continuous production and a periodic review inventory system. At every review point an order is given for the supply of the continuous demand of a period with length T, say [O, T]. This order amount is denoted by C. The supplier undertakes to deliver the amount C until the end of the period, but it is not to be forced to deliver it in a given time point. There is a typical case in which the delivery happens not at one occasion, as it is assumed by the conventional inventory models, but in random amounts in n equidistant time points of the period [O, T]. These delivery time points are usually randomly disturbed, too. The factory plans an initial stock as safety stock for each period to protect itself against the random disturbances in the delivery and demand process. The problem is how to give the minimal level of the initial stock which ensures the continuous supply in the whole period on a given service level.

We formulate a general version of chance constrained inventory models, the so-called reliability type inventory model for m different commodities as follows

$$\text{minimize } f(\underline{M}), \qquad \text{subject to}$$

$$P\left(\sup_{0 \leqq t \leqq T} \left\{\xi_j(t) - \eta_j(t)\right\} \leqq M_j;\ j = 1, \ldots, m\right) \geqq 1 - \varepsilon \tag{1.1}$$

$$\underline{0} \leq \underline{M}, \ \underline{M} \in D.$$

where ξ_j (t) denotes the cumulative amount of demand and η_j (t) the cumulative amount of delivery in the time interval [o, t] ($0 \leqq t \leqq T$) for commodity j (j = 1, ..., m), which are stochastic processes; $f(\underline{M})$ is the cost function depending on the initial stock level vector $\underline{M}' = (M_1, \ldots, M_m)$; D is an m-dimensional set, defined by the constraints (*e.g.* capacity or investment constraint). The service level is given by the prescribed joint probability $1 - \varepsilon$ of the continuous material supply in [O, T], which is formulated in the chance constraint.

The first model of this type was formulated by A. Prékopa (1965) and M. Ziermann (1963). Later on some other papers e.g. Z. László (1973), A. Móritz (1978) were published, containing solution methods for the one-commodity version of this model under different assumptions concerning the stochastic processes $\xi(t)$ and $\eta(t)$. A more sophisticated multi-commodity version of this model was published by A. Prékopa—P. Kelle (1978).

We have examined such type of problems in a textile factory and in a steel works. For the solution of the practical problems we have given new models of the demand and delivery process which will be discussed in this section.

Approximation of the Delivery Process by an Empirical Distribution Function with Random Jumps

In the published models of random delivery process it is usually assumed, that the deliveries can occur in each point of the interval [O, T] with the same probability. If there are n time points of deliveries, they are considered as the elements of an ordered sample $t_1 < t_2 < \ldots < t_n$ taken from a uniform distribution on [O, T].

This is usually an appropriate approximation in our case, too. However, for the amounts delivered at one occasion we allow any kind of distribution, so we can approximate them by help of the statistical data of earlier observations and other informations. This is a generalisation of earlier models. Here the amount delivered at the time point t is a random variable denoted by β_i / η.

Thus our model of the delivery process is

$$\eta(t) = \begin{cases} 0, \text{ if } 0 \leq t \leq t_1 \\ \frac{1}{n}\sum_{i-1}^{k} \beta_i, \text{ if } t_k < t \leq t_{k+1} (k = 1, \ldots, n) \end{cases} \tag{2.1}$$

$[t_{n+1} = T]$, which can be regarded as a generalised empirical distribution function of the uniform distribution in [O, T] with random jumps β_i / n. This stochastic process will be denoted by $F\frac{\beta}{n}(t)$.

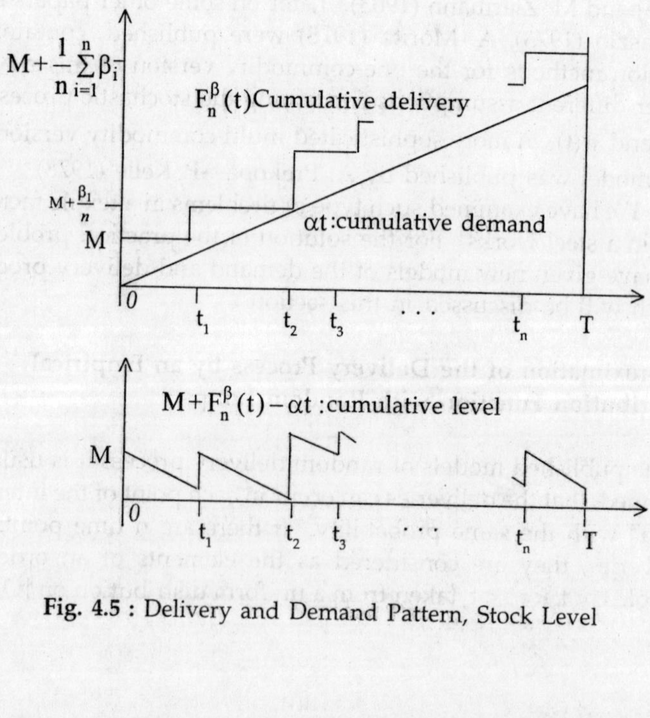

Fig. 4.5 : Delivery and Demand Pattern, Stock Level

First we consider only one commodity and a demand with constant intensity $\alpha > 0$, thus

$$\xi(t) = \alpha t \quad (0 \leq t \leq T) \tag{2.2}$$

The shape of the cumulative delivery, the cumulative demand and the stock level is illustrated on Figure 4.5.

For the solution of the model of type (1.1) the main problem is to give the probability distribution of the random variable

$$\sup_{0 \leq t \leq T} \left\{ \alpha^{t} - F_n^{\beta}(t) \right\} \tag{2.3}$$

This is a generalised version of the well-known Kolmogorov-Smirnov statistic used for statistical tests. We can prove the following theorem [owing to the extent of the proof we can only refer to P. Kelle (1979)] :

Theorem 1. If the random variables $\beta_i (i = 1, \ldots, n)$ are interchangeable, *i.e.* all of their n! permutations have the same joint probability distribution (or a special case when they are independent, identically distributed), then

$$P\left(\sup_{0 \leq t \leq T} \left\{ \alpha t - F_n^{\beta}(t) \right\} \leq M \right) = 1 - \left(1 - \frac{M}{\alpha}\right)^n -$$

$$- \frac{M}{\alpha} \sum_{k=1}^{n} \binom{n}{k} \int_0^{n(\alpha T - M)} \left(\frac{M + \frac{x}{n}}{\alpha} \right)^{k-1} \left(1 - \frac{M + \frac{x}{n}}{\alpha} \right)^{n-k} dH_k(x) \tag{2.4}$$

where $H_k(x)$ denotes the distribution function of

$$\sum_{i=1}^{k} \beta_i \qquad (k = 1, \ldots, n).$$

This model allows, that the amount ordered might not be totally delivered up to time T as it occurs sometimes in practice, too. The total fulfilment of the order can be prescribed. In this case the random variables β_i $(i = 1, \ldots, n)$ are not independent but in some cases they are interchangeable, for example in a model of A. Prékopa (1965).

The direct application of Theorem 1 is possible for planning the initial stock of a commodity if we have information concerning the distribution function of the amounts that will be delivered, and if we know the demand intensity α of the planning period [O,T]

Random Intensity of Demand

In the time point of the decision-making, the production intensity of the future planning period can often be only roughly estimated. In this case we consider the demand rate α as a random variable which has a distribution function G(x). For a random delivery process described in the previous section the initial stock level of a commodity can be given as the solution of the following equality.

$$\int_0^\infty P\left(\sup_{0\leq t\leq T}\left\{xt - F_n^{\beta}(t)\right\} \leq M \middle| \alpha = x\right) dG(x) = 1-\varepsilon. \qquad (3.1)$$

This is a special case of Model (1.1). The left-hand side of Eq. (3.1) is a monoton increasing function of the initial stock level M, thus Eq. (3.1) holds for the minimal M which ensures the continuous supply in the whole planning period with probability $1-\varepsilon$.

The demanded amount of the different commodities usually depend on each other. If we can estimate the joint probability distribution of the demand rates for a group of basic materials, then we can give a more accurate joint planning method of the initial stocks. We suppose a random supply of each material according to Model (2.1) with different parameters n_j and random variables β_i^j ($i = 1, ..., n_j$) which will be assumed to be stochastically independent for different materials (for different values of j, j = 1, ..., m). The dependence in the demand rates will be considered. Let $V(\underline{x})$ denote the joint probability distribution function of the demand rate vector $\underline{\alpha}' = (\alpha_1, ..., \alpha_m)$. The cost optimal vector of the initial stocks $\underline{M}' = (M_1, ..., M_m)$ is the solution of Model (1.1) with the reliability constraint

$$\int_{R_m^+} \prod_{j=1}^{m} \left[P\left(\sup_{0\leq t\leq T}\left\{x_j t - F_{n_j}^{\beta^j}(t)\right\} \leq M_j \middle| \alpha_j = x_j\right) \right] dV(\underline{x}) \geq 1-\varepsilon \qquad (3.2)$$

where R_m^+ denotes the positive orthant of the m-dimensional Euclidean space. The set of vectors $\underline{M}$ satisfying Inequality (3.2) is in many special cases a convex set, as it has been shown by P. Kelle (1979). This enables us to find the global optima of Model (1.1) for a convex set of constraints D and a convex cost function f ($\underline{M}$).

The above methods are too complicated and time consuming for the less important items of the production, so we want to give a simple formula for the approximate solution of Eq. (3.1). If the delivery amounts are approximately the same C/n at the different random time points of delivery, then the input process can be approximated by the empirical distribution function of the uniform distribution on [0,1] like by A. Prékopa (1965) and M. Ziermann (1963). T=1 and C=1 can be reached by an appropriate choice of the units, so this will be assumed in the following part of this section. We can apply the following asymptotic distribution well known in statistics :

$$\lim_{n\to\infty} P\left[\sup_{0\leq t\leq 1}\left\{\left(1+\frac{h}{\sqrt{n}}\right)t-F_n(t)\right\}\leq\frac{v}{\sqrt{n}}\right]=1-c^{-2v(v-h)} \qquad (3.3)$$

where F_n (t) denotes the empirical distribution function of the uniform distribution on [0,1] :

$$F_n(t)=\begin{cases}0, \text{ if } 0 \leq t \leq t_1,\\ k/n, \text{ if } t_k < t \leq t_{k+1}, \; k=1, \ldots, n-1\\ 1, \text{ if } t_n < t \leq 1.\end{cases} \qquad (3.4)$$

Substituting $\alpha = 1 + h/\sqrt{n}$ and $M = v/\sqrt{n}$ Eq. (3.3) we can get the following approximation for finite values of n

$$P\left(\sup_{0\leq t\leq 1}\{\alpha t - F_n(t)\} \leq M\right) \approx 1-e^{-2nM(M+1-\alpha)} \qquad (3.5)$$

for $0 < M < \alpha - 1$. Here α means the ratio of the demanded and the delivered amount in the planning period. Compared to the exact values calculated by means of Eq. (2.4) we have found that in the range of the usual service level 0.75 to 0.97 the approximate formula gives a probability 1 to 10 per cent less than the exact one for n=10. Here and for n<10 n numerical correction can be applied. By greater values of n we have a better approximation. Thus the solution of Eq. (3.1) can be approximated for deterministic α by the following simple formula

$$M \approx \frac{\alpha-1}{2}+\sqrt{\left(\frac{\alpha-1}{2}\right)^2+\frac{1}{2n}\,\ell n\frac{1}{\varepsilon}} \qquad (3.6)$$

which is a generalised version of the formula given by A. Prékopa (1965) and M. Ziermann (1963).

If α is a random variable, then the approximate value of the left-hand side of Eq. (3.1) is

$$1-e^{-2nM(M+1)}\,E\left[e^{2nM\alpha}\right]. \qquad (3.7)$$

where E means the expectation. For given distribution of α Eq. (3.1) can be solved by a numerical method, having the expectation , for given M. In the most important case, however as α has a normal distribution, by elementary calculations we can get the approximate solution in an explicit form :

$$M \approx \frac{m-1}{2(1-ns^2)}+\sqrt{\left[\frac{m-1}{2(1-ns^2)}\right]^2+\frac{1}{2n(1-ns^2)}\,\ell n\frac{1}{\varepsilon}} \qquad (3.8)$$

for $s<1/\sqrt{n}$, where m means the expectation m – i s means the standard deviation of α (assuming ℓ=1 and C=1). These parameters are usually easily available, they are estimated in the course of demand forecasting.

Application of the Models

The application of the above models is in progress in a big Hungarian textile factory and in a Hungarian iron and steel works. Both enterprises have had data management systems for stock control, in course of which all delivery and demand time points and amounts are registered and studied on magnetic tapes. These historical data are the ways and means to choose and to fit the appropriate model for the planned output process of each item.

We need some supplies at pro rata, such as required service level. The future suggests possibilities and demands can be only roughly estimated for most of the items mainly using past data. A statistical full-scale method and a modular programme system for planning the entire process level has been developed. The models are based on the reliability type inventory models known in literature and the ones presented here. These programme models give us the possibility to control a lot of different types of demand and supply variations. On the base of the stock level plan and order recommendation is given for the decision makers.

For the most important groups of basic materials the joint planning model (3.2) has been tested, still the difficulties in collecting the data and in having a fast working system advise the use of the simple approximate solution method of the models with appropriate numerical corrections.

IX

INVENTORY MODELS WITH ORDERING TIME LIMIT : ANALYSIS OF THE PROBLEM

Setting the Problem

In the socialist economy there exist an ordering time limit for materials in order to plan and balance basic proportion of national economic funds on the state level. According to this ordering system, up to a certain date t_0 of the current year the orders for meeting next year's demands are to be placed. It means that until t_0 it must be determined what quantities (z_k) and for which time of delivery (t_k)are to be ordered. The trouble is that at the date t_0 there is great uncertainty concerning future demand (1) for the remaining period of the current year and (2) for the next year. Therefore, the fundamental aspect of resolving the problem is the planning and modelling of requirements. Reordering and storage costs play no considerable role since—due to the great uncertainty—the prior aim is to satisfy demands.

Analysis of the Problem

Outline of the Problem : Subject of investigation is an item of materials which is needed by a company (consumer) to fulfil its economic tasks and is to be purchased from another company (manufacturer, supplier). The intermediator between consumer and supplier is a "disposer" with the following tasks:

— collecting and summarising information on material demand;
— examining future demand taking into account the available stock, as well;
— supervising of changes in stocks:
— forwarding of orders to suppliers (ordering decision);
— setting orders and supervising its performance.

Instruments of planning (methods, models, algorithms) are to be found for the disposer to make decisions of ordering.

Timing Concepts : Three consecutive periods will be taken into consideration : the year (1979), the year (1980) and the year (1981). These periods are characterised by dissimilar factors determining demands and different variables of stocks (*e.g.* production programme and plan, basic technological data, list of parts, working instruction, norms of material consumption, material demand, service level stock) concerning.

— *the previous year :* planned and actual quantities of the year before the previous year;
— *the current year :* planned stock of the previous year corrected by the figures from the beginning of year up to t_o and
— *the next year :* planning quantities (decision variable).

Ordering Time Limit and Decision Variable : Ordering time limit is the date t_0 until which normal orders are to be placed towards suppliers for meeting next year's demand. An order has to contain the following data : number of shippings (n), terms for them (t_k) and quantity (z_k) of deliveries (k = 1, 2, ..., N) for next year.

Satisfaction or Non-satisfaction of Demands : The behaviour to be followed at ordering and delivering depends on whether the demand of a certain article can be covered by the supplier for all his consumers or not :

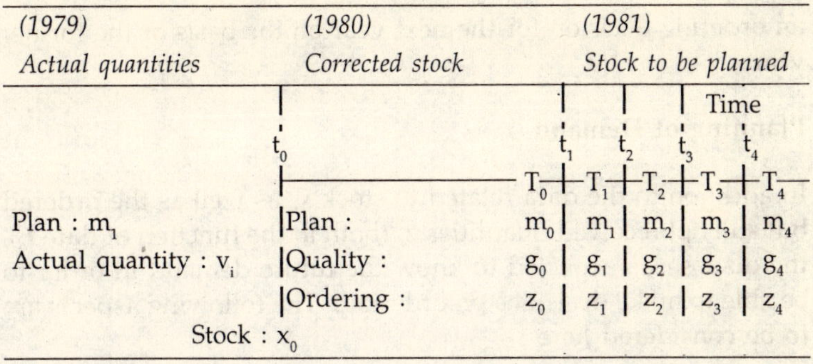

Fig. 4.6 : Timing Pattern and Variables

Quantity	*Behaviour at* *Covering* *of demands*	*Behaviour at* *non-covering* *of demands*
Actual consumption	= demand	< demand1/
Demand placed by the consumer	= demand	> demand1/
Replenishment size	= order quantity	< order quantity
Ordering decision (terms, quantities)	possible	impossible
	economic decision	administrative decision

1/ Neither of these data is suitable to estimate demands.

In the case of not satisfying demands, the order placed by consumer company cannot be directly met but negotiations are carried out in order to get an agreement—not discussed in details here—for the final solution. It is required here from an economic aspect that no higher stocks than necessary should be established (contrary to the general behaviour of the disposer).

In the following, the tasks to be solved by the company in both cases (covering or non-covering of demands) will be discussed : to estimate future demand up to date t_0 and to make an ordering decision for the next year on the basis of the former year.

Planning of Demand

In addition to the data related to stock x_0 as well as the ordered but still not received quantities z_0 (both in the function of date t_0), the disposer is expected to know the future demand in order to be able to make decisions on ordering. The following aspects are to be considered here :

— the disposer must order a great number of items of different kinds;

— items to be ordered are dissimilar as far their economic importance and, at the same time, the purchasing conditions of them are also varying, thus no unified planning method for all the items is available;

— no planning process (not even the breaking down of the list of parts) yields exact figures of demand (planned quantity);

— the quality of planning figures has a diminishing character (the so-called time dilemma of material supply—Klemm, 1979).

Because of the above circumstances, the following proceedings are recommended :

1. *Criteria of Economic Significance :*

Dissimilar features of items (from the technical point of view of planning) are to be characterised by criteria Kl—K4:

Kl : Share in Total Consumption in Value Terms (ABC-Analysis) (Magee, Boodman, 1967)

Class	*Share*	*Value of Consumption (%)*	*Quantity of items (%)*
A	High	80 - 90	10 - 20
B	Medium	10 - 15	20 - 30
C	Low	5	50 - 70

K2 : Purchasing Conditions

Class	*Significance*	*Determination by*
S	Supply is difficult (imports, bottle-neck, difficulties in delivery)	Nomenclature
NS	No difficulties in supply	

2. *Criteria of Available Information on Demand :*

K3 : Possibilities of Forecast (Schodlok 1974)

Class	*Significance*	
H	Horizontal demand pattern	predictable (v)
T	Trend-type demand pattern	predictable (v)
HS	Horizontal/seasonal demand pattern	predictable (v)
TS	Trend-type/seasonal demand pattern	predictable (v)
STR	Demands with great dispersion	not predictable (nv)
A	New items	not predictable (nv)
SP	Sporadic demands	not predictable (nv)

K4 : Share of Deterministically Calculable Demand

$$Q = \frac{\text{share of deterministically known demand (plan)}}{\text{total demand (actual)}}$$

Class	*Significance*	*Criterion*
HA	High share	Q > limit (60%)
NA	Low share	Q < limit (60%)

Thus, items have been disjunctively ranged into classes. To each class of items, the appropriate method of planning P1—P5 as well as the number n of next year's deliveries (*i.e.* the structure of scheduling) will be adjusted :

Algorithm AUSW		1	2	3	4	5	6	7
K2 :	Purchasing conditions ?	S	NS	NS	NS	NS	NS	NS
K1 :	ABC analysis ?	—	A	A	A	B	B	C
K4 :	Deterministic demand ?	—	HA	NA	NA	—	—	—
K3 :	Predictabilithy ?	—	—	v	nv	v	nv	—
	Planning method	P2 +P1	P2 +P1	P3	P4 +P1	P3	P4	P4 +P5
	Number n of deliveries	n^x	4	4	4	2	2	1

n^x = to be determined individually for each item.

Symbols :

P1 : estimated demands (by experts)
P2 : deterministic demands (*e.g.* breaking down of list of items-Group 1976)
P3 : mathematical-statistical forecast (Schodlok 1974)
P4 : average demand of the current year and the previous year
P5 : purchase in case of emergency (no planning).

Each of these planning methods given plan quantities m_k for the periods T_k, k=0(1)n, for each item. These quantities m_k are deemed forecast demands in T_k which is of course inaccurate. It is hardly possible to find regular statistic methods to estimate the quality of plan quantity m_k since

— no enough data for the individual items are available to apply traditional statistic evaluation;
— the so-called time dilemma of material management (the increasing inaccuracy of planning) is only a tendency to express groups of items;
— with the individual items, a modified method of estimation can be applied so that errors of forecast cannot be extrapolated.

Two methods are recommended for the quantification of quality g_k of plan quantities m_k, alternatively :

1. *Expert Estimation of Fluctuation for Each Method of Planning*

Examples for g %	*Period k (%)*				
	0	*1*	*2*	*3*	*4*
Constant quality	5	5	5	5	5
Decreasing quality	2	5	10	15	20
Strongly decreasing quality	5	50	60	80	100

For each item : $g_k = m_k \cdot \frac{g\%}{100}$.

2. *Statistic Calculation* : for each item, planning dimension m_i and the actually sting demands (actual consumption) v_i are used (referred to period t_0 provided that the described instruments of planning in the previous year have already been applied). Thus:

2.1. *For Each Conmmodity* : $g = \frac{1}{N} \sum_i [v_i - m_i]$, herewith the fluctuation interval is measured.

2.2. *Each Period i and Planning Method p* :

$\bar{g}_i^p = \frac{1}{N_i^p} \sum_a \left[v_i^{(a)} - m_i^{(a)} \right]$, summation over all commodities a, planning method p.

Standardizing : selection of a $\bar{g}_i^p$: $= g^x$ (e.g. the last $\bar{g}_i^p$ chronologically)

$$\gamma_i^p = \frac{\bar{g}_i^p}{g^x}$$

herewith, the chronological development of fluctuation interval for each planning method is measured.

2.3. *For Each Item* : $g_k = g - \gamma_i^p$ ($i \hat{=}$ period k of the next year).

Table 4.10

Example for Statistic Calculation

1	*2*	*3*	*4*	*5*	*6*	*7*	*8*	*Ø*	*g*	
m_i	400	400	400	400	400	400	400	400	—	
$v_i(1)$	410	380	420	420	430	350	450	408	29	item 1
$v_i(2)$	405	410	390	380	450	470	390	414	25	item 2
$v_i(3)$	395	390	410	440	450	350	450	412	31	item 3
$v_i(4)$	410	410	395	430	450	390	500	426	31	item 4
$\bar{g}_i$	4.3	7.1	6.4	15.7	25.7	25.7	24.3			
γ_i	0.18	0.29	0.26	0.65	1.05	1.05	1			
$g_k(1)$	5.2	8.4	7.5	18.9	30.4	30.4	29			item 1
$g_k(2)$	4.5	7.3	6.5	16.3	26.3	26.3	25			item 2
$g_k(3)$	5.6	9.0	8.1	20.2	32.6	32.6	31			item 3
$g_k(4)$	5.6	9.0	8.1	20.2	32.6	32.6	31			item 4

Decision Model (Outline)

The above analysis leads to the following concretising of the decision problem of a given commodity and ordering time limit t_0 :

— The algorithm AUSW establishes an adjustable planning method p which is applied to determine :
  n = Number of deliveries in the next year (and timing pattern at the same time : periods $T_0, T_1, ..., T_n$)
  m_k = planning quantity for demand T_k
  g_k = quality of the planning quantity n_k.

— Up to date t_0, the stock x_0 as well as the ordered but not delivered quantities z_0 are known.

— The quantities z_k which will be ordered for the time limit $t_k := t_{k-1} + T_{k-1}$, R = 1(1)n are yet to be known.

— The simultaneous decisions n on $z_1, z_2, ..., z_n$ are to be taken so that in each period T_k a prescribed α-service level α_0 is observed.

The few statements on future demand may be interpreted—without contradiction with the real conditions on the basis of existing information—as follows : demand $\xi[T_k]$ in period T_k is a random variable with expected value m_k and adispersion g_k :

$$P\{\xi[T_k] \leq x\} = F_k(x/T_k)$$

with an appropriate distribution function $F_k(x/T_k)$. In addition, it is to be provided that the accidental quantities $\xi[T_0]$, $\xi[T_1]$, ..., $\xi[T_n]$ are totally independent.

According to the above reasoning, there is a (S, S)—policy for each k = 1(1)n in a periodic (stationary) inventory model with delivery time lag $\lambda = T_0 + T_1 + ... + T_{k-1}$ and with lenght of period $T = T_k$, so that the α-service level is :

$$P\{\xi[\lambda + T] = S\} = F_k(S/\lambda + T) \geq \alpha_0$$

The ordered quantities are then :

$$z_1 := S_1 - (x_0 + z_0)$$
$$z_k := S_k - S_{k-1} \quad k = 2(1)n$$

Details on the above model see in Girlich, Küenle (1980) and Klemm (1980).

Safety Stocks (Sv)

Safety stocks are of special importance if the recommended strategy is followed depending on the situation of ordering time limit t_0 and uncertainty in planning. For each distribution $F_k(x/T_k)$ safety stock Sv_k can be calculated :

$$Sv_k := S_k - \sum_{j=0}^{k} m_j$$

Explicit statements on Sv are given by accepting $F_k(x \mid T_k)$ as normal distribution. Then :

$$E\,\xi[T_k] = m_k, \qquad \text{var}\,\xi[T_k] = \sigma_k = 1.25\, g_k$$

$$S_k = \sum_{j=0}^{k} m_j + k(\alpha_0)\sqrt{\sigma_0^2 + \sigma_1^2 + \ldots + \sigma_k^2}$$

$$Sv_k = k(\alpha_0)\sqrt{\sigma_0^2 + \sigma_1^2 + \ldots + \sigma_k^2}$$

with $\Phi[k(\alpha_0)] = \alpha_0$, Φ = standardised normal distribution N(0.1).

Table 4.11
Numeric Example 1

	T_2^0	T_3^0	T_4^0	T_1^1	T_2^1	T_3^1	T_4^1	T_1^2	T_2^2	T_3^2	T_4^2	ZB
m_k^0	400	400	400	400	400	400	400	400	400	400	400	1.0
$\sigma^{\%}$	2%	3%	4%	5%	10%	15%	20%					
Sv^0	8	14	22	30	50	78	112					
z_k^0	408	406	408	408	420	428	434					
$\sigma^{\%}$					2%	3%	4%	5%	10%	15%	20%	1.1
Sv^1					8	14	22	30	50	78	112	
z_k^1					408	406	408	408	420	428	434	
z_k^{-1}	with $x_0^1 = 30$						– 90	318	420	428	434	
$\sigma^{\%}{'}$			2%	2.5%	5%	7.5%	10%					1.2
$Sv^0{'}$			8	13	24	38	55					
$z_k^0{'}$			408	405	410	414	417					

$\sigma^{\%''}$			4%	5%	10%	15%	20%	1.3
$Sv^{0''}$			16	27	47	77	111	
$z_k^{0''}$			416	411	420	430	434	
$\overline{S}v^0$	8	14	22	30	30	30	30	1.4
$\overline{z}_k^0$	408	406	408	408	400	400	400	
$\overline{k}_s$	1	1	1	1	0.60	0.38	0.27	
$\overline{\alpha}$	0.84	0.84	0.84	0.84	0.73	0.65	0.61	

Table 4.12
Numeric Example 2

	T_2^0	T_3^0	T_4^0	T_1^1	T_2^1	T_3^1	T_4^1	T_1^2	T_2^2	T_3^2	T_4^2	ZB
m_k^0	400	400	400	400	400	400	400	400	400	400	400	2.0
$\sigma^{\%}$	5%	5%	5%	50%	60%	80%	100%					
Sv^0	20	28	35	203	314	449	601					
z_k^0	420	408	407	568	511	535	552					
$\sigma^{\%}$					5%	5%	5%	50%	60-%	80%	100%	2.1
Sv_k^1					20	28	35	203	314	449	601	
z_k^1					420	408	407	568	511	535	552	
z_k^1	x_0^1 =203						– 566	2	511	535	552	
$\sigma^{\%\prime}$			1%	20%	30%	40%	50%					2.2
$Sv_v^{0\prime}$			4	80	144	215	293					
$z_k^{0\prime}$			404	476	464	471	478					
$\sigma^{\%\prime\prime}$			5%	50%	60%	80%	100%					2.3
$Sv^{0\prime\prime}$			20	201	313	448	600					
$z_k^{0\prime\prime}$			420	581	512	535	552					

$\overline{S}v_k^0$	20	28	35	203	203	203	203					2.4
$\overline{z}_k^0$	420	408	407	[568]	[400]	[400]	[400]					
$\overline{k}_s$	1	1	1	1	0.65	0.45	0.34					
$\overline{\alpha}$	0.84	0.84	0.84	0.84	0.74	0.67	0.63					
m_k^1					600	600	600	600	600	600	600	2.5
$\sigma^{\%}$					5%	5%	5%	50%	60%	80%	100%	
Sv_k^1					30	42	52	304	471	673	901	
z_k^1					630	612	610	852	767	802	828	
$\overline{z}_k^1$							+51	[903]	[767]	[802]	[828]	
$m_k^{1}{}'$					200	200	200	200	200	200	200	2.6
$\sigma^{\%1}{}'$					5%	5%	5%	50%	60%	80%	100%	
$Sv_k^{1}{}'$					10	14	17	101	157	224	300	
$z_k^{1}{}'$					210	204	203	284	256	267	276	
$\overline{z}_k^{1}{}'$	$x_0^1 = 203$						– 1384	[– 1100]	[– 844]	[– 577]	[– 301]	

Table 4.13
Numeric Example 3

	T_2^0	T_3^0	T_4^0	T_1^1	T_2^1	T_3^1	T_4^1	T_1^2	T_2^2	T_3^2	T_4^2	ZB
m_k^0	250	400	150	600	200	450	150	150	700	800	200	3.0
$\sigma^{\%}$	5%	5%	5%	5%	10%	15%	20%					
Sv_k^0	13	24	25	39	44	80	86					
z_k^0	263	411	151	614	205	486	156					
$\sigma^{\%}$					5%	5%	5%	5%	10%	15%	20%	3.1
Sv_k^1					10	25	26	27	75	141	147	
z_k^1					210	465	151	151	748	866	206	
z_k^1	$x_0^1 = 39$						– 60	91	748	866	206	
$\sigma^{\%\prime}$			2%	2.5%	5%	7.5%	10%					3.2
$Sv^{0\prime}$			3	315	18	38	41					
$z_k^{0\prime}$			153	612	205	470	153					
$\sigma^{\%\prime\prime}$			5%	5%	10%	15%	20%					3.3
$Sv^{0\prime\prime}$			8	31	37	77	83					
$z_k^{0\prime\prime}$			158	627	206	490	156					

$\overline{Sv}_k^0$	13	24	25	39	39	39	39					3.4
$\overline{z}_k^0$	236	411	151	614	200	450	150					
$\overline{k}_s$	1	1	1	1	0.89	0.49	0.45					
$\overline{\alpha}$	0.84	0.84	0.84	0.84	0.81	0.69	0.67					
m_k^1				660	220	495	165	165	770	880	220	3.5
$\sigma^{\%1}$					5%	5%	5%	5%	10%	15%	20%	
Sv_k^1					11	27	28	30	82	156	162	
z_k^1					231	511	166	167	822	954	226	
z_k^1	$x_0^1 = 39$						+22	189	822	954	226	
$m_k^{1\prime}$				540	180	405	135	135	630	720	180	3.6
$\sigma^{\%1\prime}$					5%	5%	5%	5%	10%	15%	20%	
$Sv_k^{1\prime}$					9	22	23	24	67	127	132	
$z^{1\prime}$					189	418	136	136	673	780	185	
$z^{1\prime}$	$x_0^1 = 39$						−143	−7	666	780	185	

Several numeric examples (ZB) are demonstrated in Tables 4.11-4.12, where $\alpha_0 = 0.84$, *i.e.* $k(\alpha_0) = 1$.

ZB 1.0 : constant m_k, decreasing quality σ %
ZB 1.1 : continuation of ZB 1.0 in the second following year
ZB 1.2 : ordering date t_0 is 2 quarters later, quality of planning figures is better
ZB 1.3 : ordering date is 2 quarters later, quality unchanged
ZB 1.4 : modified strategy : from T_1^1 , Sv remains constant (e.g. in case of non-covering of demand)
ZB 2.0 : constant m_k , strongly decreasing quality $\sigma^{\%}$
ZB 2.1 : analogous versions to ZB 1.1—1.4
continuation of ZB 2.0 in the second following year:
ZB 2.5 : demand m_k : + 50 % in comparison to planning figures till now
ZB 2.6 : demand m_k : 50 % in comparison to planning figures till now
ZB 3.0 : fluctuating m_k, decreasing $\sigma^{\%}$
ZB 3.1—3.6 = analogous versions to ZB 2.1—2.6

The following consequences may be drawn from the above examples :

— The safety stocks are very big and are growing (1) because the increasing of inaccuracy of planning figures and (2) because the periods $T_0 + T_1 + ... + T_k$ increase.
— The shortening of periods alone (later date of ordering t_0) has no significant effect on Sv; a determinant effect is felt only if the quality of planning figures improves (what can be expected), at the same time.
— If the estimated Sv will not be ordered the service level decreases accordingly. Thus, the disturbances in production may be quantified.

References

1. Cinlar, E., "Queues with Semi-Markovian Arrivals", *Journal of Applied Probability*, 4, 365-79, (1967).

2. Cinlar, E., "Markov Reneval Theory", *Management Science*, 21, 727-52, (1975).
3. Dirickx, Y.M.I. and D. Koevoets, "Continuous Review Inventory Model with Compound Poisson Demand Process and Stochastic Lead Time", *Naval Research Logistics Quarterly*, 24, 577-85, (1977).
4. Gross, D., and C.M. Harris, "On One-for-One Ordering in Inventory Policies with State-Dependent Leadtimes", *Operations Research*, 19, 735-60, (1971).
5. Gross, D., and C.M. Harris, "Continuous-Review (s, S) Iventory Models with State-Dependent Leadtimes", *Management Science*, 19, 567-74, (1973).
6. D. Koevoets, "A Stochastic Inventory Model with Semi-Markovian Demand", *Research Report 7711*, Dept. of Applied Economic, K.U. Leuven, (1977).
7. Andres, F.M., and Emmon, H (1976), "On the Optimal Packaging Frequency of Products Jointly Replenished", *Management Science*, 22, 1165.
8. Goyal, S.K. (1973), "Determination of Economic Packaging Frequency for Items Jointly Replenished", *Management Science*, 20, 232.
9. Goyal S.K. (1974), "Determination of Optimum Packaging Frequency of Items Jointly Replenished", *Management Science*, 21, 436.

Bibliography

Andresson, H. Jönsson, H. 1979, *PICSIM I : Production Inventory Control Simulator*, Research Report 44, Department of Production Economics, Linköping Institute of Technology.

Baker, K.R. (1977), "An Experimental Study of the Effectiveness of Rolling Schedules in Production Planning," *Decision Sciences*, Vol. 8, pp. 19-27.

Bylka, S. (1979), "Optimal Policies for Dynamic Inventory Models with Discrete Stochastic Demands", Memo no. 76, Kobenhavns Universitets Okonomiske Institute.

Emskoff, J.R, Sission, R.L, 1970, *Design and Use of Computer Simulation Models*, New York, MacMillan.

Gorham, T. (First Quarter, 1968), "Dynamic Order Quantities," *Production and Inventory Management*, Vol. 9, pp. 75-81.

Grubbström, R.W., 1967, On the Application of the Laplace Transform to Certain Economic Problems, *Management Science*, Vol. 13, pp. 558-67.

Grubbström, R.W., 1967, *On the Balancing of Queueing Costs and Capacity Costs Along the Assembly Line*, 5th International Seminar on Algorithms for Production Control and Scheduling, Karlovy Vary, Czechoslovakia.

Grubbström, R.W., 1980, A Principle for Determining the Correct Capital Costs of Work-In-Progress and Inventory, *International Journal of Production Research*, Vol. 18, pp. 259-71.

Grubbström, R.W., Lundquist, J., 1977, The Axsäter Integrated Production-Inventory System Interpreted in Terms of the Theory of Relatively Closed Systems, *Journal of Cybernetics*, Vol. 7, pp. 49-67.

Grubbström, R.W., Thorstenson, A., 1980, *Evaluation of Payment Consequences from the Control and Design of Production Systems*, 6th International Seminar on Algorithms for Production Control and Scheduling, Karlovy Vary, Czechoslovakia

Johnson, E.L., (1967), "On (s, S) Policies", *Management Science*, 15, pp. 80-101.

Lundin, R.A. and Morton, T.E. (1975), "Planning Horizons for the Dynamic Lot Size Model : Zabel *vs.* Protective Procedures and Computational Results," *Operations Research*, Vol. 25, pp. 711-34.

McClain, J.O. and Thomas, J. (1977), "Horizon Effects in Aggregate Production Planning with Seasonal Demand," *Management Science*, Vol. 23, pp. 728-36.

Porteus, E.L. (1971), "On the Optimality of Generalized (s, S) Policies", *Management Science*, 17, pp. 411-26.

Sprouse, R.T., Moonitz, M., 1962, *A Tentative Set of Broad Accounting Principles for Business Enterprises*, New York, American Institute of Certified Public Accountants, p. 25 ff.

Tate, T.B., 1977, NPV, DCF and the EBQ, *Operational Research Quarterly*, Vol. 28, pp. 747-48.

Tijms, H.C. (1972), "Analsysis of (s, S) Inventory Models", Centre Tract No. 40, Mathematisch Centrum, Amsterdam.

Veinott, A.F. (1966), "On the Optimality of (s, S) Inventory Policies New Conditions and a New Proof", *SIAM J. Appl. Math.* 14, pp. 1067-83.

Wagner, H. and Whitin, T. (1958), "Dynamic Version of the Economic Lot Size Model," *Management Science,* Vol. 8, pp. 89-96.

Williams, A.C, Nassar, J.I, 1966, Financial Measurement of Capital Investments, *Management Science,* Vol. 12, pp. 851-64.

5

Optimising Productivity in Organisation : Role of the Manager

Productivity has been a concern to all managers, administrators, bureaucrats, politicians and in general to all interest groups of business. Traditional approaches to increasing productivity no longer gives the desired results. Increasingly industrial engineers, systems analysts and behavioural scientists are joining together to devise new strategies to combat increasing costs through inflation and meet competition from more successful business practices.

In this chapter we have attempted to obtain a clear understanding of what productivity is about and its relation, in the context of an organisation and study the role of the manager in balancing/optimising the productivity factors in relation to his organisation, attempt to conclude that:

- — human resource is the most basic tool of productivity;
- — managers at both functional and top levels play key roles in productivity optimisation;
- — top management's commitment and seriousness in optimising productivity has to be a part of corporate philosophy;

— productivity is a wholistic concern and not a segment affair;

— productivity is a way of life and it is the people and their attitudes that go to improve productivity.

Definitions and Understanding

While talking to company executives and organisational leaders, considerable time was spent in interpreting/crystallising the basic meaning of productivity in the context of organisational objectives and health. Therefore, it is wise to first put down the basic understanding of the key terms:

(a) Organisation

It is basically a human order in society. For most adults, the work scene is the most meaningful community, not because we spend most of our working hours there but because the relationship to other people there are both structured and highly plastic. And the workplace gives us instant identification, which is the first step in following Maslow's theory of motivation and satisfaction. Hence, man is the most important factor in the organisational process.

Considering the organisation as a whole, where capital resource is the first step in evolution of the organisation itself and man and his capabilities are the basic foundation as well as the medium, productivity is the common objective of survival. By focusing management's attention and employee attention on productivity, not only can profits rise but enough revenue can be generated for wages to rise also. Profit of the organisation is its cost for tomorrow's risk and therefore for an organisation to sustain, profits have to be generated and productivity is the most important means of achieving the same.

(b) Productivity

It is a complex idea, unlike efficiency which is a simple quotient of output by input. A comprehensive definition would be to express outputs as a ratio to all inputs or resources:

Inputs are:

(i) known inputs like plant, machinery, capitals etc.

(ii) invisible inputs like culture of the orgn., etc. as listed in Table 5.1.

(iii) external factors like climate of industrial relations, political changes, etc.

While efficiency can be related to known inputs, productivity can be considered as a measure of the visible and invisible system, *i.e.*, a ratio of the overall output to the visible and invisible inputs.

(c) The Manager

The meaning of the Manager or his role is critical especially due to the sanctity of setting norms for monitoring productivity improvement and its implementations. Traits of a Manager must be properly considered/corrected/discounted in order to have effective implementation and control of any optimisation plan concerning productivity in an organisation. In the Indian context, some trait-based classification of managerial functions can be made as follows:

- Zamindar Managers
- Game Player
- I.A.S. Managers
- Clerical Managers
- Executive Managers
- Leaders

Their relevance to a productivity exercise is given below:

(a) Zamindar Managers

It can include people who are in employment as a second alternative only and not necessarily for their daily bread and butter. They continue in the job as a matter of choice and not as a necessity. They have personal resources that gives them monetary benefits equal to or more than what the person gets through employment. With this background, they carry the magnanimity-cum-carelessness of the resourceful family circle, to the office/factory work.

Such people are likely to set/accept high productivity norms and will sincerely desire to achieve the same, generally with high visibility. However, during execution, they would themselves give concessions or make compromises in case of a major problem and try to defend the actual limited achievements as the real optimum level.

(b) Game Player

While he may show occasional brilliance, be is well past his prime productivity. He has either lost interest and enthusiasm, or has come to a level where he expects the problem to come to him for rescue. They are insecure, invariably defensive and resistant to change.

Game Players avoid risk by predicting the "right side" of an issue based upon who supports it. Insecure managers who are Game Players themselves—find the Game Player to be a comfortable couch. They will influence others to do tasks they consider risky, then carry the successfully completed task forward under the illusion of being the producer. They will be reserved if they are not sure of the reaction to their comments/suggestions to improve productivity.

(c) I.A.S. Manager

He is generally found in the administrative ranks and identifies himself as a typical bureaucrat. He is classically the "organisation", pre-occupied with preserving the current structure. He is a very low risk-taker and is indecisive when change is called for. They rely on paper-work and strict routings of information. Their work rate is constant, their behaviour predictable. Leaders often find them a joy to manage. Consequently more such I.A.S. managers are created.

He will follow something new only when he is sure it is a solution and also ensures protection. A true picture of productivity improvement effort can't be expected of them, as we fear any small change in productivity or result will be explained away as the desired result in achieving higher productivity.

(d) Clerical Manager

They are so much bothered about the details that they are called as "clerks". Their queries on finer details have no relevance to productivity. The leader should identify and allot "one best task" for him to obtain the best possible productivity. Yet he revels in the systems or products of his work more than their output or efficiency. He never sees his work as finished and revises and revises.

(e) Executive Manager

He can be tuned by a manager, yet can act independently in adopting to new situations—while retaining a positive commitment to the organisation. He follows the leader yet also does what is best for the organisation as he sees it.

They are mature and have humility. They have fairly balanced amount of different qualities described above for different managers. They can be the true torch-bearer for productivity optimisation in an organisation.

(f) The Leader

He has interesting leadership styles and employees look to him for inspiration, counter-ideas. He will give timely warning/ reminders and shoulder upon himself many of the tasks under vacuum.

Leaders are honest in admitting failure and can be depended upon. For productivity optimisation efforts, leaders are to be first identified, groups made around them before expecting fruitful execution and success.

The managerial traits determines the leadership styles adopted by individuals. In general, leader-behaviours are characterised by the tasks to be accomplished and the building or maintaining of relationships between themselves and the followers.

The above list of managerial attitudes considers a limited spectrum of behaviour patterns of leadership. No person adopt a single style. The patterns are dynamic and are changing with different situations. Different leadership situations require different leader styles.

We feel that Managers are agents of change with no single or best leadership style; that successful leaders are those who can adapt their leader behaviour to meet the needs of the followers or group members and the particular situation.

In managing for effectiveness, a manager should be able to diagnose his own leader behaviour in the light of his own environment. Some of the variables other than his followers which he shall consider are the organisation, superiors, associates and job demands.

The different managerial styles that we have considered are not exhaustive. The fact is, the Manager rightly is the protagonist in the issue under discussion.

Factors Affecting Productivity

Productive/counter productive factors are essentially responses to the environment. But for tackling the questions of what can be done to create a highly productive organisation, it is useful to list down the characteristics which make an organisation so. These are found in the organisational climate, in its structure and relationships between workers and their jobs.

Conducive	*Counter-Conducive*
¤ *Autonomous work group and integrated support functions*	¤ Absenteeism
	¤ Accidents
¤ Challenging job assignments	¤ Tardiness
¤ Job mobility and rewards for learning	¤ Manpower turnover
¤ Facilitative leadership—innovative styles	¤ Poor industrial relations
¤ Availability of decision-making information	¤ Inventory shrinkage
¤ Self-government	¤ Machine downtimes
¤ Organisational reputation	¤ Poor quality products
	¤ *Insensitivity to informal organisation channels*

THE SINGLE MOST IMPORTANT REASON FOR AMERICA'S DECLINING PRODUCTIVITY

Reason	*Per cent Selected*
Management's ineffectiveness in addressing this problem within separate organisations	30
Management's excessive concern with short-term results	30
Decline in the work ethic	8
An adversary relationship between business and government	7
Insufficient participation by the work force in decisions affecting production	7
Inadequate tax incentives for saving and investment	6

HBR Vol. 60, No. 5, Sept-Oct 1982—Truth about Productivity—Arnod S. Judson.

In order to derive meaningful results in optimising productivity through any production plan, the manager should keep the above factors in mind, apart from those highlighted in Table 5.1.

Table 5.1
Factors that Affect Productivity

Primary Factors		
Task capacity (potential performance)		
Individual effort		
Secondary Factors		
Raw materials		Capital investment
Task design		Individual capacity
Individual Factors		
Knowledge	Skills	Attitudes
Organisational Controlables		
Products and process design		Communications
Selection		Peer relationships

(Contd.)

Training	Qualitative rewards
Supervision	Monetary rewards
Demographics of the Organisation and its Individual Members	
Volume	Informal organisation
Labour market	Individual preconceived attitudes
Labor union	Organisational climate
Individual health	
Files of Information	
Industrial engineering	Personnel knowledge
Money market	Technology
Human relations	Comparison of pay scales

Source: Adapted from Ruch and Hershauer, *Factors Affecting Worker Productivity*, Tempe, Arizona State University, 1974.

Role of Functional Manager

In this part of the chapter, we have attempted to look at the principal functions of any organisation from a productivity measurement perspective.

A caveat to all productivity modification efforts is that attempts by management to stabilise production and pay for host opportunity to earn bonus are fraught with difficulties which create excess costs. Frequently, the benefits, though difficult to quantify on financial terms, is the reduction in negative thinking, rather than an increase in positive thinking. More often than not, an incentive approach that encourages a cooperative attitude to producing high levels of quality output at the right cost is desirable. It is especially important that workers are convinced that improved productivity will increase their job security and job satisfaction.

Productivity indicators are easier to arrive at all levels in functions where physical work is done or where value is added. Thus productivity indicators are easier to contemplate for production, marketing etc. Functions such as service or staff function have relative productivity indicators which tend to be less objective. Further, lower levels of all functions lend themselves more easily to measurement and hence productivity indicators are easier to arrive at.

Efforts to change productivity standards largely depend on:

(a) The problems to be solved and the size of the organisation.
(b) The commitment and involvement of the top management in such efforts, such as allocation of funds.
(c) The timing of the introduction of efforts to improve productivity.
(d) The scope and area of the effort. It should be neither too narrow nor over-ambitious.
(e) The participants to the effort—their numbers, experience and attitudes to change and most important of all choice of indicators to measure the productivity efforts.

As in any other aspect of management, it is important to first identify areas where it is felt that productivity levels are below par. This requires constant internal scanning and periodic assessment to avoid *ad hoc* and reactive measures to rectify areas of low productivity.

In Table 5.2, lists of key task areas (indicators) measuring the productivity efforts at different levels in various functions are given. These quantifiable and objective factors form the pivot for efforts to change or monitor productivity.

Table 5.2
Some Key Task Areas

Production Function

1. Quantity production
2. Quantity rejected
3. Scrap value
4. Equipment downtime
5. Absenteeism
6. Maintenance cost
7. Adherence to schedules
8. Variance from fixed overhead
9. Variance from variable overhead

(Contd.)

10. Variance from budget expenses.

Marketing Function

1. Order value
2. Quantity
3. Market share
4. Margin
5. Finished goods inventory turnover
6. Outstanding collections
7. Advertising expenses
8. Distribution expenses
9. Personnel expenses
10. Contribution.

R & D Function

1. Supply new products to marketing within specified period
2. Maintain/bring out competitive leadership in X years
3. Decrease research effort ratio of feasible marketing to actual marketing products
4. Decrease product complaints to X ratio
5. Regular feedback to the top management on products having declining life.

Finance Function

1. Cost of funds
2. Interest charges
3. Taxes paid
4. Adherence to MIS schedules
5. Utilisation of banking/credit facilities
6. Suppliers.

Personnel Function

1. Employees turnover
2. Adsenteeism
3. Employee grievances
4. Welfare activities
5. Union-Management relationship
6. Suggestion scheme
7. Self-development programme for the employees and managers.

A productivity programme can take the sequence of steps elucidated below:

- The areas for improvement are located.
- The work groups identified (The participants shall be representative of the employees constituting the problem area).
- The responses scrutinised to ascertain whether this problem can be solved internally or through the hiring of an outside consultant.
- The possible reasons for low productivity ascertained (through means such as personal interviews or questionnaires).
- The participants shall through their initial discussion arrive at a common perspective of the problem
- Through further detailed discussions arrive at a list of feasible recommendations (This list shall consider recommendations that are not practically difficult to execute and which are financially viable).
- The group chooses the indicators or operating statistics to be measured and mechanisms to review periodically and monitor it.
- The participants allocated specific job responsibilities with a team of managers who shall ensure adherence to modification plans.
- All the employees and connected interest groups interacting with them shall be intimated of the group's findings. The general course and time of intended action and the reasons for the same shall be made known.
- Finally the results of the new plan shall be monitored and reviewed periodically (corrective action taken in case of serious variation from set targets).
- Based on productivity improvement result, rewards can be given to all concerned.

Productivity modification efforts depends to a great extent on the reinforcement or rewards gained through the achievement of desired productivity levels. It should be explicitly spelt out as to what will happen if the revised targets are met. Rewards such as praise, recognition, advancement, modified work schedules, pay increase and rescheduled breaks could be some of them. All improvements may not be quantified, but where improvisations achieve tangible savings these could be shared on a basis devised in accordance with accepted principles. The one time "buy back" system, says Fein, "offers employees an opportunity to exchange their ingenuity for cash". Table 5.3 indicates some of the possible ways this can be achieved. Another way is to tap the employees' ingenuity and reward them (Scanlon Plan) which combines features of a suggestion system and çosts sharing, though it is different from both. Inasmuch as the reward system is important, the timing of rewards such as recognition is vital for the success of any behaviour modification programme.

Table 5.3
Alternatives for Sharing Savings Through the Productivity Buy-Back

Savings to be distributed through buy-back : $7000 (10 per cent of the payroll of 10 employees each earning $7000 a year)

Case 1	
Group shares equally Saving	$ 7000.00
— 5% to go to a plantwide productivity pool	–350.00
Amount shared by group	$ 6650.00
Each member's share ($ 6650/10)	665.00
Case 2	
Two employees make the innovation	
To innovators : 75% of $ 7000	$ 5250.00
To group : 20% of $ 7000	1400.00
To productivity pool : 5% of $ 7000	350.00
Each innovator receives : $ 5250/2	2670.00
Plus $ 1400/10	140.00
Total to each innovator	$ 2810.00
Each other group member receives	140.00
Plant pool receives	350.00

Source : Adapted from Mitchell Fein, "Restoring the Incentive to Wage Incentive Plan", in *The Conference Board Record*, November, 1972 pp. 17-22.

Summarising this part of the chapter, it can be said that productivity can be measured against its norms at the lower level of management and the same becomes difficult to measure in a tangible manner at higher levels of the hierarchy where effectiveness is more important. When effectiveness is good at the top, productivity automatically optimises or tends to optimise at the functional or unit level.

Role of Top Level Manager

The Chief Executive/Top Level Manager is the key member in an organisation for affecting its productivity at various functional levels, merely through his attitudes and the importance he imparts to the efforts in improving productivity. Unfortunately in the Indian context these have been generally lacking, resulting in poorer levels of productivity when compared to the Japanese and Western organisations.

Looking at developments in a global context it is seen that since World War II, productivity in Japan has increased two to three times as fast as it has in the United States/Europe. This fact is to illustrate the buoyancy and growth of the Japanese economy, which has adopted Western technologies, assimilated their techniques and improved on them to pose serious threats to the traditional businesses of the developed world. The staggering gains of the Japanese, to many, is miraculous; what makes this enigmatic is that Japanese business techniques and systems have remained largely traditional in spite of the absorption of advanced western technologies. For these results, besides social systems etc., the credit can be given to the Chief Executives who have given the required importance and desired support to the efforts towards higher productivity rather than just thinking about it.

One of the most intriguing lessons of the art of Japanese Management is the quality control circle or QC Circle. The explanation is that they share with management the responsibility for locating and solving problems of co-ordination and productivity. Statistical techniques are used to identify problems of quality and productivity by the "front line" employees; who are then delegated the power to influence changes to bring about improvements. This combination of statistical techniques with the human side of the organisation has resulted in the magic of

Japanese productivity levels. As the Union has put it, the fundamental purposes of the QC Circle are to :

- "Contribute to the improvement and development of the enterprise.
- Respect humanity and build a happy, bright workshop which is meaningful to work in.
- Display human capabilities fully and eventually draw out infinite possibilities."

These adaptations and changes reflect the seriousness/ interest shown by the Chief Executive Officer without which they are not possible.

A Chief Executive Officer of an Indian enterprise would do well to remember that atleast culturally we are closer to the Japanese thank the Occidents. Our values and societal norms could be rated as closer. Any economic activity that relates closely to societal norms and values tends to promote the productivity of the economic activity. Some basic ideas that the Corporate Management should be encouraged by a Chief Executive Officer to adapt can be the following.

- Recruit and develop people who have a drive to improve themselves.
- Initiate effective measures of productivity criteria though they may be hard to come by.
- Compensation must be perceived by the employees to be adequate. Once they do, pay will lose motivational effectiveness, and non-monetary consideration will become more important.
- Be conscious of "*Likert's System* : Participative Management" ideals. *System* 4 leaders are interested in their subordinates and treat them in a supportive manner; they have high, no nonsense goals; they provide their subordinate with good equipment, good planning, training and other help with their work; and finally, build their subordinates with skills and have them tackle the work problems faced by the group.

Most studies have repeatedly shown that the human element of the enterprise holds the trumps. Japanese business practices as mentioned earlier has incorporated their societal norms in their organisational culture sincerely. (Please refer Table 5.4. Indian businessmen have so far relied on western business models and ideologies alone without any assimilation of Indian societal norms/systems.

Table 5.4

Comparison of Organisational Characteristics

Japanese Organisations	*Western Organisations*
— Life-time employment	— Short-term employment
— Slow evaluation and promotion	— Rapid evaluation and promotion
— Non-specialised career paths	— Specialised career paths
— Implicit control mechanisms	— Explicit control mechanisms
— Collective decision making	— Individual decision making
— Collective responsibility	— Individual responsibility
— Wholistic concern	— Segmented concern

As the Chief Executive Officer encourages greater participation and co-operation within the functions and between the functions of his organisation, it is inevitable that groups will be formed. These groups have been identified to serve the formal functions (the needs of the organisation), and the informal functions (the need of the individuals). The effective integration of the two is a complex process. The leadership style of the Chief Executive Officer calls for maturity and deep understanding of group problem-solving, "group-think", and the factors that serves as assets and liabilities for group action. It is well known that individuals can solve their problems individually. In collective decision-making various pressures are inflicted upon the members of the group through their inter-actions. It is not without reason that some groups are more unified in their action than others, and are able to "establish a problem solving process that capitalises upon the total pool of information and provides for great interstimulation of ideas without any loss of innovative creativity due to social restraints."

Summarising, it can be said that it is the Chief Executive Officer who can contribute most to optimisation of productivity through encouraging group action and participation of the employees in the organisation's management process. The approach to this group process places the leader in a particular role in which he must "avoid evaluation, and refrain from thinking about solutions. Instead he concentrates on the group process, listens in order to understand rather than to appraise or refute, assume responsibility for accurate communication between members, be sensitive to unexpressed feelings, protect minority points of view, keep the discussion moving, and develop skills in summarising."

Conclusions

There are many approaches that go to improve productivity such as higher capital investment, effective financial controls, management information systems, good communications, etc. The key to productivity increases in future will be the integration of societal norms into business and employment ethics. Management should evolve towards this goal and promote such leadership styles. The freedom amongst people to be a party to the decision making process and implementation of their ideas promotes co-operation and productive efforts. Awareness of the harmony produced through decision making by consensus and creating a conducive environment to tap the potential of the innovativeness of group action will promote a higher commitment to quality work at all levels.

Japan's success stories evoke emulation the world over. However, Japanese business practices cannot be transplanted anywhere with the same amount of success. Indian culture having more in common with the Japanese, hazards us to guess that we are better placed to adapt Japanese business concepts than those of the traditional western models we are used to.

Productivity is a complex idea; but it can be simplified in many ways to become comprehensible. It is possible to measure productivity and to encourage behaviour modification plans amongst employees to achieve higher standards. The Chief Executive Officer through the culture and norm he perpetuates and the environment he promotes to create at the various levels, will matter enormously.

As the slogan goes, "Efficiency is doing a thing right; Effectiveness is doing the right thing; Productivity is both."

Industrial Robots : Japanese Experience

The use of industrial robots in Japan over the past 10 years or so has produced a number of economic and social advantages. Among them are an improvement in productivity, greater humanisation of working life, prevention of industrial accidents, improvement of product quality, and early return on capital investments.

These economic and social effects stemmed from the fact that the industrial robots are flexible and versatile, featuring a greater freedom of movement similar to that of the upper limbs (arms and hands) of human beings. This has enabled the automation of small-batch production, and the introduction of industrial robot has changed the production system from a man-machine system to a man-robot-machine system. This change in production system means that people have been released from dangerous, unfavourable work.

The practical utilization of industrial robots made outstanding progress in Japan throughout 1970's with a total of 57,000 industrial robots being in use at the end of 1979. It is predicted, however, that substantial popularisation of industrial robots in Japan will occur after 1980's.

Production of industrial robots in Japan amounted to some Yen 78.4 billion in 1980 and Yen 107.8 billion in 1981. Demand for industrial robots in the manufacturing industries in 1985 and 1991 is forecast as approximately Yen 290 billion and Yen 520 billion, respectively.

Furthermore, it is expected that there will be substantial demand for industrial robots in the future in non manufacturing industries such as nuclear energy, ocean development, and public works and construction, as well as in service trades such as medical services and transportation.

Industrial robots at present are those devices which provide versatile and flexible moving functions similar to those of human limbs and which provide flexible moving functions through their sensing and recognising capabilities. The Terminology Standardisation Committee (TSC) of the Japan Industrial Robot

Association (JIRA) worked out the classification and definitions of industrial robots in 1977.

This classification was officially incorporated into the Japanese Industrial Standard in February 1979. Along with the anticipated technological progress, however, there may come into being those which are able to perform such motional functions as for animals like snakes and crabs. Hence the classification and definitions of industrial robots will have to be modified as technology continues to progress. For this reason the TSC prepared a draft definition to the effect that "the industrial robots are those devices providing flexible moving functions similar to those of the moving parts of organisms, and/or providing intellectual functions, so that they can operate in compliance with human request. Here the intellectual functions means the ability to govern any of the functions like judgment, recognition, and learning, by means of sensing, memory and other capabilities."

There have been a number of factors affecting the diffusion of industrial robots throughout the country. First, the development of industrial robots and their practical application were touched off by a serious labour shortage in late 1960's a decade which witnessed the nation's high economic growth. GNP showed an average 12 per cent growth annually during this period; shortages of labour, particularly skilled labour, became more acute and widespread, reaching as many as 1.8 million in 1965. This eventually promoted the concerted efforts to develop industrial robots and put them into practical use.

Second, the first oil crisis in October 1973 forced the nation to shift its direction to low economic growth. As a result, the strain on the labour market eased to a remarkable degree, but the country's higher oil and other natural resources bills pulled up commodity prices drastically and hence labour costs. Fighting against this cost-push inflation inevitably required a dramatic improvement in productivity, encouraging private businesses to invest more in automation.

Third, Japan's population shows a 1.1 per cent increase per annum, whereas the growth rate of its labour force has been levelling off at 0.7 per cent due chiefly to the mounting ratio of students going to higher educational institutions. This has increased the need for higher productivity to achieve the 5 per cent annual economic growth target. The need is particularly felt in the manufacturing sector where, unlike the tertiary industry, an increase in labour force is not expected.

Fourth, shortage of skilled labour have again reached considerable proportions due to a growing number of young people moving on to a school of higher grade. As of June 1980, skilled labour shortages amounted to about 840,000.

Fifth, a need has been more and more strongly felt to prevent industrial accidents and occupational diseases due to dangerous and hard work as well as unfavourable working conditions. To meet this need, great pressure has been brought to bear on management to increase the use of industrial robots.

Finally, labour unions in Japan are primarily not craft unions but industrial unions or unions organised on a company basis, making it much easier to introduce industrial robots and relocate workers.

There is also an evident need to prevent industrial accidents and occupational diseases and to upgrade the quality of human labour and precluding the tendency to loss of humanities which is turning mankind into a slave of machinery as exemplified in the conveyor system. In fact, the provision of agreeable working environments and the humanisation of working life represent an important key to promoting industrial and social welfare.

Industrial robots play their roles not only in improving productivity and welfare as mentioned above, but also in upgrading product quality, saving resources and energy based on more effective capital investments and a reduced rejection rate, improving production control, stability of employment, solution of skilled manpower shortages, creation of new technology, development of new industrial sectors, so forth.

Industrial robots are capable of continuous operation without any interruption. This helps improve productivity by a considerable degree. Moreover, industrial robot introduction changes a "man-machine system" into a "man-robot-machine system" in which robots serve the conveyor directly in place of human operators.

Improved productivity is required firstly for the purpose of strengthening international competitiveness and corporate profitability. Nonetheless, diversified social needs are in turn bringing about diversification of the product mix. In Japan's machinery industry, for example, approximately 80 per cent of total output comes from multiproduct small or medium batch production, the automation of which leads to drastic improvement in productivity. If goes without saying that productivity improvement is also needed to meet the tendency toward wage hike.

The second reason why improved productivity is needed consists in the supply demand situation of labour force. While efforts are being made to shorten working hours, Japan is tending toward a highly educated society, although the anticipated annual growth rate of labour force in the year ahead is as low as 0.7 per cent. It will therefore be increasingly difficult to recruit blue-collar workers.

It is also expected that the percentage of the overall working population represented by those engaging in the tertiary industry, which was 52 per cent in 1980, will gradually increase following the pattern of the United States, where it was already as high as more than 70 per cent in 1979. Since a significant growth of the work force in the secondary industry sector can hardly be expected, productivity improvement will no doubt play an important part in the development of this sector.

At present, industrial robots are gradually taking over those dangerous, severe, trying, or monotonously repeated works which human beings have so far been forced to engage in because of difficulty in achieving automation. This tendency will go a long way toward preventing industrial injuries and occupational diseases resulting from such unfavourable jobs.

Meanwhile, increased robot utilization could play an important role in promoting the employment of aged people looking for jobs in a society like Japan which is marked by greater longevity.

Efforts are also being made to develop care-taking and fire-fighting robots. In addition to reducing the work load of nurses and other helpers taking care of the bedridden, these could help enable the physically handicapped to perform occupational functions along with ordinary workers or could take over the role of leader dogs serving the blind. Thus industrial robots could turn out to make greater contributions to the promotion of social welfare.

Dangerous, severe, trying, and monotonous repeated works are disliked by workers, thereby leading to a greater mobility of labour. If industrial robots are to conduct these unfavourable works with a view to levelling up the quality of man's labour, it would be possible to promote labour stability and to provide increased employment opportunities for white-collar and aged workers. Here too is the significance of industrial robot application.

Needless to say, it would be possible to promote ocean development by applying industrial robots to those underwater operations which are difficult for human being to carry out. It would likewise be possible to facilitate the development and use of nuclear energy by using these robots for reactor operation and maintenance, which entail the danger of radiation injuries. The resultant improvement in plant capacity factor could spur the progress of the nuclear energy industry. Thus great expectations are entertained of robot application to these new industrial sectors. No doubt, the progress of these sectors will lead to a higher growth rate of the economy, increased employment opportunities, and improved manpower utilisation.

People do not want to work at night. For this reason, it is presently a common practice to work during the day time on a single work shift basis except in steel mills, automobile plants, and other special cases. In a "man-robot-machine system", as distinguished from the conventional man-machine system, "man" represents the minority intellectual side of the labour, and the freedom from physical pain enables a two-shift or three-shift working system to be employed. Consequently, it is quite possible to reduce the amount of money required for a given output to a factor of two or three as the case may be. The net effect of this cost saving would be an increased return on capital investment and resource conservation.

Other impacts brought about by industrial robot utilization include : (1) improved stability of product quality; (2) resources conservation resulting from reduced rejection rates and materials saving; (3) improved production control; and (4) solution of the skilled work force shortage.

Bibliography

Performance Appraisal Manual—Larsen & Toubro Ltd.
Theory Z. by William G. Ouchi—Avon Publishers.

Improving Busines Results by John W. Humble—Pan
The Incredible Japanes by M.K. Rustomji & S.A. Sapre—Macmillan (India) Ltd.
Office and Administrative Management (3rd Edition)—by C.L. Littlefield, Frank M. Rachel and Donald L. Caruth—Prentice Hall.
Assets and Liabilities in Group Problem Solving : The Need for an Integrative Function by Norman R.F. Maier—Psychological Review, Vol. 74, No. 4.
Groups and Inter-group Relationships by Edgar H. Schein—Organizational Psychology , Prentice Hall.
Groupthink by Irving L. Jains—Psychology Today 'Magazine, Nov. 1971.
Truth About Productivity by Arnold S. Judson—Harvard Business Review, Vol. 60, No. 5.
Productivity—Why We Must Improve—by David S. Brown—Pitt and Quarry, Vol. 75, No. 4.

6

Production Shopfloor : Time Studies Techniques

I

Classification of Work

For the purpose of classifying time studies all work falls into two main categories. The first is where the work is of a repetitive nature when the Work Study Officer is able to stand in one place and obtain all the required observations of the particular elements. The second is where the Work Study Officer follows a worker around a plant taking observations of a series of elements which are essentially non-repetitive.

The first type of a study enables the elements to be written down on the Time Study Observation Sheet before the study commences, but the second type of study demands that the Work Study Officer should be able not only to enter the time and rating for each element, but also to write a brief element description as and when each element occurs. However, if the work being measured has been planned in detail before measurement, then it is unusual for studies of a long series of consecutive non-repetitive elements to be made. The Work Study Officer will be selecting specific elements to build up his 'stock' of data which he will later synthesise to obtain the times for the job or operation.

Commencement of Study

Before starting the study make a note of the details required to complete the Study Summary Form. When taking the Time Study enter the details of the elements using any form of shorthand or abbreviation which is satisfactory. The rating for each element should be assessed about the middle of each element and must be entered on the sheet before entering observed time. With training it is possible to write in the observed times and ratings without looking at the board or with only a quick lance to locate the position for writing. This procedure ensures the maximum amount of time that is available for actually observing the operator at work. The observed time is entered in 'centiminutes', not decimal minutes.

During the study any ineffective time should be entered in the appropriate column and because ineffective time is usually unexpected it is sensible always to be ready for the unexpected to happen when taking a Time Study. The stop watch should be fully wound before commencing the study, and it should not be wound up in front of the operator. Lastly, always carry two sharp pencils or ball point pens because nothing is so irritating as to find oneself in the middle of a Time Study with a broken pencil and nothing else with which to write.

Because the observer when taking a Time Study comes in close contact with the operator there are several problems of human relations. Understandably, the floor supervision and the workers may be somewhat suspicious and fearful of the initial application of Time Study in their department. The purpose of Method Study is usually obvious to everyone. The purpose of a Time Study is less obvious, and unless it is very carefully explained to everyone concerned its objects may be completely misunderstood.

If the ultimate purpose of the Time Study is to apply any incentive scheme, the initial approach to introducing Work Study to the supervision and operators would have explained the principles involved. However, the Work Study Officer, before taking his first Time Study should ensure that everyone with whom he is likely to come in contact has a reasonable understanding of the simple procedure of taking the studies.

The Work Study Officer should make an endeavour to gain the confidence of all concerned. He should make every effort to foster understanding amongst floor supervision and workers that he is completely impartial and that his purpose is to measure work and to measure it correctly.

Before starting a study explain to the worker what you are doing, and if he is not familiar with the procedure of Time Study be prepared to go into details as described previously. Ask his permission to take the study, and if there are objections be sympathetic and don't just brush them aside. Encourage workers to explain their jobs because most men when given a chance to talk about something with which they are familiar will open up and become more friendly. Instruct him to carry on working in his normal way, not trying to hurry the work or slow down, but just carry on as if he were not being watched. Most workers quickly settle down to a normal working pace, but a nervous worker sometimes has a tendency to work unnaturally fast in front of the observer and this may cause him to fumble and make errors. Such methods of working are usually obvious to the observer and he should be prepared to waste some of the study whilst the worker settles down (which he usually will do in a very short time) or else stop the study and chat with him. Discuss the situation with him frankly pointing out that there is no need to work at anything other than his normal pace, and that his actions are more likely to create errors in timing than anything else.

If the worker knows the purpose of the Time Study, he is less likely to deviate from the elements or works which are connected with the specific job which is being measured. However, being human, he is very likely to do the unexpected, and once again this warning is given, be ready for the unexpected in a Time Study. Wherever possible the observer should stand where the worker can see him, and he should show interest in the worker's task by his actions; he must not launge about, lean against walls or girders nor sit down whilst the worker is standing. Take the trouble to thank the worker after doing a study.

The work Study Officer should remember that he is allowed on the plant floor by the sanction of the Plant Manager, and in consequence he should follow any rulings which appertain to recording his presence on and off the plant. If there are no specific rules it is always a good practice to contact the manager or foreman (if only to pass the time of day), and let him know you are going to be engaged on the plant.

Trainees in Work Measurement should make an elapsed time check for every study while under training, and the trained Work Study Officer should make such checks periodically to ensure that they are not deteriorating in efficiency. Remember to check the accuracy of stop watches periodically.

II

RELAXATION ALLOWANCES

Definition

Relaxation Allowance (RA) is an addition to the normal time intended to provide the worker with the opportunity to recover from the physiological and psychological effects of carrying out a specified work under specified conditions and to allow attention to personal needs. The amount of RA given depends upon the nature of the job and is given as a percentage of the normal time.

Factors for Computing RA

The principal factors for which the RA per cent is computed are:

A. Personal Needs including Basic Fatigue
B. Posture
C. Motions
D. Energy Output
E. Visual Fatigue
F. Thermal Conditions
G. Atmospheric Conditions
H. Other Influences of Environment.

Personal needs including basic fatigue are common to all work, and hence are termed as constant allowances.

Factors A to G are described as physiological and factor H as psychological.

Guide to RA

Table 6.1 is intended as a guide for assessing RAs of individual elements. The appropriate allowance for any factor present in the element should not be given until the influence of other factors is also considered. Separate allowance for women need to be given for factors A and D only. When special protective clothing have to be worn by the workers, care should be taken in making allowances under factors B, C, D, E, F, and G to compensate for additional fatigue. It is a general practice to allow for a minimum overall allowance of 10 per cent for men, and 12 per cent for women.

RA for Atmospheric Conditions

The Effective Temperature Chart (Chart 6.1) and Effective Temperature Curve (Chart 6.2), offer means of determining RA to be allowed for atmosphere conditions. The steps involved in determining this RA are :

(i) Obtain readings of wet and dry bulb temperatures. Place a ruler on the wet and dry bulb temperature/ readings, and read off effective temperature on the Effective Temperature Chart.

(ii) Decide which line on the Effective Temperature Curve most nearly represents the type of work under consideration. From the point where the effective temperature cuts the selected curve, read off the RA required to be given.

Calculation of RA

For arriving at an appropriate RA per cent for each element, the assessor should consider each factor on the RA table in turn, and determine whether it applies to that element. If it does, then he assesses how much allowance is to be given, working within the

Chart 6.1

Effective Temperature Chart

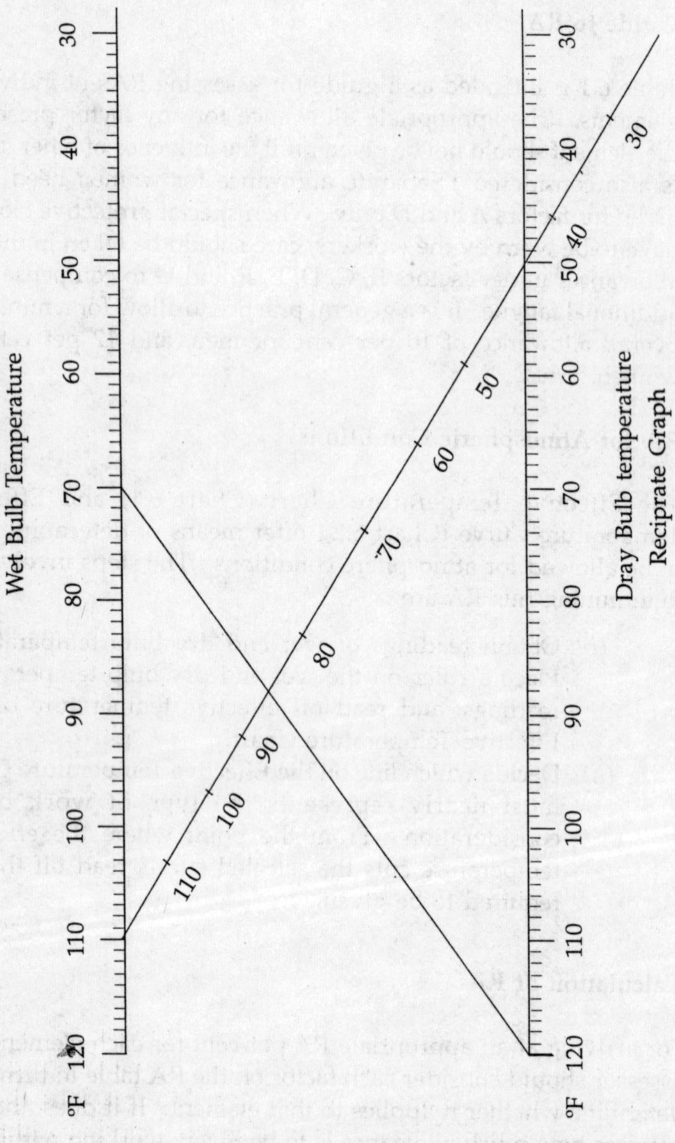

Chart 6.2

Effective Temperature Chart

● ● ● ● ● ● Light Physical Work Floor Sweeping
Light Bench Work Etc. 21 A.K. Cols./hr.

. . . . Walking of 4M.P.H. 328 K. Cols/hr.

———— Medium Physical Work : Floor Polishing, Hacksawing, Etc. 292. K. Cols/hr.

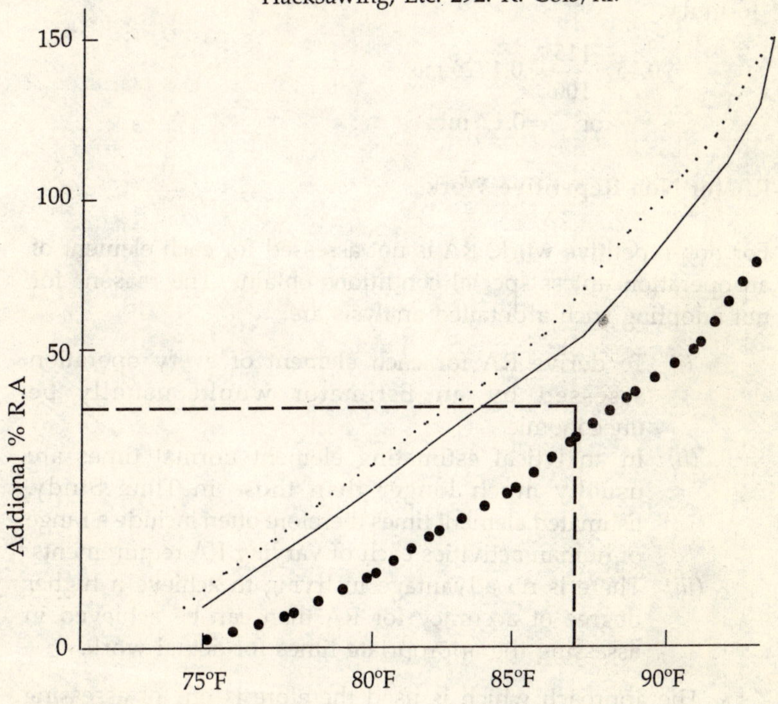

maximum and minimum range listed. Having considered each factor in relation to the element, the assessor should add up the percentages of the various factors. These should preferably be done in the following manner :

Element Ref. No.	Element Description	Normal Time	RA % Factors A B C D E F G H	Total

Having obtained the RA percentage, the work content for each element is found as follows :

Normal time (say) = 0.15 mts.
RA % = 15

RA Time = $0.15 \times \frac{15}{100} = 0.022$ mts.

Work Content = 0.15+0.02=0.17 mts.

The work content could also be obtained by the use of the formula

$$0.15 \times \frac{115}{100} = 0.1725 \text{ mts.}$$

or =0.17 mts.

RA for Non-Repetitive Work

For non-repetitive work, RA is not assessed for each element of an operation unless special conditions obtain. The reasons for not adopting such a detailed analysis are:

(i) To derive RA for each element of every operation assessed by an Estimator would usually be uneconomic.

(ii) In analytical estimating element normal times are usually much longer than those in Time Study. Estimated element times therefore often include a range of human activities each of varying RA requirements.

(iii) There is no advantage in trying to achieve a higher degree of accuracy for RA than can be achieved in assessing the appropriate times for actual work.

The approach which is used therefore is one of assessing RA (using the guide table) for the operation as a whole, the RA being allocated in the form of a 'blanket' allowance. It is not pretended that 'blanket' allowances as they exist at present are the final answer to RA for non-repetitive work. On the contrary, the field is still open to further improvement, but it should be emphasised that the 'blanket' allowance has proved itself reasonably satisfactory in practice.

RA for Short Cycle Repetitive Work

Short cycle repetitive work normally requires a slightly higher

RA than long cycle work of a similar nature. This is due to the fact that the repetitive use of a given set of muscles requires a longer period of time for complete recovery from accrued fatigue.

In every short cycle work (where the complete cycle may take less than 15 centiminutes), monotony becomes a factor of considerable importance. However, it is often possible to reduce the relative effect of monotony by introducing small alternative duties which can be performed by the operator at periodic intervals (such as an operator obtaining his own materials from stock). Where this is not possible, a higher RA percentage for monotony must be allocated in computing the RA percentage for the element, than where a regular break can be introduced into the repetition of the work cycle.

RA in Operations Involving Heavy and Light Work

For operations involving alternating periods of heavy and light physical work (for example, a storekeeper who handles light and heavy equipment) recovery from the fatigue resulting from heavy work may be accelerated as a result of changing over to work of a lighter nature. This is a result of the recuperative effect caused by the changeover of the groups of muscles being used. Assessments for elements incurring high allowances, therefore, may require reduction when followed by elements incurring less fatigue or when followed by periods of waiting.

Higher Allowances

Where RA greater than 50 per cent is necessary, it may often be regarded as criticism of management (and of designers in particular, since mechanical aids might have been provided or alternative methods investigated. Unfortunately, there are still cases in industry where relaxation allowances of more than 50 per cent must be allotted. It is hoped that the now increasing use of Work Study in plant design will accelerate the trend towards the elimination of such work.

Rest Periods

It is generally true to say that, when operatives are left to take their allotted RA at their own discretion, they do not choose properly balanced rest periods. For example, they may work for too long a period before taking a rest thereby incurring avoidable cumulative fatigue. Hence, it is sometimes necessary for management to predetermine set rest periods, so that the operatives will derive the maximum benefit from their RA.

However, from the psychological angle, completely organised rest periods have obvious disadvantages. A suitable compromise, therefore, is to give a proportion of the RA in the form of fixed rest periods, and to allow the operator to take the remainder at his own discretion. This has the attendant advantages of enabling management to plan the provision of tea breaks, etc.

The effectiveness of an operative tends to increase after the start of a working day, up to a point where the increase is balanced by accumulating fatigue. Hence his effectiveness tends to decline until the lunch break is reached. After lunch, a similar cycle takes place, but it is pitched at a somewhat lower level. Therefore, if maximum benefit is to be derived from the set rest periods they should be placed just after those peak points, where operator effectiveness is highest.

RA and Job Appraisement

In job appraisement one of the main heads under which a job is assessed is 'working conditions'. One of the factors under which RA is assessed is also 'working conditions'. There it might appear, at first sight, that allowances were being made twice for the same factor. In other words, it might seem that an operative was being paid twice for the working conditions connected with his job. This is not the case.

The object of job appraisement is to fix differential job rates above the base rate, so that each job is paid on its merits in relation to other jobs. If each job is correctly assessed, the job differential should be sufficient to reward people adequately for the nature of their work whatever the conditions of the job.

When a man is working, it is only right that he should be given sufficient rest to enable him to work at standard normal performance without suffering at the end of the day from more than normal healthy fatigue. Furthermore, the man must be enabled to maintain his work level, not only throughout the day, but also throughout the week and throughout the months. In order to do this he is allotted RA which, as explained above, is a part of the allowed job time. Hence it is apparent that working conditions as a factor of job appraisement are something apart from working conditions as the basis for RA.

In short, job appraisement is additional reward for the nature of the job and the general conditions under which it is performed; while the RA enables him, when once on the job, to continue working at the normal performance.

Table 6.1

Tables for Relaxation Allowances

Factors	*Range of RA %*	
	Men	*Women*
A. *Personal Needs and Basic Fatigue*	9.0	11.0
B. *Posture*		
1. Sit	0.0	0.0
2. Stand on both feet	2.0	2.0
3. Stand on one foot (using a foot control)	2.5-4.0	2.5-4.0
4. Lying down	2.5-4.0	2.5-4.0
5. Bending	4.0-10.0	4.0-10.0
C. *Motions*		
1. Normal (free swing of hammer)	0.0	0.0
2. Limited (limited swing of hammer)	0.0-5.0	0.0-5.0
3. Awkward(carrying heavy load in one hand)	0.0-5.0	0.0-5.0
4. Confined—limbs only (working with arms above head)	5.0-10.0	5.0-10.0
5. Confined—whole body (working on a thin coal seam)	10.0-15.0	10.0-15.0
D. *Energy Output*		
1. Light bench work, either seated or standing equivalent to no load handing.	0.0	1.0

2. Light shovelling—equivalent to	2 kg. handling	0.0	1.0
	" " 4 kg. "	1.0	2.0
	" " 6 kg. "	2.0	3.0
	" " 8 " "	3.0	4.0
3. Hacksawing or filling	" " 10 " "	4.0	6.0
	" " 12 " "	5.0	8.0
	" " 15 " "	7.0	10.0
	" " 18 " "	9.0	13.0
4. Swinging heavy hammer	" " 20 " "	11.0	16.0
	" " 25 " "	15.0	20.0
5. Loading weights—equivalent to handling in range of 30 kg. to 50 kg.		20.0	30.0
		Women are generally not expected to lift heavy weights.	

(*Note :* Above 50 kg., special consideration needs to be given)

E. Visual Fatigue

1. Intermittent eye attention reading meter or gauges	—*(a)* under good light	0.0	0.0
	—*(b)* under poor light	1.0	1.0
2. Nearly continuous eye attention Precision machine work	—*(a)* under good light	1.0	1.0
	—*(b)* under poor light	2.0	2.0
3. Continuous eye attention with varying focus	—*(a)* under good light	2.0	2.0
	—*(b)* under poor light	5.0	5.0
4. Continuous eye attention with fixed focus	—*(a)* under good light	4.0	4.0
	—*(b)* under poor light	8.0	8.0

F. Thermal Conditions

	Temp. °F		*Humidity %*	
			Normal	*Excessive*
1.	Freezing	Below 30	over 10	over 12
2.	Low	32 - 55	10 - 40	12 - 5
3.	Normal	55 - 75	0	5
4.	High	75 - 100	0 - 40	5-100
5.	Excessive	above 100	over 40	over 100

(*Note :* Make use of chart for assessing RA for Thermal conditions as given later).

G. Atmospheric Conditions

1. Good—well ventilated or fresh air	0
2. Fair—Badly ventilated or presence of non-toxic or non-injurious fumes	0 - 5
3. Poor—Presence of toxic dust or heavy concentration of non-toxic dust requiring breathing filters.	5 - 10
4. Bad—Presence of toxic fumes requiring respirators.	10 - 20

H. Other Influence of Environments

1. Continuous repetitive and short cycle	0 - 3
2. Absence of company—in day	1
—in night	2
3. Excessive noise, intermittent and loud	2 - 5
4. Vibration of floor or machines	5 - 10

III

OTHER ALLOWANCES

Introduction

The other allowances include:

(i) Periodic Activity Allowance
(ii) Contingency Allowance
(iii) Unoccupied Time
(iv) Interference Allowance.

Periodic Activity Allowance

It is an allowance to compensate workers for waiting time for activities carried out at definite intervals, or in the course of a batch or order of production, or may be for change over of production line. The actual work of periodic activity, other than the waiting time, should never be given as a form of an allowance, but it should be measured and time issued for it.

Contingency Allowance

It is an allowance of time which may be included in a standard time to meet legitimate and expected items of work or delays which are uneconomical to measure. The extent of contigency allowance should be determined either by Production Study or Activity Sampling. Contingency allowances are of two types:

(i) for work, and
(ii) for delay.

The total allowance given under this head should never exceed 5 per cent otherwise methods should be improved. A complete record should be kept of the work for which this allowance is given. Further contingency allowance is not a permanent feature. It should be reassessed at specified intervals.

Unoccupied Time

In an automatic process or in an operation carried out by a group of workers, a few definitions are to be reckoned with.

Governing Time: The elements or cycle time controlling the output of one or more workers, machines, or processes.

Machines/ Process Cycle Time: The actual time a process or machine runs when it is governing or controlling the output of a worker or group of workers.

Outside Work: This is carried out before or after the machine or process cycle, such as loading prior to starting it and unloading the machine after its machine cycle.

Inside Work: This is the actual control or attention worked out during the machine or process cycle.

Unoccupied Time: This is the difference between the machine or process cycle time and the inside work expressed as work content.

The Method Study techniques should be fully made use of for minimising unoccupied time is unproductive time.

Unoccupied time is a loss to a company; it is unproductive time, and it is the duty of a Work Study Officer to seek means of utilising that. There are many ways of doing this, and the following questionnaire will act as a guide :

(i) Can the machine or process controlled time be reduced?

(ii) Can the sequence of elements forming the outside work be changed so that some can be done as inside work?

(iii) Can the worker control additional items of plant or additional machine?

(iv) Can any other useful work be given to the worker?

Interference Allowance

Interference allowance is akin to unoccupied time. The unoccupied time is the waiting time for the operator till machine or process cycle is over. Interference is the waiting time for the machine or process, when an operator attends to more machines at a time and the work on a given machine or process remains incomplete till the worker attends to it. This means more time for completing the work, and the worker is compensated through interference allowances.

Consider an automatic operation which involves:
Outside work (OW) = 3 mts. (work content)
Machine Time (MT) = 8 mts.
Inside Work (IW) = 4 mts. (work content)
Then unoccupied time (UT) = MT — IW = 8 – 4 = 4 mts.

This can be shown diagramatically as follows :

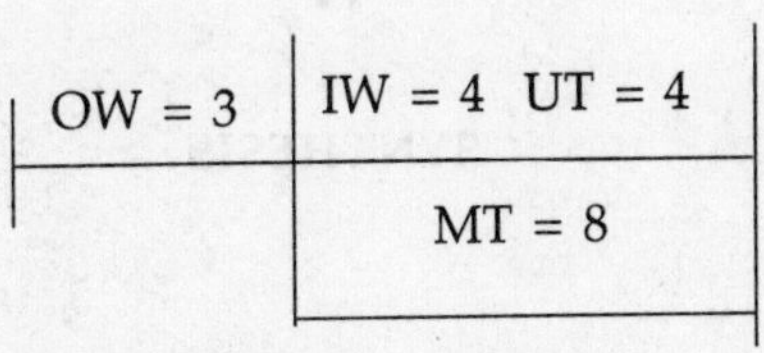

In order to minimise UT, an operator is given another machine to operate similar operation. He carries out the work in the following sequences :

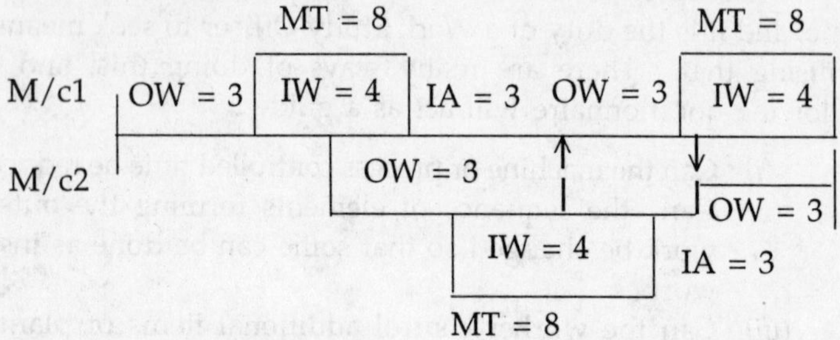

Now unoccupied time (UT)

= Machine Time—Inside work on all machines *plus* outside work on all machines *less* the first.
= 8 – (2 × 4 + 3)
= 8 – 11= - 3

UT is —ve and this is equivalent to Interference Allowance (IA). It means that while the operator is fully engaged, the machine cycle time has gone up by 3 minutes due to interference.

This perhaps is too simplified an illustration of interference. In the earlier example it was assumed that 4 units of inside work on a machine would be attended to simultaneously. This may not be the case in actual practice. Interference acquires a complex problem when it is of a cycle or random nature. Cyclic interference occurs on machines at fixed intervals of time on different machines and random interference occurs at random intervals of time on different machines.

IV

SYNTHESIS

Introduction

The main purpose of the synthesis stage of the Work Measurement is to take the measured constituent parts and build them together again. The building is done in stages: basic motions are built into basic elements, basic elements into composite elements, and finally composite elements into times for operations or jobs. This procedure of synthesis is commonly called as setting-up. All set-up forms are designed in one of the two basic principles:

(i) The single-column form
(ii) The multi-column form.

It cannot be emphasised too strongly that all information which will help to describe the work being set up should be detailed on the set-up form. Quite a lot of this information can be given in the element description, and indeed it is often necessary to include it in the element description even though it is listed elsewhere. It has been pointed out that good work measurement results in 'data' that is, times for elements or work which occur frequently. There may exist in company data elements for operating valves on pipelines. In order to use this data it is necessary to specify the type of valve, the diameter of the handwheel, the resistance to turning and the number of turns. This information needs to be entered against the element description, and the same is true of many items of tools and equipment handled.

Both the single-column form and the multi-column form should contain a column for the Element Number and a wider column for the Description of the Element. The Work Study Officer should keep in mind the necessity to make his element description in such a way that another person can read it and understand what work is done so clearly that he could duplicate it exactly in actions. It is often helpful, and saves words, to define the breakpoints between elements. Reference to an accompanying plan often reduces the number of words needed. The following two examples illustrate first a poor and secondly a good example of element descriptions:

Poor :

(i) Walk from foremen's office (temporary office on ground floor of No. 4 building) to stocks of powder X.
(ii) Pull over drum for keeling.
(iii) Keel drum to scale.

(*iv*) Weigh drum
(*v*) Move drum aside from scale to temporary stock area.

Correct :

(*i*) Walk from foreman's office to Area B.
Breakpoint : hand touches drum.
(*ii*) Pull over drum for keeling.
Breakpoint : drum begins to roll.
(*iii*) Keel drum to Scale No. 3 (17 metres) and position on the scale.
Breakpoint : and releases drum.
(*iv*) Weigh drum (check of gross)
Breakpoint : Hand touches drum.
(*v*) Slide or keel drum aside to area J (approx. 2 metres).

Both single and multi-column forms should have a number of columns in which the normal time for each study (or group of studies) can be entered and there should be space for the Study Summary reference number to be quoted at the top of the appropriate column. Up to the Study Summary Sheet all times have been expressed in centiminutes: on the set-up form the times should be converted to minutes expressed to three decimal places.

The average normal time for each element is entered in the appropriate column in single or multi-column form. Then RA% is entered against each element. The procedure of setting up now varies with the type of form used.

Single-column Set-up Form

The aim of a single-column set-up form is to condense the work content times for each element into one column. In order to achieve this, the work content of each element must be multiplied by the frequency at which the element occurs in the job or operation for which the total work content is required. If it is necessary to set up a simple job of trucking six sacks one at a time from place A to place B and for each job the sack truck has to be collected and replaced after use, then by the single-column procedure it is necessary to decide whether the total work content will be for a job of trucking six sacks, or a work content for the operation of trucking one sack. This decision must be made before the frequency for the first element can be entered on the set-up form. As the decision regarding frequency is not required at this stage on the multi-column form, it can be said that this is a weakness of the single-column form, although it does not invalidate its use for certain types of setting-up.

If it is decided to set up the sack trucking job in such a way as to obtain a work content for a job of trucking six sacks, then the element of collecting the sack truck occurs at a frequency of one. The element concerned with loading the sack to the truck and unloading the sack from the truck occurs at a frequency of six. The element of trucking the sack from A to B also occurs at the frequency of six, but the element of going back with the empty truck from B to A occurs at a frequency of five. The last element of replacing the sack truck after use occurs at a frequency of one.

If it is decided to set up for one sack, that is to obtain the work content for an operation of trucking one sack, the elements and frequency will be as follows:

		Frequency
(i)	Collect sack truck	1/6
(ii)	Load sack to truck	1
(iii)	Push load to B	1
(iv)	Unload	1
(v)	Push empty to A	5/6
(vi)	Aside truck	1/6

With the frequency decided, the 'Average Normal Time' is increased by the relaxation allowance to obtain 'Standard Minutes' which are entered in the column headed with the title 'Work Content'. Again the entry is made in minutes to three decimal places. Now the work content is multiplied by the frequency to obtain the 'Work Content per Work Cycle Minute' which is again entered in minutes to three decimal places in the extreme right-hand column on the set-up sheet. The total of this last column will give the total standard minutes for the elements of work in the job or operation for which the frequency was selected.

On the reverse of the single-column form are spaces for the calculation of allowances. The summations of all the information on the set-up form is made in the block 'Standard Time' on the reverse of the form, where the work content in minutes, and the

Element No.	Description of Element (See Plan for Area Locations)	AS 1	TY 3	AS 3	Basic Time	R.A.	Per Job	Per Sack	Per Journey Loaded	Per Journey Empty
1.	Walk from Foreman's Office to Truck area	20	yards	.0085	.170	10	.187			
	B.P. Hand tourches truck									
2.	Take Sack truck to area A	.210	.220	.230	.220	10	.242			
	B.P. Hand touches sack									
3.	Load Sack to truck (Pullover action)	.060	.055	.065	.060	15		.069		
	B.P. Truck commences move									
4.	Push loaded truck to Area B	.330	.350	.340	.340	12½			.383	
	B.P. Truck moves up from trucking position									
5.	Unload Sack—Tip against wall	.043	.045	.044	.044	15		.050		
	B.P. Truck commences move									
6.	Push empty truck back to area A	.310	.300	.320	.310	10				.341
	B.P. as Element 2									
7.	After last bag, push empty truck back to truck area									
	B.P. Release Truck	.210	.230	.220	.220	10	.242			
8.	Return to Foreman's Office	20	Yards	.0085	.170	10	.187			
							.858	.119	.383	.341
					Add for 6 sacks					.714

	Add for 6 journeys loaded	2.298
	Add for 5 journey empty	1.705
		5.575
	Use 5.6 Standard Minutes per Job of Six Sacks	
Alternative :	Add 1/6 Job Time	.143
	Add Per Sack Loaded	.383
	Add 5/6 Sack Empty	.284
		.929

USE 0.93 WORK CONTENT PER BAG

MULTI-COLUMN
SET-UP FORM

minutes of allowances are entered and totalled to show the standard time in hours and minutes for the particular job or operation.

Multi-column Set-up Form

The multi-column set-up form is a simple form compared to the single-column form, and it is designed to be as flexible in use as possible. It is used particularly for the setting up of process type work, although it can be used to set up any kind of work. The form allows for element number and description and then consists of vertical columns covering the remainder of a double foolscape size form. The first few vertical columns are used for the entry of normal times from the studies, and in order to separate the columns used in this way from the remainder of the form two columns are selected about the middle of the form, and the following headings are written in them:

(i) Normal time
(ii) Relaxation Allowance percentage (or RA %).

The general principle of using this form is to use the remaining vertical columns to pull out the 'standard minutes' for the elements according to the fundamental frequency at which they occur. Using the same simple job of trucking sacks; the elements of collecting and replacing the sack truck which occur once per job would be entered into a column which is headed 'Per Job'. Loading and unloading the truck occurs for every sack, and hence these elements would be entered in another column headed 'Per Sack'. The elements of trucking loaded and trucking unloaded do not occur per job or per sack, although there is a loaded journey for every sack. The elements for trucking loaded would be put in a column headed 'Per Journey Loaded,' and likewise the element of trucking empty occurs in column 'Per Journey Empty'.

Each of the separate columns is now totalled separately to obtain the total standard minutes for elements occurring at the fundamental frequencies. It is now possible to turn these totals into a grand total of work content expressed for one job of six sacks, or one operation of one sack.

It should be appreciated that in the simple example of sack trucking, there are very few elements, with the result that some of the columns have only one element entered in them. Longer set-ups will have many more entries in each column. The advantages of the multi-column procedure over the single column are many, but one advantage that should be obvious at this stage is that the calculation at the bottom of the set-up could be done for a job of any number of sacks. The basic information is available to do this.

A separate column is used for the unoccupied time against the element which lists the time for the machine or process element. A series of elements which form the inside work can be given a separate column so that the total of the column gives the total work content of the inside work. If necessary several columns may be used for unoccupied time, one column for each type of machine or process cycle, etc.

Where more than one worker works at a particular job, such as a team, there is nearly always unoccupied time between members of the team, and further there may well be changes in the load or governing worker. Separate columns can be used for the work content and unoccupied time for each worker so that the totals of the columns will give the work content separately for each worker, and also the unoccupied time for each worker.

V

STANDARD TIMES

Steps

Observed Time : This is the time taken to perform an element or combination of elements by means of direct measurement.

Normal Time : The observed time is extended to normal time by the rating factor:

$$\text{Normal time} = \frac{\text{Observed time} \times \text{Observed rating}}{\text{Normal rating}}$$

Work Content: After adding RA% to normal time, work content is arrived at. Sometimes contigency allowance for work and delay as percentage of work content is also added at this stage if it has not been possible to measure them economically.

Standard Time: This is the total time in which a job should be completed at a normal performance, *i.e.* work content contingency allowance for work and delay, unoccupied time and interference allowance where applicable. Standard time may be expressed in minutes or hours.

Measured Work Performance (MWP)

$$\text{MWP} = \frac{\text{Standard Minutes}}{\begin{array}{c}\text{Minutes of attendance time } \textit{Minus} \text{ waiting time,} \\ \text{unoccupied time, uncontrolled work, diverted time.}\end{array}} \times 100$$

Attendance Time : The total time spent by a worker at the place or places of employment whether working or available for work for which payment is made. During attendance time the worker is likely to be occupied by 'Working Time', 'Diverted Time', or 'Waiting Time'.

Working Time: The time taken to do the work, including authorised relaxation.

Diverted Time: That part of attendance time when a worker is engaged on other than productive or ancillary work, e.g. committee work, accident prevention, etc.

Waiting Time: That part of attendance time other than unoccupied time during which a worker is available, but is prevented from working. Waiting time may be analysed under the heading: 'Department Responsible' (DR) and 'Department Not Responsible' (DNR).

Controlled Work: Work for which standards have been set as a basis for control.

Uncontrolled Work: Work for which no control standards have been determined.

---

* The concept of basic time may be used in place of normal time by extending the observed time by applying standard rating factor instead of normal rating. The work content or standard time so arrived at will be completed at standard performance.

DIAGRAMMATIC APPROACH TO STANDARD TIME

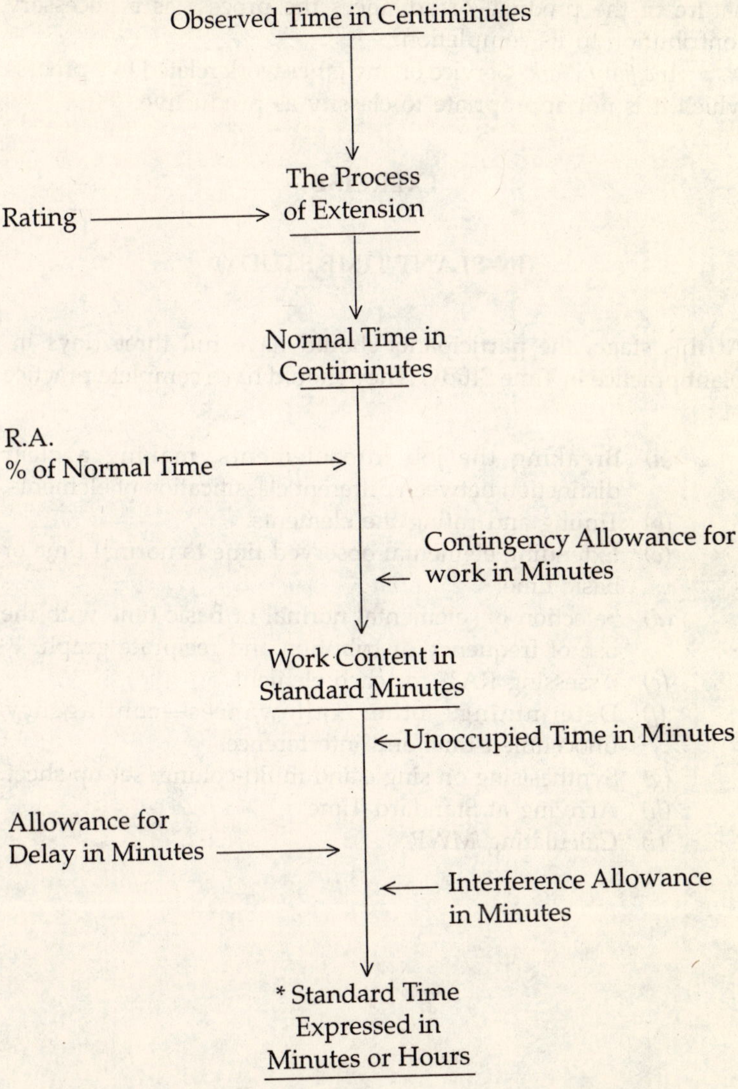

---

* When standard time is calculated by using the concept of basic time and standard performance this is converted into "Allowed Time" by adding 33½% extra time. The allowed time is issued when operatives are put on financial incentives.

Productive Work: Work which alters the physical or chemical nature of the product, or advances the process as a necessary contribution to its completion.

Ancillary Work: Service or any other work related to a process which it is not appropriate to classify as productive.

EXERCISE

(IN-PLANT TIME STUDY)

At this stage, the participants should have full three days in-plant practice in Time Study. They should have complete practice of :

- *(a)* Breaking the job into elements, making a clear distinction between different classification of elements.
- *(b)* Timing and rating the elements.
- *(c)* Extending elemental observed time to normal time or basic time.
- *(d)* Selection of elemental normal or basic time with the use of frequency distribution and reciprate graph.
- *(e)* Assessing RA% for each element.
- *(f)* Determining other allowances—contingency, unoccupied time and interference.
- *(g)* Synthesising on single and multi-column set-up sheet.
- *(h)* Arriving at Standard Time.
- *(i)* Calculating MWP.

7

Process of Technological Innovations

I

CASE OF TELECOMMUNICATIONS AND ELECTRONICS IN JAPAN

The Nippon Electric Company was founded in 1898 as a joint venture with the Western Electric Company of the United States. The first company of its kind in Japan, Nippon Electric started by importing, manufacturing and selling telephone sets and switching equipment to the Japanese government; which was responsible for operating the telephone business at that time. Since then, the company has made progress in line with the technological development of telecommunications in Japan.

On November 10, 1928, the Emperor's coronation was held in Kyoto. Two large newspaper companies, publishers of *The Mainichi* and *The Asahi*, planned to transmit photographs of the ceremonies from Osaka to Tokyo. *The Mainichi* used the Belin system of France and *The Asahi* used the Siemens system of Germany. However, the success of the Belin system was doubtful, since experiments had not been satisfactory. Consequently, it was changed over to the Nippon Electric facsimile system, then under development by Dr. Y. Niwa and Dr. M. Kobayashi. This episode was helpful in expediting the completion of the system. The Nippon Electric system proved superior to the Siemens system in speed and clearness, and the transmission was successful. This event was a motivating force on the subsequent rise in the promotion of domestic technology in telecommunications in Japan. A year later, in 1929, I joined Nippon Electric with the expectation of becoming a pioneer of new communications technology. I suppose it was my young blood and ambition that drove me to the dream.

One of the activities that further promoted domestic technology in Japan was the proposal in 1932 by Dr. S. Matsumae and Dr. N. Shinohara of the Ministry of Communications for a nonloaded-cable carrier system. It was innovative in two ways. First, it applied multiplex carrier to cable lines, and such a system had so far been used only on open-wire communication lines; and second, it abolished loading coils, which were commonly used for cable lines at that time. Prior to the proposal, from 1930 to 1932, Dr. T. Kajii and Dr. Matsumae carried out an important experiment in which I participated. It was a transmission experiment of multiplex telegraph and voice telephone using a 200-kilometer direct current submarine telegraph cable that had been placed under the Korean Straits many years earlier by a Danish company. Such a nonloaded cable line had a great deal of line loss, but compared with the loaded line, the cut-off frequency problem was almost eliminated. If the line loss is compensated by a vacuum-tube amplifier of good quality and uniform wide-band characteristics, it is possible to use it as a telephone transmission line. This experiment was successful, and the new proposal was made with confidence.

Some active engineers thought that it was unbearable to put new ideas into an old leather bag, and they tried to promote a domestic communications technology based on their own ideas. With the Institute of Telegraph and Telephone Engineers as its center, a committee for domestic technology was organized to study the status of technologies, both domestic and foreign, and to develop a plan for promoting the domestic technology.

As a result of the study, it was discovered that 90 per cent of the patents used in Japan's communications technology were owned by foreign corporations. In view of this, the Ministry of Communications established a policy that no process or equipment covered by patents owned by foreign corporations could be used in developing the nonloaded-cable carrier system. For example, the system of optimum allocation of carrier frequency, which is widely used today, was covered by a German patent. Accordingly, in compliance with the Ministry's policy, a different frequency allocation was employed, despite the inconvenience. The frequency was changed after the war to that recommended by the International Telegraph and Telephone Consultative Committee.

It was my conclusion that there was no amplifier better suited for nonloaded-cable carrier systems than the negative feedback amplifier invented by Dr. H.S. Black of the Bell Telephone Laboratories. I was developing a repeater based on this principle, but it was not adopted because of the patent-origin restrictions. I was forced to resort to the next best means. A triode having less distortion was developed for exclusive use. Thus, a 3,000-kilometer 6-channel nonloaded cable line between Japan and Manchuria, probably one of the longest lines in the world at that time, was completed in 1939. This was a milestone, and it gave us confidence in developing Japan's own technology.

It is true indeed that Japan's own technology was developed to avoid using equipment and processes covered by foreign patents. However, I cannot help feeling that this technological isolation went too far and was unreasonable. From the international stand-point, I believe that cooperation in the form of give-and-take is the best method of development.

Other example of the movement to develop Japan's own technology in which Nippon Electric participated include the development of coaxial-cable carrier systems, the completion of the 100-kilowatt radio broadcast equipment installed at Changchun, Manchuria, and the development of a VHF 6-channel multiplex radio-telephone system for linking the 60-kilometer span between Japan's main island, Honshu, and Hokkaido Island across the Straits of Tsugaru. The latter system was proposed between 1937 and 1939 by one of the young engineers of the Ministry of Communications, Dr. S. Yonezawa (now the president of Nippon Telegraph and Telephone Public Corporation). At that time, it was a noteworthy multiplex radio-telephone system that was put into commercial use.

In 1937 and 1938, I visited the United States and Europe to study the status of technology there. As a result, I recognized that there were great technological gaps between Japan and these countries. For instance, in Japanese technology, even if the concept were creative, its peak always fluctuated because of the lack of integration of the related technologies and because of the low industrial level in general. It could be said that the American and European technologies were standing on the vast base of Mt. Fuji, while Japan's technology could be compared to the sandstone spires in Colorado's Garden of the Gods. Needless to say, one of the major factors in such gaps might be ascribed to the difference in scale of the national economy. I think also that the gap resulted from shortages in the quality and quantity of Japanese engineers. In the period of postwar restoration, Nippon Electric retained many capable engineers in its research laboratory. We were able to make these engineers a motive power in reconstructing our company by transferring them to important line positions. I believe that this was an important factor in the rehabilitation of the damaged industry.

Let me now refer to a patent policy formulated by the Japanese military command just before World War II. In this policy, all inventions would belong to the state and would not be turned over to private industries' own rights. Private industries were asked not to file any patent applications for their own inventions. Thus, there was a blank period for Japanese patents that lasted for several years. In contrast to this, the effective period of all those patents owned by allied nations in Japan after World War II was extended for a period of ten years, which resulted in a large gap in the field of patents between Japan and these countries. This extension period was one of the major factors in causing a large-scale postwar introduction of technologies from foreign countries into Japan. After the war ended, every technology in Japanese industries had to be started afresh. For their postwar rehabilitation, the industries adopted modern management and control technologies that had been developed mainly in the United States. The Nippon Electric Company was the first to apply statistical quality control to industrial production. In 1946, Mr. W.S. Magill, a staff member in General Douglas MacArthur's headquarters and a quality control engineer of the Western Electric Company, proposed to commend statistical quality control methods to all Japanese industries. As the first model case, our company was advised to adopt it. I promoted it for immediate practice under his guidance, and the results were successful. Two or three years later, MacArthur's headquarters opened a quality control course. Japanese academic circles cooperated, and thus statistical quality control gradually spread over the whole industry.

The quality control technology, including statistical quality control and total quality control, contribution greatly toward the improvement of products in Japanese industry. Quality control methods made it possible to combine manufacturers with customers in a feedback loop, which had considerable influence upon the concept of quality of merchandise. Up until that time, it was considered necessary only to produce good products to meet the initial delivery specifications. Today, however, the emphasis is on making a product that will continue to satisfy the customer. In this way, constant efforts were made to improve the reputation of products "made in Japan."

During the period of Japan's occupation by Allied Forces, research on television was prohibited. Fortunately, however, no prohibition was placed on microwave technology. Consequently, technological innovations began in the field of microwave communications systems after the war.

As I mentioned earlier, Nippon Electric participated in the development of a VHF multiplex radio-telephone system during the period from 1937 to 1939. After the war, we resumed research on microwaves, based on our experience in radar research during the war and on the knowledge obtained from the United States and Europe. We looked to the area of private communications as the first market for microwave systems. We supplied, without cost, a complete one-route microwave communications system to a certain electric power company that was very much interested in introducing technological innovations. This was in 1952 when the financial recovery of our company was still incomplete and when the electric power company was provided with only a 3-channel power-line carrier system for business communications facilities. With the addition of our microwave system, the power company's communications capacity was expanded to 24 channels, which was a substantial contribution to smoother operation of the power utilities. Eight other electric power firms later adopted such a microwave communications system. Further, it found its way into the national railways and into many private enterprises, such as private railways and gas and electric power companies. Its application was extended from communications to telemetering, telecontrol, and data transmission. Thus a broad market was exploited for the system.

The ban on research in television was finally removed, and in 1950 the Radio Law and the Broadcast Law were enacted. Radio frequencies monopolised by the Japanese military government were opened to public use, and television broadcasting began. The realisation of commercial broadcasting was accelerated by the release of broadcasting from the monopoly of the Japan Broadcasting Corporation. The start of television broadcasting necessitated the installation of a nationwide relay network for television programmes. We knew that in the United States a coaxial-cable system and a microwave system were used together for this purpose. However, the Nippon Telegraph and Telephone Public Corporation (NTT), which was established in 1952 as a result of the release of the telecommunications business from government operation, chose the microwave system, which requires shorter installation time and is more economical in construction cost. Travelling-wave tubes were adopted from the beginning.

NTT decided to use this microwave communications system for super-multiplex telephone relay as well as for relay of television programmes and proposed to carry out developments of the system as a special project of NTT's Electrical Communication Laboratory. Nippon Electric was asked to cooperate fully with NTT in this project, and NTT encouraged us with its readiness even to import components of foreign make if necessary. We added what we learned from the Bell System and the International Telephone and Telegraph Corporation of the technology created by our own research and development. Some representative examples of our developments are a combined oscillation and amplification system using travelling-wave tubes, solid-state technology and a high-sensitivity receiving system using phase-lock threshold extension and 2,7000 channels.

Increases in nationwide radio and television network broadcasting were supported by a rapid growth in the number of radio and television subscribers. At the end of 1967, the number of contracted households for television alone was 20 million and the percentage was 83 per cent. If radio is included, the figures are 22.5 million and 93 per cent. This number of households is the second highest in the world, following the United States.

Such increases in the number of radio and television subscribers brought about a rapid expansion of the receiver manufacturing industry. The semiconductor industry, especially, was built up through technology from the United States. This created a new market for the so-called "handbag radio" and accelerated the growth of Japan's whole electronic industry. The desire to create a new market, coupled with the efforts made to develop new technologies required for its realisation, is considered one of the important reasons for the rapid growth of Japan's economy.

Dr. T. Kajii, the first president of NTT, shaped the basic policy that all technological innovations were to be adopted in order to rapidly develop a modern telecommunications network in Japan. In the early 1950's, telephone subscribers amounted to only 1.55 million. The Nippon Telegraph and Telephone Public Corporation worked out its four consecutive five-year expansion programmes, planning for 20 million subscribers by 1972, and tried to erase all waiting lists. In an effort to accomplish their goals, NTT personnel asked communications equipment manufacturers to cooperate with them. This was an epoch-making event for manufacturers, and it encouraged us to proceed with technological innovations. Most of those American and European engineers and manufacturers of communications equipment who visited Japan expressed their views that the progress of the communications industry in Japan was a result of not only the efforts of manufacturers, but also of the forward-looking policy of NTT as users. I fully agree, and I believe that the positive, mutually cooperative attitude of users and customers is the most important factor as a background for stimulating technological innovation.

NTT's first requirements for innovation were improving carrier transmission equipment and developing microwave systems to meet the expansion of toll telephone lines. In carrier transmission equipment, cost reduction by miniaturisation was required. We had many expensive failures, but after ten years we were able to manufacture equipment of a high technological level through the development of filter design theory and magnetic materials of high performance and through the adoption of solid-state technology. Speaking of size only, it was merely halved during the ten years before the war while it was made to be one hundredth of its former size during the 20 years after the war.

Earlier, I mentioned the progress in the development of microwave equipment. It was important that both the microwave system and the coaxial-cable carrier system were developed in competition. Within our company, the two engineering groups worked independently of each other and stimulated each other. This resulted in further developing both systems to show their respective features. Thus, equipment provided with 2,700 channels per system was completed for both systems, and today a pulse-code modulation system has been developed for each of them. I assume that the microwave system and the cable system will compete keenly with each other in the immediate future, but I think that in the long-run they will find a complementary position and will be linked to television networks, satellite communications and millimetre wave systems.

In parallel with such expansion of toll lines, a new crossbar system has made rapid progress as a switching system for both local and toll calls, getting rid of the step-by-step system that had remained unchanged for more than 40 years. Telephone sets have also been improved from the old No. 3 type to the newest No. 600 type. We manufacturers jointly cooperated with NTT's Electrical Communication Laboratory in these developments.

In this way, NTT's five-year programmes have proceeded satisfactorily. This year is the first year of its fourth programme. Fifteen years ago, we had to wait for hours to complete a call from Tokyo to Osaka—much longer than the three hours and ten minutes that it takes the new Tokaido Railroad to travel between these two cities. Today, direct automatic dialling networks connect more than 3,000 cities and towns in Japan. According to an estimate of NTT, these technological innovations resulted in reducing the cost of plant facilities by about $1.1 billion at the middle of the third five-year programme.

NTT next took up both electronic switching and data communications systems as major subjects for development. Manufacturers are cooperating with NTT in these projects. We have ideas for many new telegraph and telephone services, and various types of customer equipment are being developed to meet these ideas. One example is the development of a television telephone. Many technological problems have yet to be solved before television telephony is made available to the public, but it is expected to be in use shortly on a private-line basis. One of the corporate communications systems we developed and began marketing was a television telephone called the Executive Videophone, to be used in communications among executives in office buildings.

Apart from the progress of technological innovation at NTT, I believe the electronic computer to be most important. The computer industry in Japan started later than that in the United States. The only experience that Nippon Electric had in this field was the development (in cooperation with Tokyo University) of a sorting and tabulating machine using electromagnetic relay. Skipping over the first generation of vacuum-tube computers the electronic computer industry started by using parametrons invented by Dr. E. Goto in 1954 as logical elements. The parametrons were put into commercial use and many of these computers were supplied to the market. Later, there was remarkable progress in transistors of high reliability for industrial use. In 1958, after a prototype transistorized computer (MARK IV) had been developed by the Electro technical Laboratory of the Ministry of International Trade and Industry, we further developed it and put it into commercial use. The first computer of this type was delivered by plane to the AUTOMATH Exhibition held in Paris in 1959 where it was successfully operated. Our engineers were very much encouraged by the high reputation that it earned.

In the late 1950's, I visited major computer manufacturers in the United States and Europe to study the electronic computer business. As a result, I found that the computer industry is quite different in nature from other industries. Frankly speaking, I realised for the first time that this industry is designed to sell soft-ware, such as information processing services, rather than hard-ware like computers, and that it represents new industrial concept that places the economic value on knowledge and information. Such then I have endeavoured to promote this industry in Japan for more than ten years. We have completed a series of computers ranging from small types to fairly large ones; several that use integrated circuits are included in the series. In 1967 we delivered a time-sharing system, the first in Japan, to Osaka University.

The special feature of the Japanese computer industry is that it has been developed mostly by the communications industry, whereas in other countries it has generally evolved from the business-machine industry. It should be quite interesting to observe the technical innovations resulting from these differences.

Nippon Electric is also involved in satellite communications. One day in July 1962, I switched on a television set in a Chicago hotel and watched a programme relayed from Paris via Telstar I. I was deeply impressed by the telecast because I have always attempted to inspire our engineers with the thought that in order to pave the way for future development of our company, they must look for technological innovation in the area of international communications. I had emphasised that it is essential to have a direct communications network throughout the world. The development of the over-the-horizon relay system based on the invention of a high-sensitivity receiving system using phase-lock threshold extension was one of the results of this encouragement. However, I was not satisfied with only this development. As I watched the television relay via Telstar I, I felt that the satellite communications field was what the Nippon Electric Company had been seeking for a new project area.

On my way home from Chicago, I visited Hughes Aircraft Company in Los Angles—which had developed the SYNCOM satellite—to see Dr. L.A. Hyland, vice president and general manager. From our meeting a setup was established between our two companies for the development of satellite communications equipment. The first product of this joint development was the STAR (Satellite Telecommunication by Automatic Routing) System. In 1965, public simulation experiments using a transponder similar to the one in the Early Bird satellite were carried out in Tokyo. The basic concept of this system is to consider the satellite as switching equipment installed in space and not to regard it merely as repeater equipment.

I should like to mention the high-sensitivity receiving system a little further. The over-the-horizon radio-relay system, first developed in the United States, required a high transmitting power of more than 10 kilowatts. Economic considerations and disturbances arising from the use of such high-powered transmitters limited its application to isolated islands and mountainous borders. In an attempt to minimise transmitting power, studies were made, and the high-sensitivity receiving system using phase-lock threshold extension was invented in our laboratory. We found means of improving remarkably the signal-to-noise ratio, and we were able to reduce the transmitting power needed to less than 100 watts. This over-the-horizon system could thus be used for domestic communications in combination with line-of-sight communications systems, and as a result, the market for microwave communications was expanded to an even greater extent.

When a computer system is combined with an electronic switching system, a satellite communications system and a satellite broadcasting system, a worldwide communications network can be realised. It will include data communication and information processing. As I look forward to telecommunications at the beginning of the twenty-first century, I like to emphasise that "communication" is beginning to mean talking, listening, and seeing between two or more persons at any place and at any time. I think that this definition is rather meaningful in helping us plan for the future.

Competition in the export market with manufacturers from various countries was new stimulation to our company in promoting technological innovations. In the telecommunications field, NTT is very influential domestically, but there is an unavoidable limit within so small a land as Japan. So it is necessary to develop larger markets in foreign countries though there will be keen competition. We should be able to overcome international competition through the efforts of technological innovation. For instance, it was difficult initially for us to export our microwave communications equipment from the standpoint of price. However, through full transistorisation and many other innovations, we were able to realize reasonable cost reductions and, thus, could enter the world market successfully.

Finally I should like to mention the concept of the "knowledge industry" It is very important for a company to have a proper business image for carrying out its activities and for encouraging innovation. The Nippon Electric Company's business image has undergone various changes. Until 1925, we were simply a manufacturer of telegraph and telephone equipment; between 1935 and 1955 we were a manufacturer of telecommunications equipment. Later, the development of computers coupled with software, automatic control systems, and data communications made it necessary for us to develop another new business image. Once the term "4C" (communication, control, computer and components) was proposed, but it was not satisfactory because of lack of flexibility and dynamism. Around that time, I read the book *Production and Distribution of Knowledge in the United States*, by Professor F. Machlup of Princeton University, and was very much impressed with his concept of the knowledge industry. His theory is too pick out such parts of knowledge and information as will be of economic value and to regard them as industry. This idea gave me the framework for which I have searched. I believe that offering the most useful electronic technology in support of the knowledge industry will be a business image most suited to our company. As I am not a scholar, I would not want to explain precisely what is meant by "knowledge industry" Speaking about it from the management standpoint, I might consider it to be a new field of industry backed by a combination of information science, systems engineering, and electronic technology. What is needed is brain-power. Japan is lacking in natural resources but abounds in diligent and well-educated brainpower. I think that we should carve out a hopeful future in this area and that this will be the road we should follow.

Technological innovation has much to do with the economy of a nation. I sometimes compare the Japanese economy to a top with small mass and the United States economy to a top with large mass. The top with large mass can spin either fast or slow, while the top with small mass falls down when it rotates either too fast or too slow, because of its decentralisation. Needless to say, the United States economy has a wider range of stability than does Japan's economy; therefore, we need to pursue technological innovation in such a way that fits well into the economy of our country.

Japan is one of the countries located in the so-called Pacific Economic Region. There are many countries whosc economies are fairly stable, like ours, and many countries whose economies are more unstable than ours. I think that in promoting technological innovations, Japan should find a proper role in such a regional economy as well as in the world economy.

II

INNOVATION IN PRODUCTION TECHNIQUES : R & D IN PRIVATE BUSINESS IN USA

Inherent in this symposium on "The Process of Technological Innovation" is the conviction that innovation generally is not only beneficial to mankind but is also essential for its welfare. Obviously, this does not mean that invention and innovation do not create problems. One need only think of the atomic bomb, the contamination of our environment, and the traffic jams in any large city to realise that in solving one set of problems technology can create others as a by-product. There has also been a vocal minority expressing fear that technological change would in the relatively near future cause increasing unemployment and that automation would eventually eliminate all but a few jobs.

This concern was a key factor in the establishment in 1964 by Congress of National Commission on Technology, Automation, and Economic Progress. I was among the 14 members of the Commission along with two other members of the National Academy of Engineering, Edwin Land and Philip Sporn. The complete report of the Commission, *Technology and the American Economy*[1] was published in 1966 and should be of interest to all who are concerned with the process and the problems of technological innovation.

Key sentences from the report are: "Technical change and productivity are primary sources of our unprecedented wealth.... The basic fact is that technology eliminates jobs, not work... It is unanimously held conviction of the Commission that the most important condition for successful adjustment to technological change is an adequate level of total income and employment."

These are conclusions with which, I believe, most of us can readily agree. Yet Messrs. Land and Sporn, and I—and undoubtedly many of the other members of the Commission as well—regretted that preoccupation with the problems of technology prevented adequate discussion and recommendations on how the process of technological innovation might be augmented to meet the pressing needs of society.

There can be little doubt that the need is for more innovation, not less. For example, consider what should be required to bring the year 2000 Gross National Product (GNP) per capita of the non-Communist world, excluding the United States, up to the level prevailing in the United States in 1966. Table 7.1 shows that the GNP per capita of the United States in 1966 was $3,770 and that the GNP per capita of the rest of the non-Communist world in that year was $490. Assuming that the population grows 2.2 per cent each year in the rest of the non-Communist world, increasing GNP per capita to $3,770 would require a compound growth rate of 6.2 per cent against the 2.7 per cent actually achieved since 1950. The formidable nature of the task, however, is made much more obvious when one looks at the total gross national product this would require. In the year 2000 the United States would have a total gross national product of $2,600 billion, an increase of three and one-half times. For the rest of the non-Communist world, however, it requires growth from just about

Table 7.1
Requirements to Provide Non-Communist World, Excluding United States, with Equivalent of 1966 Per Capita U.S. Gross National Product in Year 2000*

			Compound Growth per Year	
	1966	*2000*	*1966-2000*	*1950-1966*
Population, millions of people United States	197	316	1.4%	1.7%
Non-Communist World, excluding United States	2,044	4,227	2.2%	1.9%
GNP per capita, U.S. dollars United States	$ 3,770	$ 8,200	2.3%	2.2%
Non-Communist World, excluding United States	$ 490	$ 3,770†	6.2%	2.7%
GNP, billions U.S. dollars United States	$ 743	$ 2,600	3.8%	3.9%
Non-Communist World, excluding United States	$ 998	$15,936	8.5%	4.7%

* Constant 1966 dollars.
† Same as United States in 1966.

$1,000 billion to nearly $16,000 billion and a compound growth rate of 8.5 per cent, compared to the 4.7 per cent actually achieved since 1950. Yet, even these statistics do not portray the problem in its full complexity.

If the statistics of Japan and the 13 nations that make up the European Economic Community (EEC) and the European Free Trade Association (EFTA) are segregated from those of the rest of the non-Communist world, excluding the United States, a different picture develops. Assuming that their population will grow at 0.5 per cent year—which seems reasonable—these 14 nations need only increase their gross national product from $594 billion to $1,659 billion, a compound growth rate of 3.0 per cent (Table 7.2). However, the remainder of the non-Communist (world excluding the United States), with population estimated to grow at 2.4 per cent per year, must grow at a rate of 11.1 per cent and attain a GNP of $14,277 billion in order to attain by the year 2000 the same $3,770 GNP per capita enjoyed by the United States in 1966.

Table 7.2
Requirements of EEC, EFTA, and Japan Compared to Rest of Non-Communist World, Excluding United States, to have Equivalent of 1966 Per Capita U.S. Gross National Product in Year 2000*

	Billions U.S. Dollars		*Compound Growth per Year*	
GNP	*1966*	*2000*	*1966-2000*	*1950-1966*
EEC, EFTA, and Japan	$594	$ 1,659	3.0%	5.5%
Rest of Non-Communist world, excluding united States	$404	$14,277	11.1%	3.7%

* Constant 1966 dollars.

Of course, the gross national product cannot be equated completely with need and certainly most with the quality of life in a nation. Still, the disparities and needs are so great that there can be little questions that our concern must be that however effective innovation may be throughout the world, it will not be effective enough. The task for the foreseeable future is so large that even our best efforts will not be sufficient to attain desirable goals.

There are problems within problems. The United States is a country with a very high standard of living. We pay ourselves more for our hours of work than does any other country in the world. Yet the United States must sell to and compete with the rest of the world. If this nation is to sustain its high standard of living, then its over-all industrial effectiveness must be sufficiently higher than that of any other nation so that when the high wages we pay ourselves for our hours of labour are multiplied by our relatives effectiveness, we still come out in total as competitive.

Those of us who are engaged in developing, manufacturing, and selling products and services around the world know that in many respects this has become increasingly difficult over the past decade. For example, even though hourly earnings of manufacturing employees in Japan have been increasing at a faster rate than in the United States, the absolute difference has increased from about $1.78 per hour in 1957 to nearly $2.14 in 1966; for Italy, from $1.72 per hour difference in 1957 to $ 2.08 in 1966; for West Germany, from $1.55 per hour difference in 1957 to $1.61 in 1966; and for the United Kingdom, from $1.30 per hour difference in 1957 to $1.48 in 1966 (Figure 7.1).

A look at Taiwan's hourly salary differential (Figure 7.2) is helpful in making a comparison with another Far Eastern nation that is striving with considerable success to move into the modern industrial world. In 1957 Taiwan's manufacturing employee received an average of $1.98 per hour less than a similar worker here in the United States; in 1966 that difference had increased to nearly $2.60 per hour.

In an absolute sense, this comparison in terms of hourly cash earnings exaggerates the difference because not all indirects are included. This would not, I believe, change the relative and expanding differences in cost per hour and, indeed, might even increase the absolute differences in some cases because of the marked upturn in indirects in the United States in recent years.

Although all these examples are made with respect to hourly earnings of manufacturing employees, the relative differences, I believe, would be only moderately less if the comparison were made for professionals and managers.

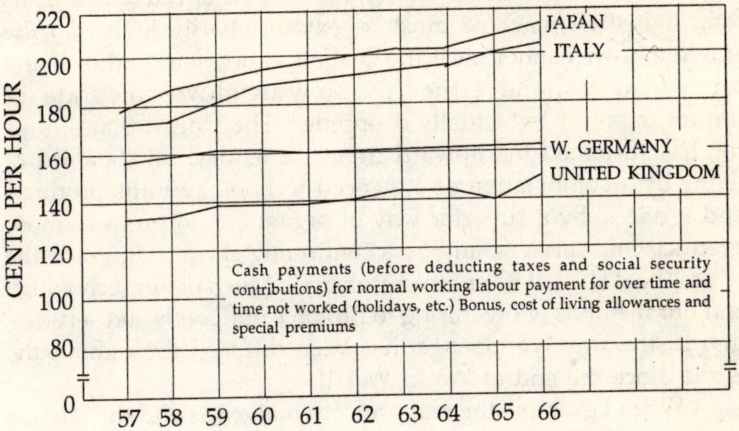

Source : Date from Bulletin of Labour Statistics, International Labour Office

Fig. 7.1 : Difference between Hourly Earnings of Manufacturing Employees in the United States and Other Industrial Countries.

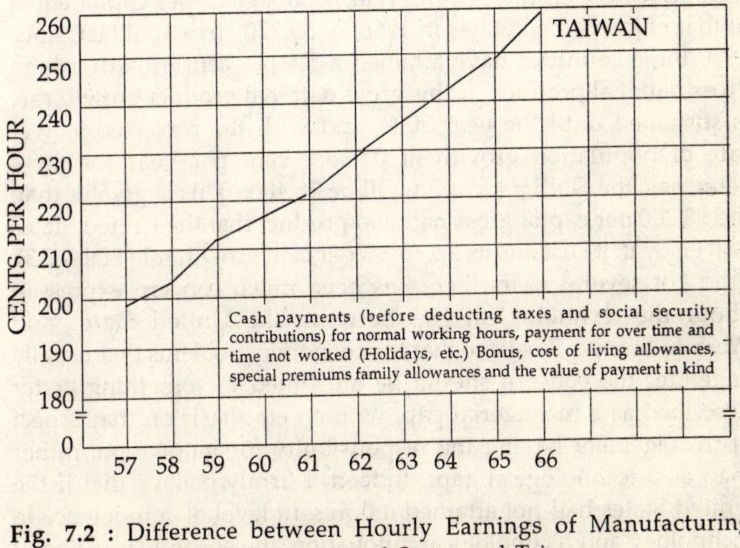

Fig. 7.2 : Difference between Hourly Earnings of Manufacturing Employees in the United States and Taiwan.

Obviously if the United States is to compete with wage and salary differences such as these, the over-all effectiveness of its total industrial machine must be extraordinarily high. To the extent that we cannot meet the challenge, our standard of living must also respond either by slowing down the rate of improvement or by actually dropping. The United States, thus far, has sustained the upward trend of its over-all standard of living by a combination of advanced technology in its products and services, by a superior way of organizing to produce those products and services, and by a continuing effort to upgrade the educational level of its entire population. Much of our technology and our methods of organising to produce our goods and services, that is, the way we manage, has been diffused throughout the world since the end of World War II.

When I examine the real problem that exists and the relative level of effectiveness that we must maintain in the United States to compete, my own concern is whether we can apply the admittedly excellent technology available now and in the future with sufficient innovativeness to continue improving our standard of living.

As Table 7.2 indicates, a 3.0 per cent increase per year in the gross national product of Japan and the 13 industrial countries of Europe would produce in the year 2000 a GNP per capita equal to that of the United States in 1966, or $3,770. In actual fact, since 1950 these countries have attained a 5.5 per cent growth rate in gross national product. If this gross national product growth rate is sustained until the year 2000, and with the projected slower rate of population growth of 0.5 per cent per year for these countries, the GNP per capita will be $8,400. This is greater than the $8,200 per capita gross national product that the United States will enjoy it, it sustains its 2.2 to 2.3 per cent growth rate (Table7.3).

For several years there has been much concern expressed about the technological gap between the United States and Western Europe. I believe that the economic problems that usually engender the concern should be attributed to something better described as a managerial gap, with an emphasis on that aspect of management having the responsibility for innovation, rather than as a technological gap. Indeed, I firmly believe that if the United States had not attained its present level of competence in technology and technological innovation, the absolute position of the remainder of the industrialised world would be lower than it is, even though the relative difference might be less.

Table 7.3
Gross National Product Per Capita, in 1966 U.S. Dollars

GNP	*1966*	*2000*	*Compound Growth per Year 1966-2000*	*1950-1966*
United States	$3,770	$8,200*	2.3%	2.2%
EEC, EFTA, and Japan	$1,580	$8,400†	5.0%	4.5%
Rest of Non-Communist world, excluding United States	$ 242	$ 367	1.2%	1.5%

* U.S. projection from Table 7.1.

† GNP in year 2000 (based on 1950-1966 rates of growreh)divided by projected population in year 2000.

Thus I believe that many of the restrictive practices in Japan with respect to non-Japanese-controlled industry and the growing economic nationalism in some European countries (generated by concern for such things as the strength of United States companies around the world and the so-called "technological gap") are ill-founded. Also, there is real danger that the effect of such actions is to slow down technological innovation in the United States through the limitations on markets and effectiveness thus imposed, particularly since the balance-of-payments problem of the United States is producing self-generated restrictions on trade, which, I believe, will be serious if long continued. The absolute level of GNP per capita of our European and Japanese friends, whether they be customers or competitors, will likely be lower, whatever the relative difference, if the United States is hindered in its efforts to sustain its economic growth.

Similarly, the underdeveloped countries continually express concern about their relative gains in standard of living with respect to the industrialised world. This is understandable, because even though their growth in gross national product since 1950 has been a respectable 3.7 per cent per year, their population has been growing at 2.2 per cent per year. Hence, their net gain in GNP per capita has been only 1.5 per cent per year. If a gross national product of 3.7 per cent per year is continued through to the year 2000, and with the projected change in population, the GNP per capita will still be modest, going from $242 to $367. Yet I think that the absolute position of the underdeveloped countries would be still poorer if the industrialised nations were less prosperous, even though the relative difference might be less. They, indeed, have problems, both in the need for increasing innovation and in the control of population; but if the whole industrialised world stumbles and does not continue to achieve technological innovation at a rate commensurate with its immediate past, then the underdeveloped nations are also going to be worse off in the year 2000 than they otherwise would be. Technology knows no boundaries, and the science and engineering on which it is based are soon readily available anywhere in the world. Many of these underdeveloped countries would be far better off if they made it easier for the companies of the industrialised countries to establish themselves there. The generation of the kinds of institutions necessary to comprehend and use that knowledge and of a national environment that encourages its use is much more difficult.

It is here that a really vital private enterprise system can provide the essential energy and drive required. No cumbersome or drawn-out government approvals are required. A vital private enterprise system makes it possible for an individual or a small group of men to solve a problem by applying new technology or by combining old technology in a new way to pursue that end and to obtain the necessary funds within the system. Further, such a system can make the rewards for success very high and can make the years of effort, high risk, and pay seem worthwhile. Also, the system creates a number of potential customers whose views and needs are sufficiently different that there will almost always be someone venturesome enough—seeing gain for his own institution from the innovation—to become a paying customer and to try the new product or service. A vital private enterprise system encourages the generation of corporations of all sizes, including many very large organisations that are absolutely necessary to handle the large-volume or large-scale tasks so essential to a modern industrial economy. A vital private enterprise system allows the enterprising innovators with the new product or services to choose whether to seek reward for success by growing into an organisation of sufficient size, whether to make and market the product or service on a scale commensurate with the opportunity and the need, or whether to merge with a larger organisation or sell out to it. For the men who are enterprising innovators, this latter course is frequently far better both for them and for society. Yet the antitrust policy of the United States often makes this kind of acquisition difficult or impossible for the very organisations where the end results would be most productive.

The contributions of the private enterprise system to the furnishing of highly innovative products and services to meet United States government needs, especially for space and national defence, are obvious. Certainly, every new piece of military equipment from strategic missiles to helicopters is based on technology and innovation. I have said the contributions are obvious, but this was not really true before World War II. Then the collaboration among government, university and industry radically changed the tools of war. This new approach was initiated by the British, for example, in their development of radar, and led to an effective and lasting collaboration here in the United States. The cooperative approach, if not the prototype, suggests at least what is probably a productive course to follow in tackling such major problems of modern industrial civilisation as traffic control in our crowded cities, the pollution of our environment and the preservation, distribution and control of water resources.

Even when the government is the end customer, the private enterprise system has advantages. To name just one, it is often easier to get a new product or service on the market by selling it to a contractor who wants to improve his own competitive position than it is by going directly to the government agency, where the individuals concerned may lack the knowledge, the authority, the stimulus, and often even the immediate funds to launch the new product or service.

In 1964, President Johnson directed the Department of Commerce to explore new ways for "speeding the development and spread of new technology."[2] In response, Secretary of Commerce John Connor appointed an *ad hoc* Panel on Invention and Innovation. The panel report, *Technological Innovation : Its Environment and Management*,[3] was published in January 1967. Time taken to examine this report is worthwhile. For example,

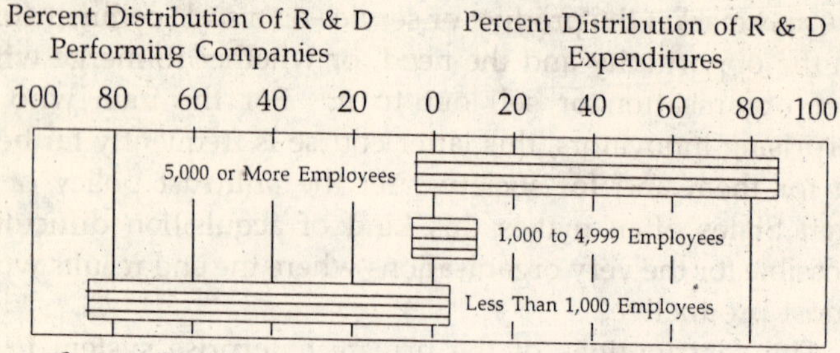

Source : Basic research applied research and development in industry 1962, NSF 65-18, 1965.

Fig. 7.3 : Variations in Research and Development, by Size of Company

the panel examined research and development in industry and attempted to correlate it with invention and innovation. As is shown in a chart from the panel report (Figure 7.3), based on National Science Foundation data, a comparatively few large companies having 5,000 or more employees performed almost all the research and development in industry in 1962. Important inventive contributions of independent inventors and small organisations were pointed out in the panel report (see Table 7.4).

Table 7.4
Some Important Inventive Contributions of Independent Inventors and Small Organizations in the Twentieth Century*

Xerography	Chester Carson
DDT	J.R. Geigy & Co.
Insulin	Frederick Banting
Vacuum tube	Lee De Forest
Rockets	Robert Goddard
Streptomycin	Selman Waksman
Penicillin	Alexander Fleming
Titanium	W. J. Kroll
shell molding	Johannes Croning
Cyclotron	Ernest O. Lawrence

(Contd.)

Cotton picker	John and Mack Rust
Shrink-proof knitted wear	Richard Walton
Dacron polyester fiber "Terylene"	J.K. Whinfield and J.T. Dickson
Catalytic cracking of petroleum	Eugene Houdry
Zipper	Whitcomb Judson and Gideon Sundback
Automatic transmissions	J.F. Hobbs
Gyrocompass	A. Kaempfe, E.A. Sperry, S.C. Brown
Jet engine	Frank Whittle, Hans Von Ohain
Frequency modulation radio	Edw in Armstrong
Self-winding wristwatch	John Harwood
Continuous hot-strip rolling of steel	John B. Tytus
Helicopter	Juan De La Clerva, Heinrich Focke, Igor sikorsky
Mercury dry cell	Samuel Ruben
Power steering	Francis Davis
Kodachrome	L. Mannes and L. Godowsky, Jr.
Air conditioning	Willis Carrier
Polaroid camera	Edwin Land
Haterodyne radio	Reginald Fessenden
Ball-point pen	Ladislao and Georg Biro
Cellophane	Jacques Brandenberger
Tungsten carbide	Karl Schroeter
Bakelite	Leo Baekeland
Oxygen steelmaking process	C.V. Schwarz, J. Miles, R. Durrer

* U.S. Department of Commerce, *Technological Innovation : Its environment and Management*, U.S. Government Printing Office, Washingtion, D.C., 1967, p. 18 :

After analyzing a number of studies of invention and innovation, the panel reported as follows :

> These studies were unusually consistent in indicating that independent inventors (including inventor-entrepreneurs) and small technologically-based companies are responsible

for a remarkable percentage of the important inventions and innovations of this century—a much larger per centage than their relative investment in these activities would suggest.

Professor John Jewkes, *et al.* showed that out of 61 important inventions and innovations of the twentieth century, which the authors selected for analysis, over half of them stemmed from independent inventors or small firms.

Professor Daniel Hamberg of the University of Maryland studied major inventions made during the decade 1946-55 and found that over two-thirds of them resulted from the work of independent inventors and small companies.

Professor Merton Peck of Harvard studied 149 inventions in aluminium welding, fabricating techniques and aluminium finishing. Major producers accounted for only one of seven important inventions.

Professor Hamberg also studied 13 major innovations in the American steel industry—four came from inventions in Europeans companies, seven from independent inventors, and none from inventions by the American steel companies.

Professor John Enos of the Massachusetts Institute of Technology studied what were considered seven major inventions in the refining and cracking of petroleum—all seven were made by independent inventors. The contributions of large companies were largely in the area of improvement inventions.

Obviously, caution is required in correlating the single year of research and development distribution by company size with studies of invention and innovation over more than half a century, but I suspect that the inverse relationship persists.

Some legitimate reasons why the absolute amount of research and development increases in big companies far more rapidly than do inventions and innovations are as follows:

1. If invention is going to lead to significant innovation, it must have a major impact on the society and it must involve, ordinarily, large-scale manufacture and use. Thus, medium-sized or big companies almost inevitably execute all or a major part of this extension into use.

2. In a number of cases the same organisation is involved in both the invention and the extension to the full market; that is, the company was small at the time of the invention or innovations but grew larger in the process of exploiting it into a successful full scale effort.

3. It usually takes many more development dollars and some more research dollars to extend the initial invention or innovation to full exploitation than it does simply to prove feasibility. Much more research and development money is involved in exploitation than in initial invention.

4. Individuals and small companies ordinarily do not become involved in the inventions or innovations that, by their nature, require large numbers of people and large resources. Thus a natural sorting operation is taking place, and a considerable proportion of the large company's research and development effort is involved in the multidisicipline research and development requiring extensive laboratories and equipment. Often, the result of the large-scale effort can still be identified as only a single or a small number of inventions or innovations even if successful.

Nevertheless, I think that those of us who have been involved in invention and innovation, both in small and large organisations, agree that it often becomes more difficult as the organisation grows and that a disproportionate effort seems to be involved in achieving the same amount of invention and innovation that occurred when the institution was younger and smaller. This recognition of increasing difficulty in bringing about innovation as the institution grows is usually accompanied by an acute feeling of frustation because it is so obvious that it should not be that way. As the organisation grows, it has more resources more knowledge, more qualified people, more contacts with customers, more opportunities, and greater need for innovation. Innovation ought to be getting easier instead of harder. Why is it not?

Here are what I believe to be some of the reasons:

1. As the organization grows it becomes more complex. Hundreds and then thousands of people are involved, often at several locations. The number of customers grows. Operations extend into many states and frequently into many countries. Governments add complexities of reporting and regulation—some

of them necessary but irksome and some of them unnecessary and cumbersome. To fully exploit the invention or innovation and to attain broad distribution, the price must come down. The margin between price and cost narrows. At a relatively early stage in the development, as far as this invention or innovation is concerned, it becomes far more important that the principal managers be good administrators than good innovators. The administration in a technologically based business may often require good or even highly advanced technical skill, but at this stage what counts is the aid that knowledge brings to administration rather than to innovation.

If the organisation is going to develop and grow, it must do so profitably. This can be exceedingly difficult, of course. Quite understandably we begin to get a preponderance of what I will call "administrative managers." They can exploit the innovation, but the skills they need and admire in themselves, in their peers, and in their superiors and subordinates are skills of administration, including leadership. Hence, the people they need and select are, in turn, predominantly administrative managers.

After a while, the cycle of exploitation of the innovation approaches maturity. However competent they may be and however secure they may feel in operating and adding to the organisation, most of the good men now in positions of responsibility do not really comprehend the process of innovation. Often they have succeeded or displaced the original innovators, and sometimes they have suffered justifiable despair at the inability of the innovators to perform adequately the increasingly difficult administrative tasks. At the same time, however, many an innovator fails to recognize how poor an administrator he really is. His own experience and value system simply do not qualify him to comprehend what is involved, how difficult it is to get the administrative management job done, and how justified the administrative manager is in his despair.

As a consequence the administrative managers have no basis on which to judge and respect the contribution that the innovator can make. All they are able to see is his often inadequate ability to administer. So, they help to develop the organisation by accretion, adding the products and services that flow naturally from the business they are already in, supplementing the markets in which they are already engaged, doing effective work in cutting costs and lowering prices. All of these factors are essential, but none is likely to provide the step function in product and service that is necessary for dynamic growth.

Aware of the desirability and pressure for growth at this stage, or even earlier, they begin to go down the acquisition and merger route. Because they are efficient administrators, the net result is often constructive and usually results in a more effective organisation that is more profitable and more useful to society. But, at the same time, the merger makes the organisation still more complex and decreases the relative number of those who know how to innovate, so innovation becomes increasingly harder. At some point the growth rate slows down or falls below that of the industries in which the organisation exists.

2. For the reasons enumerated, most of the status symbols—department managerships, administrative staff managerships, officerships, and perquisites—go to the administrative managers. The innovators around the organisation begin to believe, with some justification, that the way to be promoted is to succeed at administration. Some do succeed and become good administrators, and their knowledge of both innovation and administration may make the crucial differences in whether the organisation stagnates or continues to innovate and grow. However, with the system as it is, many of these men will not fit the pattern that the administrative manager recognises, and all too rarely will they get the time and the right kind of experience to succeed at administration. Too often they will "top out" well down in the management hierarchy; or if they do progress, just because they are not very good at administration, they have to work frantically to keep up and therefore will possess neither the energy nor the opportunity to innovate.

3. As the technologically based organisation grows, even when it succeeds in making the innovators into good administrative managers, it can confuse continued and competent technological development and commercial exploitation of its initial innovation with successful continued innovation. Where there are many scientists and engineers doing good science and engineering, accompanied by technically trained managers—all working long hours and running the business at a profit and with some growth—and the tasks being performed are difficult

and require all their professional skills, it can be difficult to recognise that there is no longer the requisite amount of really innovative effort going on to provide a step function in growth. In essence, the company is being consumed by its own success. After all, if the innovation is to be exploited to the degree necessary to bring all advantage due, every, proper technical and commercial potential must be turned into a reality. To do so and yet to remain competitive and profitable can consume more time and energy than all the organisation's best people, including the innovators, can find.

4. So, to handle the growth and the increasing complexity, the organisation decentralises into groups, divisions, departments, and branches. The total job is divided into a size that allows a good administrative manager to get his arms around it. This is logical and good management practice, but unless each general managers understands his job thoroughly, the company is in danger of becoming no more than the sum total of the decentralization parts loosely governed, from a financial point of view, at the corporate level. Then, the biggest job the corporation can handle has to be related to the biggest job that one or, at the most, a few of the decentralised units working together can handle. The only way that this can be prevented is to tie the decentralised entities together strongly at the top. Top notch general managers, aided by strong functional organisations in marketing, research and development, personnel, and control, must knit together the decentralised line units. Every manager must understand that the frequently enunciated management rule about responsibility and authority always going together is just not so.

The correct rule is that responsibility and authority must go together to the maximum extent possible. However, in a decentralized organisation the span of responsibility practically always exceeds the span of authority, and each manager has an authority that extends only to his own decentralised unit but a responsibility that extends only across the corporation. Without some countervailing force, even when good innovative managers develop in a decentralised organisation, their innovations are generally restricted only to the entity for which they are responsible or, at most, barely beyond it. Hence, although the organisation as a whole may have far more of the tools, the opportunity, and the skilled people needed for innovation, the exposure of any one manager is restricted, and he simply fails to see those larger opportunities to solve problems that are the right scale for the whole corporation or a large part of it.

Because the innovative efforts, even when they exist, tend to be restricted by the size of the decentralised units, there are few or none of what I call "breakthrough strategies". In other words, there are few strategic and innovative courses of action that, if they succeed, will have a major impact on the whole corporation—the sort of single strategy, the success of which can produce 10 per cent growth rates per year all by itself, even in a large corporation.

5. For every good man in a successful organisation, there is always more work than he can possibly do. Consequently, the personal discipline involved in balancing how much of the organisation's limited time shall go into exploitation and how much into further innovation is exceedingly difficult. This is particularly true because when one must choose between the hazy and uncertain high-risk future associated with a major innovative effort and the tangible, quantifiable future of exploiting present technological and commercial possibilities, the temptation is almost irresistible to stress the latter and postpone the former. If one is an administrative manager whose accomplishment is unquestioned, the necessity for choice may not even suggest itself.

If an innovative effort is to be of such significance that, if it secedes, it will have a major impact on a big company—a true breakthrough strategy—then at some critical time in its development the risk will be very large and the general management must understand both the risks and the potential rewards. Such examples of breakthrough innovations can be seen in RCA and colour television, IBM, and the 360, Xerox with at least two major inventions, Texas Instruments and its early breakthroughs in semiconductors, and Boeing and the 707. If management does not understand the choice, the applied resources simply will not be adequate and the strategy will fail; no innovation will result, not because it was not potentially there but because management lacked the comprehension and the courage to proceed.

Yet, for all the reasons outlined previously, it may be difficult for executives to determine with certainly what their company's policy is with respect to specific innovation effort.

The Boston Consulting Group has published a paper called *The Price of Uncertainly*,[4] which, although not specifically aimed at innovation in the large organisation, has great pertinence:

> Few things can paralyze an organization more than uncertainty about the strategy and the value system of the chief executive. Such uncertainty paralyzes initiative, inhibits adaptation to change and makes long-range planning impossible.
>
> Many of the committee meetings, staff conferences and even ceremonial occasions within a company serve primarily to reinforce and strengthen the assurance that "these are our objectives; this is how we propose to reach them; that is the area in which initiative will be acceptable." In the absence of such reassurances, initiative is a very dangerous thing.
>
> No member of management can afford to propose courses of action very often which will be rejected. Nor can he afford, even once, to start on a major plan or programme which at some point in the future will be dependent upon uncertain management support or approval. The intermediate manager who leads his subordinates in a plan of action which will be vetoed at a critical phase of implementation seriously jeopardizes his own future acceptability as a leader and a manager to his subordinates....
>
> There is genuine dilemma here. The chief must either make all the decisions or be completely predictable. Yet, he can't make all the decisions because the channels of communication are too limited almost by definition. Neither can he be predictable because that by definition does mean he can make no decisions except those already predicted.
>
> The solution to this organizational dilemma lies in policy. A policy is a statement of how a class of decisions will be made...the value of policies is that they remove uncertainty. Without them no one would dare take the initiative except in routine and repetitive areas.

The art of policy making is one of the most difficult and essential in business.

I would like to add that establishing policy is especially difficult when it applies to major innovative effort. Few large organisations manage to create a policy for innovation on a scale that is commensurate with their size and that, in turn, can result in major impact on the institution.

I have had the good fortune to be associated with Texas Instruments for most of my professional life, having joined the company in late 1945. The company is a good example of an organisation founded on innovation and developed by its founders over the years through exploitation of that innovation. It was first founded as Geophysical Service Inc. (GSI) in 1930. The first president, Dr. J.C. Karcher, and a succeeding president, Eugene McDermott, who though now retired is still an active director of Texas Instruments, are credited with playing principal roles in the invention and development of the reflection seismograph for oil exploration. By 1946, sixteen years later, GSI had grown into a good small organisation doing $2.25 million per year, practically all of it generated by competent technical and commercial exploitation of the initial innovation, but with no subsequent innovation of consequence.

After World War II we began an effort—at first halting and uncertain but later deliberate and relatively successful—toward growth through innovation. At any rate, Texas Instruments growth since then, from $2.25 million for the entire year of 1946 to over $50 million per month at the present time, has been due primarily to a series of inventions and innovations generated quite deliberately and with some consistency since 1946.

Introduced in 1954 were the first silicon grown-junction transistors and the germanium grown-junction transistors that made possible the first pocket radio.

The first semiconductor integrated circuits ever made was developed in our company's laboratories in the summer of 1958, just ten years after the transistor itself was invented at the Bell Telephone Laboratories.

In 1963, with contribution from Texco and Socony-Mobil, Texas Instruments introduced commercially a new oil exploration process based on the application of communications theory to seismic data processing.

In 1965, Texas Instruments clad metals helped to solve the shortage of silver coins in the United States.

In 1968, large-scale integration (LSI) components from Texas Instruments will go into prototype equipment. LSI is a technology for combining many hundreds, even thousands, of transistors, disorders, and similar electronic devices in a single slice of silicon. An integrated electronic component part of a computer memory providing storage for thousands of bits of information along with the auxiliary circuitry required to get in and out of the memory unit.

At the same time that we have been growing because of a series of successful innovations like these, we have had an uncomfortable recognition that growth can be accompanied by a decreasing innovativeness. Furthermore, in our work on semiconductors, we had the striking example that when the transistor was invented at the Bell Telephone Laboratories in 1948 or, even later, when the celebrated Bell Laboratories/Western Electric symposium on transistors was held in the spring of 1952, none of the three presently leading companies in the field—Texas Instruments, Motorola, and Fairchild—could have in any sense been expected to be logical organisations to occupy a leadership position. Certainly, they could not have been if success were measured by the size of research and development effort, extensive background in the solid-state and applied science and engineering, organisational know-how in similar componentry, and well-established relationships with all major customers.

As we grew, we continued to innovate but we knew that there had been even more opportunities that we had failed to seize. We could have done still better. To one degree or another, we found ourselves suffering from the inhibitions to innovation that I previously described as tending to go along with growth.

Senior management at Texas Instruments has been increasingly preoccupied with the process of innovation, and we have made a serious attempt to institutionalize it by developing a system for the management of innovation. This consists of a formal statement of business objectives, a detailed summary of the strategies that will be followed to attain the objectives, and a series of tactical programmes in such functions as research and development, manufacturing, and marketing, with emphasis on the invention and innovation required—all of which, if pursued effectively, will ensure the success of the strategies.

In 1965 I had the privilege, along with Dr. Casimir of Philips Industries, of participating in a European/North American conference on research management sponsored by the Organization for Economic Cooperation and Development (OECD). In my paper I examined in some detail the genesis of what we call our "(Objectives—Strategies—Tactics" system (OST) for managing innovation.[5]

Incidentally, Texas Instruments is now nearly twice the size it was when that paper was presented, and all the growth has been accomplished without acquisition or merger. This is significant only in that we were preoccupied then with managing innovation for growth. Today, with an over-all billings rate of more than $600 million per year, we feel that we have made some progress in the management of innovation and the development of our system. Yet we are still struggling to comprehend the process of innovation, to improve the environment for innovation, and to install and operate this OST system for the management of innovation on an equally effective basis across our entire company.

Let me illustrate one technological business area where the operation of the OST system has been carried out effectively. A forward-looking infrared system (FLIR) made by the Government Products Division of our Equipment Group for the United States government. It provides real-time images in a TV format with obvious implications for its significant contribution to the solution of night vision problem in high-speed military aircraft.

The development of this FLIR equipment is significant in that it required deliberate technological innovation and, in a number of cases, invention from a wide variety of decentralized and organizationally separated research and development, engineering, and manufacturing units on tight schedules.

The key technological innovations were initiated in fulfilment of a Government Products Division strategic plan and then combined to satisfy a series of military requirements. The research and development work on a special infrared window glass, including significant invention, was done in the Materials Science Research Laboratory of our Central Research Laboratories; the engineering and production work was conducted in the technical development area of our Components Group. At the upper right is a 400-element linear detector array. Detectors sensitive to the infrared energy are obtained both by doping single-crystal germanium with mercury and by forming single-crystal detectors out of mercury, cadmium, and tellurium. The required research and development (again including invention) was carried on in the Advanced Components Research Laboratory of our Central Research Laboratories; the engineering and production work was done under the Advanced Infrared Systems Components Group programme.

Another crucial invention is the monolithic array of 400 gallium-arsenide emitters. The research and development work was carried on in the Semiconductor Research and Development Laboratory of our Components Group, and engineering and production was done in the Advanced Infrared Systems Components Group programme. Yet another is a new type of electronic camera tube that we call the TIVICON, another key element in this FLIR system. Here we built on original research and development done at the Bell Telephone Laboratories and subsequent research and development in our Central Research Laboratories emphasizing the infrared spectrum. In the light-sensitive area of the tube is a monolithic array of almost half a million semiconductor diodes. The semiconductor diode array itself required research and development in our Semiconductor Research and Development Laboratory. The engineering and production of the entire assembled tube was carried on in the Components Group.

How does the OST system help to specify and coordinate the technological innovations required from these decentralised and organisationally separated entities? First of all, there is an intracompany objective on electro-optics. It covers all businesses and exploratory research in Texas Instruments founded on electro-optics technology. Its purpose is to push back existing internal boundaries to extend the electro-optics part of our business.

In addition to the intracompany objective, there is a specific strategy that describes the course we intend to pursue in the design, manufacture, and marketing of electro-optics systems. A strategy manager is responsible for seeing that all elements of the strategy are pursued adequately, not only within his own area but everywhere in the corporation.

We also have tactical action programmes. A part of one of the crucial components called for the development of three of the critical components previously mentioned—the TIVICON, the infrared glass, and detector array. A tactical action programme manager is responsible for all these developments being carried on adequately, even though a majority of the work is done in other research and development laboratories over which he has no immediate authority.

The OST system attempts to remove the uncertainty about objectives and strategies previously noted as inhibiting and to establish policy with respect to invention and innovation required in general business and technological areas. When innovation is managed properly using the OST system, the over-all accomplishment and the amount of significant invention and innovation is remarkable.

The FLIR system was one output of well-managed strategies and tactics, and it required little or no interventions on the part of top company management other than that involved in establishing the original objectives, strategies, and tactics. On the other hand, many of our earlier innovative successes, such as the digital seismic system, demanded positive and frequent top management intervention because our OST system was then in a rudimentary and much more informal state of development.

I wish I could state that all our strategic and tactical programmes were as successfully conducted as the FLIR system. As might be anticipated, in too many cases the strategies are not well-conceived, and the resources required are neither properly assessed nor subsequently applied and managed adequately. For the last year we have been making progress in systematizing and improving our capability in this regard. Indeed, we must succeed in the effort if significant invention and innovation are to continue to be basic to our growth.

Yet, considering the pressures on the United States previously, discussed, the gains required are so large that it seems doubtful whether they can be attained by professionals and managers alone, however effectively they may perform. Hence, after some experimentation over the past few years, Texas Instruments in 1967 launched a programme to involve most employees in team efforts to manage and improve their own jobs in the company and, through these efforts, to upgrade themselves, to add to the over-all level of innovativeness, and to markedly improve company productivity.

In one of our Annual Reports we stated the following:

> In November, we announced a major change in pay practice for U.S. hourly paid TI employees, to be effective January 1, 1968. They now receive a salary instead of pay by the hour.
>
> The step recognized the increased responsibility being extended to TI employees for managing their own work. It is part of a long-term effort directed toward having people at every level in the company more involved in planning, doing, and controlling their own and the work of their natural work group to solve problems and match and achieve personal and company goals...
>
> Texas Instruments is taking a "team" approach which calls for working groups to analyze their own jobs and suggest improvements., set individual and group performance goals, measure their own achievements against these goals—and learn from their own mistakes.
>
> The results are striking where team improvement efforts have been established. Over an 18-month period, operators on a germanium transistor manufacturing line exceeded by 20 per cent their own performance goals for reducing production costs and increasing output. These goals were higher than standards previously set by supervisors. Absenteeism during the period averaged less than 1 per cent of scheduled work hours. Team members on another mechanized assembly line introduced equipment improvement which cut labour costs at their point in the process by 40 per cent. Assemblers working on magnetic and rotary components for radar equipment cut production time from 2.5 to 1.2 hours per unit over a 15 month period. Members of these groups reported interest in their work increased sharply.
>
> This team approach to work, however, must be developed. In 1967, we established training programmes to educate managers and supervisors for the broader leadership role the approach requires, and we began to encourage employees at all levels to participate as team members in individual and group goal-setting and problem-solving

activities. Our goal is to have approximately 10,000 TI men and women involved in the team improvement efforts by the end of 1968, or early 1969.

In the final analysis, it is the corporation's Board of Directors that is legally and morally responsible for its policies, and there is no more complex or important corporate policy than that relating to corporate self-renewal. Texas Instruments has established a net-sales-billed goal of $3 billion, accompanied by a corresponding increase in earnings, to be accomplished in the next two decades. It is for this long-term goal, and even more generally for the years beyond, that our Board of Directors has been examining its responsibilities, structures, and practices. We recognize that, as a Board, our responsibilities include not only attaining the corporation's long-range objectives, but also determining what kind of corporation we are while our goals are being attained. Our deliberations have convinced us that our prime responsibility as a Board of Directors is to ensure our corporate self-renewal.

Thus, as a Board, we must prepare ourselves not only to attain a multibillion-dollar level in the coming decades, but to govern as institution of that size and to ensure that it continues to be a viable, constructive, self-renewing corporation dedicated to changing the world around it by creating, making, and marketing really useful products and services that will satisfy needs and solve problems for customers around the world.

Without interfering with the heavy and inevitably complete operating responsibilities that fall upon our principal executives, we feel that our Board must evolve mechanisms that will allow us to examine and influence and, in the final sense, take responsibility for corporate self-renewal by ensuring that

1. The corporate structure, policies, and practices are realistic, sufficiently elastic, and yet powerful enough to couple with the national and international environment as it now exists, and as it will be through future years over the entire corporate span of interests.

2. The corporation's products and services are truly innovative and are really contributing in a major way to constructive change in the world around it.

3. An innovative, aggressive, properly educated, and experienced staff of professional managers, scientists, engineers, and other specialists is available and is being generated in sufficient depth and talent to meet the corporation's long-range goals.

We are still in the process of discussing how we can best fulfil this responsibility for self-renewal, but tentatively we have concluded that, in addition to the usual outside directors who participate primarily through monthly board meetings and the full-time operating officers who serve as directors, it would also be desirable to have directors for whom this would be a principal occupation. Such a plan would ensure our having high-level capable people who have the time to study, to consider, and to comprehend the impact of the rapidly changing internal and external environment and the relationship of both environments to our corporate self-renewal. These directors would have no operating responsibilities; their duties would relate entirely to their function as directors and advisers to the Board. We have added one such director whose principal experience has been developed as a senior executive of Texas Instruments. In the future we shall, no doubt, add one or more additional directors whose principal experience has been within the company. We also want to add to the Board at least two individuals whose principal experience will have been developed outside the company.

Will all the efforts described be adequate? One believes so, but obviously cannot know for certain. Our struggles to comprehend and manage the process of technological innovation are the only ones one can discuss with any confidence. Of course, many other individuals and institutions also are grappling with the problems of innovation—some of them, no doubt, more effectively than we are. We do not believe that this is the only way to comprehend and manage innovation in a technologically based business institution; it is just our way. It is still too early to determine whether these programmes will be sufficient to ensure our corporate self-renewal. If, in the absence of external catastrophic events, the growth rate is sufficient to approach its net-sales-billed goal of $3 billion at an adequate profit level in the general time periods of the near future and if, as in the past, this has been accomplished primarily through internally generated products and services, then these programmes will have played a major role in attaining that goal and we can assume that a reasonably comprehensive system for managing corporate resources to ensure innovation has been established.

References

1. *Technology and the American Economy,* Report of the National Commission on Technology, Automation, and Economic Progress, U.S. Government Printing Office, Washington, D.C., 1966.
2. *Economic Report to the President of the Congress of the United States,* U.S. Government Printing Office, Washington, D.C., 1964.
3. U.S. Department of Commerce, *Technological Innovation: Its Environment and Management,* U.S. Government Printing Office, Washington, D.C., 1967, p. 16.
4. The Boston Consulting Group, *The Price of Uncertainty,* Organization Series, 1968.
5. Patrick E. Haggerty,"Strategies, Tactics, and Research", Paper presented at the European/North American Conference on Research Management, sponsored by the Organization for Economic Cooperation and Development, Monte Carlo, February 1965, pp. 89-110.

8

Production Inventory Models

I

AN ANALYTICAL INVENTORY MODEL WITH STOCHASTIC LEAD TIME

Introduction

The inventory model presented in this chapter is to a great extent similar to that of Liberatore [2]. The most important difference is that, in the model to be presented, distribution of the lead time is given in a finite interval, contrary to that in [2]. Interpretations of ordering cost and lot size are also different. Besides, this model is the cost optimisation version of the simplest member [4], [5], or the model-group of Prékopa and Ziermann.

Analysing this model, we succeeded in proving in an analytical way that if some assumptions are fulfilled, there exists an optimal solution. A new result is, compared with those in [2], that limits can be given to the optimal values of parameters. Structure of the limits is the same as in the model given by Gerencsér [1], which assumes continuous reviewing and stochastic demand.

In the last part of this chapter we also show an approximative solution, which is easier to treat.

1. Model Formulation

The model is based on the following assumptions:

(1) The model deals with stocking of a single item.
(2) Demand is deterministic, with the uniform rate x.
(3) The amount ordered is delivered in a single lot.
(4) Date of delivery, denoted by ρ, is a random variable in the interval $[0,\gamma]$, with the known probability distribution $G(\rho)$. Let M_1 and D^2 designate the expected value and variance of the distribution, respectively.
(5) There is a continuous reviewing.
(6) Shortagès are allowed; all the shortages are to be made up.
(7) Costs taken into account are [$] :
c_1—holding cost per unit quantity, per unit time
c_2—shortage cost per unit quantity, per unit time
c_3—ordering cost per order.
(8) The decision variables are as follows:
s—safety stock; we order when the inventory level reaches this value (*i.e*, s: reorder point), $s \geqq 0$.
q—lot size, $q > 0$.

Before writing down cost function of the model, we also need the following assumption :

$$q \geqq \gamma x \tag{1}$$

This assumption ensures that there can be only one ordered lot that has not been delivered.

Now we can compose the cost function showing the expected total costs per unit time

$$K(s_1 q) = c_1 \frac{q}{2} + c_1 s - c_1 M_1 x + (c_1 + c_2)\frac{1}{2q_{s/x}} \int^{\gamma} (\rho x - s)^2 \, dG(\rho) + c_3 \frac{x}{q} \tag{2}$$

In the following section of this chapter we deal with the optimisation of cost function (2).

2. The Optimal Solution

Analysing cost function (2) with the classical methods of analysis, we arrive at the following statement:

Theorem 1 :

If $G(\frac{s_0}{x}) < \frac{c_2}{c_1 + c_2}$, the optimal value s_0 can be obtained by solving the following equation :

$$c_1(c_1 + c_2) \int_{s_0/x}^{\gamma} (\rho x - s_0)^2 \, dG(\rho) + 2c_1c_3x$$

$$= (c_1 + c_2)^2 [\int_{s_0/x}^{\gamma} (\rho x - s_0) dG(\rho)]^2 \quad (3)$$

In turn, the optimal q_0 can be calculated in the following way :

$$q_0 = \sqrt{\frac{c_1 + c_2}{c_1} \int_{s_0/x}^{\gamma} (\rho x - s_0)^2 dG(\rho) + \frac{2c_3}{c_1} x} \quad (4)$$

Proof : Let us calculate partial derivatives of cost function (2), with respect to s and q, respectively :

$$\frac{\delta K(s_1 q)}{\delta q} = \frac{c_1}{c_2} - \frac{c_1 + c_2}{2q^2} \int_{s/x}^{\gamma} (\rho x - s)^2 dG(\rho) - \frac{c_3 x}{q_2}$$

$$\frac{\delta K(s_1 q)}{\delta s} = c_1 - (c_1 + c_2)\frac{1}{q} \int_{s/x}^{\gamma} (\rho x - s) \, dG(\rho)$$

Having these derivatives to be equal to zero and solving the system of equations gained in this way, we get (4) from the first equation, and (3) from the second one.

In order that the solution of the equation system should really be an optimum, it is necessary that the Hessian matrix of function (2) should be a positive definite one. It assumes the derivatives of second order to be positive, and determinant of the Hessian matrix to be greater than zero.

Let us check these assumptions, one by one.

$$\frac{\delta^2 K(s_1 q)}{\delta q^2} = \frac{c_1 + c_2}{q^3} \int_{s/x}^{\gamma} (\rho x - s)^2 dG(\rho) + \frac{2c_3 x}{q^3}$$

This is obviously positive, when

$$s < \gamma x \tag{5}$$

This condition formulates the economically reasonable assumption that one should not hold safety stock of amounts greater than the total demand occurring during the maximum lead time.

This is so much an evident assumption that even the optimum of function (2) will be sought only in interval $[0, \gamma x]$.

$$\frac{\delta^2 K(s_1 q)}{\delta s^2} = (c_1 + c_2)\frac{1}{q} \int_{s/x}^{\gamma} dG(\rho)$$

Again, this term is positive if the condition (5) is fulfilled.

$$\frac{\delta^2 K(s_1 q)}{\delta q \delta s} = (c_1 + c_2)\frac{1}{q^2} \int_{s/x}^{\gamma} (\rho x - s)\, dG(\rho)$$

On the basis of the above, we can determine that value of determinant of the Hessian matrix belonging to cost function (2):

$$\left(\frac{c_1 + c_2}{q_0^3} \int_{s_0/x}^{\gamma} (\rho x - s_0)^2\, dG(\rho) + \frac{2c_3 x}{q_0^3}\right)(c_1 + c_2)\frac{1}{q_0} \int_{s_0/x}^{\gamma} dG(\rho) -$$

$$-(c_1 + c_2)^2 \frac{1}{q_0^4}\left[\int_{s_0/x}^{\gamma} (\rho x - s_0)\, dG(\rho)\right]^2 > 0$$

This, by small alterations, can be transformed to the following form :

$$(c_1 + c_2) \int_{s_0/x}^{\gamma} (\rho x - s_0)^2 dG(\rho)\, [(c_1 + c_2) \int_{s_0/x}^{\gamma} dG(\rho) - c_1] +$$

$$+2c_3x[(c_1+c_2)\int_{s_0/x}^{\gamma} dG(\rho)-c_1]>0$$

This term is positive, if

$$(c_1+c_2)\int_{s_0/x}^{\gamma} dG(\rho)-c_1>0$$

from which the condition $G(s_0/x)<\dfrac{c_2}{c_1+c_2}$ can be gained immediately.

Q.e.d.

That is, if there is an s_0, corresponding to Theorem 1, we know that this and q_0 belonging to it are optimal solutions of cost function (2). Now it only remained to study the problem: on what conditions has equation (3) a root in the interval $[0, \gamma x]$. Regarding this, the following theorem can be proved.

Theorem 2 : Let s* denote the value of s, for which

$$G(\frac{s^*}{x})=\frac{c_2}{c_1+c_2} \tag{6}$$

Then, if the condition

$$\frac{2c_1c_3}{c_1+c_2}<[c_2\,M_1^2-c_1\,D^2]\,x \tag{7}$$

is fulfilled, equation (3) has one and only one root (s_0), in the interval $[0, \gamma x]$, for which : $0 < S_0 < s^*$.

Proof : Let L(s) denote the following function :

$$L(s)=c_1(c_1+c_2)\int_{s/x}^{\gamma}(\rho x-s)^2\,dG(\rho)+2c_1\,c_3\,x-$$

$$-(c_1+c_2)^2[\int_{s/x}^{\gamma}(\rho x-s)\,dG(\rho)]^2$$

Let us calculate the first derivatives of this function.

$$L'(s) = 2(c_1 + c_2) \int_{s/x}^{\gamma} (\rho x - s)\, dG(\rho) \left[(c_1 + c_2) \int_{s/x}^{\gamma} dG(\rho) - c_1 \right]$$

Sign of this term is obviously determined by the sign of function

$$L_1(s) = (c_1 + c_2) \int_{s/x}^{\gamma} dG(\rho) - c_1$$

As $L_1(s) = 0$, when $s = s^*$, $L_1(s) > 0$, when $s < s^*$, and $L_1(s) < 0$ when $s > s^*$, the following can be stated about the behaviour of function : L(s) is monotonically increasing in the interval $[0, s^*]$ monotonically decreasing in the interval $[s^*, \gamma x]$ and has a maximum at s^*.

It results from this that if L(s) is negative at $s = 0$, and is positive at $s = \gamma x$, then L(s) has only one root in the interval $[0, \gamma x]$ and this root is in the interval $[0, s^*]$.

That is :

$$L(\gamma x) = 2c_1 c_3 x > 0$$

$$L(0) = (c_1 + c_2)\, x^2\, [c_1 D^2 - c_2 M_1^2] + 2c_1 c_3 x$$

By transforming $L(0) < 0$ we get condition (7).

Q.e.d.

It is worth to compare equation (6) defining s^* with a result of L. Gerencsér [1], who, in the case of stochastic demand process used $s_0 < s^*$ where s^* is defined by the following equation.

$$F(s^*) = \frac{c_2}{c_1 + c_2} \tag{8}$$

where F(x) is the distribution function of demand.

Structural and essential identity of equations (6) and (8) is clear-cut. The question arises whether the models with continuous reviewing have an unchanging property of giving similar limits to optimal values of parameters, independently of the nature of stochastic process which is influencing it.

Thus far we treated this model in its most general form. We had not even assumed that the probability distribution is continuous; the statements made so far are valid for both discrete and continuous distributions.

However, in order to exceed equation (3) in solving this problem it is necessary to specify the distribution function. In the case of equation (3), this hardly seems to be a practicable way, because assuming even the uniform distribution, one arrives at an equation of fourth degree in s_0. This is why solution of equation (3) can rather be achieved by using a computer. In doing that, Theorem 2 may prove to be useful, since the root-seeking procedure can be limited to the interval [0, s*].

At the same time, however, demand of finding an approximative solution, easier to be treated, is also arising. In the following section of the chapter we deal with this problem.

3. Approximative Solution

Basis of the approximative solution is to assume : $q_0 = \gamma x$. This is a reasonable assumption, when the demand rate is uniform and known.

Having altered all the equations according to this assumption, we gain that optimal s_0 should satisfy the following equation :

$$\frac{c_1}{c_1 + c_2}\gamma x = \int_{s_0/x}^{\gamma} (\rho x - s_0)\, dG(\rho) \qquad (9)$$

For solving this, we can make use of the following theorem.

Theorem 3 : If $M_1 \geq \frac{c_1}{c_1 + c_2}\gamma$, equation (9) has one and only one root in the interval $[0, \gamma x]$.

Proof : Be now

$$L_{2=}(s) = (c_1 + c_2)\int_{s/x}^{\gamma} (\rho x - s)\, dG(\rho) - c_1 \gamma x$$

As $L_2(s) = -(c_1 + c_2)\int_{s/x}^{\gamma} dG(\rho) < 0$, so $L_2(s)$ is a monotonically decreasing function. Now $L_2(\gamma x) = -c_1\gamma x < 0$, so if

$L_2(0) = (c_1 + c_2)x \int_0^{\gamma} \rho dG(\rho) - c_1 \gamma x > 0$ – which is equivalent to the condition in the theorem – the existence of the unique solution – because of the monotony of the function – is guaranteed.

Q.e.d.

This model is really easier to treat. Let us take an example now, where we suppose that $G(\rho)$ is a distribution function of a random variable, uniformly distributed in the interval $[0, \gamma x]$. In this condition in Theorem 3 takes the following form:

$$\frac{\gamma}{2} \geq \frac{c_1}{c_1 + c_2}\gamma$$

and it is fulfilled, when $c_2 > c_1$, a relation which is quite reasonable to assume.

Now the equation corresponding to (9) is of form :

$$c_1 \gamma x - (c_1 + c_2)\frac{1}{\gamma} \int_{s_0/x}^{\gamma} (\rho x - s_0)\, d\rho = 0$$

Solution of this is :

$$s_0 = \left[1 - \sqrt{\frac{2c_1}{c_1 + c_2}}\right]\gamma x \qquad (10)$$

When examining this result, we find that it is always smaller than 1, that is, it should never be stocked as a safety stock, an amount of inventories equal to the total demand during the maximum lead time. In addition, we see that the right side in (10) is an increasing function of c_2, that is, the inventory level s_0 is increasing when c_2 is increasing, the probability of not having any shortages is increasing, too.

Let us take a numerical example. One might demand that the probability of the stockout should not exceed 5 per cent. Then, if the probability of stockout is approached by the ratio $c_1/(c_1 + c_2)$, a feasible solution of equation $c_1/(c_1+c_2) = 0.05$ is *e.g.* $c_1 = 1$ and $c_2 = 19$. The value of s_0 belonging to this is $s_0 = 0.75\ \gamma x$.

Let us compare this result with that of the simplest model of Prékopa and Ziermann. This model is based on conditions that are definitely the same as in our model. Solution of that model is $M = [1-\xi]\,\gamma x$, where M is the initial inventory, ξ is the probability of stockout. When substituting the above data into this model, we get $M = 0.95 \quad x$.

It can be seen that using the cost optimization version of the model results in nearly 20 per cent inventory level reduction.

Simulation tests of this model are to demonstrate whether is true or not.

II

OPTIMUM EXECUTION OF STOCK KEEPING PROCESSES

1. Problem

The solution of a series of economical problems like those of the stock keeping and operating type, for instance, cause to study stochastic systems, whose essential system qualities are characterised by a parameter vector c. Supposing Q to be the characteristic value of efficiency, we will deal with the following stochastic optimum problem :

$$J(c_0) = \min \{J(c) / c \in C \wedge h(c) \geq 0\} \tag{1a}$$

$$J(c) = E_z\{Q(z,c)\},\ h(c) = E_z\{g(z,c)\}. \tag{1b}$$

The mathematical structure obtained is often too complicated to permit any analytical solution at all or under restrictive conditions only.

Especially the development of computer engineering brings about some possibilities of extending the scope of the mathematical model analysis beyond the limits of performance of the mathematical optimisation procedures, provided that the mathematical model is realised by a computer and that an approximation solution of the problem concerned is found out by means of planned model tests.

Instead of a simple comparison of variants aimed at solving this problem, test planning intended for reaching the admissible target zone by as few tests as possible becomes necessary.

The amount of rules for choosing the system out of the system family given, which the suitable dimensional variable is to bè determined for by means of the model test, is called a search plan. This article is intended to demonstrate, how to apply sequential and simultaneous search plans to the execution of production and stock keeping processes. Therewith sequential search plans lay down the following test on the basis of the results obtained by the tests carried out hither to, where methods of planning optimising tests and search methods, respectively, are adequate to establish them in addition to heuristic statements.

2. Stock Keeping System to be Studied

Conditions

A stock is being considered. Let the demand R for a definite article within the order period [th, (t+1)h] be a time-independent random variable $R=R_1+R_2$, in connection with which R_1 and R_2 are independent random demands at the intervals [th, $(t+1-\lambda)h$] and [$(t+1-\lambda)h$, (t+1)h], respectively, with the probability density functions $f_1(R_1)$, $f_2(R_2)$. Orders for recharging the stock are possible to be passed at fixed order times $(t+1-\lambda)h$, let the order time be constant λh. The stock keeping causes the expenditure of storage costs k_L, which are proportional to the mean stock, as well as that of procurement costs k_B. The normal procurement costs consist of a constant part k^0_B, which has to be expanded for each supply and of a part k^1_B, which is proportional to the amount ordered.

If the stock is empty, the demand has to be met by a special procurement and the costs k^1_F for special supply are proportional to the mean stock shortage.

Aim of the Study

It is required to establish an order rule (s, S), whose application at the interval The keeps the mean costs for stock keeping and procurement per period of order as low as possible, with s being the critical stock and S the order level. Therewith J(S, s)=E {Q(T, S, s)}, in connection with which Q(T, S, s) are the random total costs to be expanded at the interval [0, Th] applies to the expected value of the total costs at the interval Th. It holds true :

$$Q(T,S,s) = \sum_{t=0}^{T-1} Q(\, x[th],\, R_1^t, R_2^t,\; S,s),$$

in connection with which x[th] is the stock at the beginning of the order period [th, (t+1)h], R_i^t (i=1, 2) is the realisation of the demands at [th, (t+1−λ)h] and [(t+1−λ)h, (t+1)h], respectively. Therewith to the stock x[th] applies x[(t+1)h]=x[th] + p(t+1, h)− $R_1^{t-} - R_2^t$, in connection with which are p(t+1, h) = {S−x[th] +R_1^t} H{x[th] −R_1^t −s} as well as H(z)=1 for z > 0 and H(z)=0 for $z \le 0$.

There are even with simple probability density functions $f_1(R_1)$ and $f_2(R_2)$ obvious considerable difficulties in the analytical solution of the stochastic optimum problem. That is why an algorithmic model was programmed in ALGOL and PL 1, respectively, and was realised by the computer R 300 and EC 1020, respectively.

3. Adaptive Trial Solution

The model (in general an algorithmic one) of the stock keeping system to be studied, is realised by the computer. As a result of the model tests a realisation of samples taken at random of the model state development is yielded for each realisation of samples taken at random of the influencing variables. Depending on which efficiency criterion is choosen, we will get a realisation $Q(z^r, c)$, in connection with which $Q(z^r, c)$ is a random variable of an unknown partition. The optimum problem Eq. (1a, 1b) to be solved turns out to be a stochastic optimum one of an insufficient a-priori-information. If the complexity of the model does not permit sequential search plans to be supplied, it is possible to make use of the well-known regular search methods, provided that they are combined with a suitable statistic test. For this purpose a combination was made between

- *(a)* the search algorithm after Nelder/Mead and a sequential test for equality to two mean values (NS),
- *(b)* the gradient methods and a statistic estimation of the gradient (orthogonal test planning) (BW).

In addition to this, stochastic search methods are adequate, whereby a modified algorithm of the stochastic approximation (S) was applied to the case in question.

In conformity with these possibilities, programmes were developed in PL 1 and were realised for different problems of the stock keeping and operating type.

For the purpose of illustration (Müller, 1978) indictates the mean optimum strategies for the example by means of stochastic simulation and by the application of sequential search plans (NS, BW and S) to different partition functions and model parameters.

4. Probability Theory Approach

Another possibility is offered by the probability theory approach of the simulation (–, 1971), which does not use any realisations of the random variables unlike the stochastic simulation, but makes use of their probability functions as original information. The transformation of the probability functions in the way adequate to the system logic, yields the desired probability functions of the state variable concerned. Thus the solution of the optimum problem does not differ any longer from the solution of the deterministic optimum problem Eq.(1a).

The task of the algorithmisation is to determine the transformation of the probability functions and to realise them by the digital computer. Therewith it becomes evident, that a small number of typical operations, which can be pre-programmed as macro-orders, will have to be carried out, if circumstances are favourable. A suitable programme is available, with the most important macro-orders being in PL 1.

This programme was applied to the study of operating and stock keeping problems. In order to determine the optimum critical stock and the optimum order level in a stochastic demand of the example, the stock keeping system was modelled in the specified way and was combined with the search method after Rosenbrock.

For the determination of the expected value of costs we need the probability function of stock (and stock shortage, respectively), that of ordered quantity as well as the probability of an order to be passed. These variables can be determined by realising the following operations:

X(5, L) = SUB [X(3, I), X(4, K)]
X(L) = SUB [S, X(5, L)]
X(1, L) = SCW [S–s, X(I), 0]
H(L) = SCW [s, X(5, I), S]
X(3, L) = SUB [H(I), X(6, I)],

in connection with which the following probability functions are used :

- X(1, L) —Consignment at the beginning of the order period $p_t = (t, t+h)$
- X(3, L) —Stock at the beginning of the order period
- X(L), H(L) —Auxiliary variables
- X(4, L) —Demand in $[t, t+(1-\lambda)h]$
- X(5, L) —Stock at the time of order passing
- X(6, L) —Demand in $[t+(1-\lambda)h, t+h)$.

Besides this there is the following meaning of the operators:

SUB [Y(L) = SUB {X(I), Z(I)}] :

$$Y(L) = \sum_{M} X(I)\, Z(K), \qquad M = \{(I,K) / I - K = L\}$$

as well as

SCW [Y(L) = SCW {P, X(I), R}] :

$$Y(R) = \sum_{I=x_{min}}^{P} X(I), \qquad Y(L) = X(L) \text{ for } L > P.$$

Basing on the defined initial state, the probability functions of the desired stable state are yielded after an adequate number of iterations.

The programme for the realisation of the given operations was combined with a regular search method after Rosenbrock (T). The mean optimum parameters (s_0, S_0) for $T \to \infty$ (stationary state), which were obtained, are shown in (Müller, 1978).

5. Application of Simultaneous Search Plans

The partially considerable computing times needed by the electronic data processing equipment EC 1020—for one example, even the determination of the mean optimum order strategies for the stock keeping system shown in (Müller, 1978) (2 decision variables) took 5 to 20 minutes depending on the search method and the model parameters – reveal the bounds of the application of such sequential search plans to complicate algorithmic models and to a great number of decision variables, respectively. In many cases, however, simultaneous search plans are adequate to attain a desired improvement of the characteristic value of efficiency.

Generally, the application of simultaneous search plans is aimed at approximating to the complicate functional J(c) Eq. (1b) by a simpler one, *e.g* by a polynomial in c. Therewith the number of test points has to be fixed until active model test is started. Within the scope of the theory of test suitable search plans, which are used to avoid systematic errors in the experimental arrangement, were developed. If it is known in advance, that not all the decision variables (factors) exercise an equally strong influence on the characteristic value concerned, use can be made of the method of random balance (Nalimov, 1971), which eliminates the essential factors relative to a given characteristic value from the totality of influencing factors. The method of random balance is here a heuristic one.

The application of such simultaneous search plans is necessary in order to determine optimum order strategies within the stock keeping system concerned, if several storage goods are considered. To give further information, let us study a stock in conformity with passage 2, but of M storage goods. In this case the order strategy includes 2 M variables (S_i, s_i) [i = 1 (1) M]. Let the optimisations of every storage article in ones be excluded, as the storage capacity K_0 of the stock is restricted. If the storage demand is $B = \sum_{i=1}^{M} f_i S_i > K_0$, there will be additional costs of rent $c_L(B - K_0)$ due to the removal of a portion of storage goods. Therewith f_i is the specific storage demand of the i-th storage article, c_L the costs of rent per storage unit.

The function of costs obviously turns out to be

$$J(S, s) = \sum_{i=1}^{M} J_L(S_i, s_i) + c_L\left(\sum_{i=1}^{M} f_i S_i - K_0\right) \text{ sign } \left(\sum_{i=1}^{M} f_i S_i - K_0\right).$$

In this case the following approach is to be recommended:

A. Repetitive combination of the method of random balance with the orthogonal test planning (Martin, 1980)

For the stock keeping system of M storage goods an algorithmic model is set up. Active model tests in the original state by means of the random balance permit to choose N_1 factors, which have an particularly strong influences on the costs, J(S, s) from among the 2M factors S_i, s_i [i = 1 (1) M]. The use of the orthogonal test planning for the N_1 factors will result in an analytic (linear and quadratic, respectively) model, by means of which it is possible to determine a zone close to the optimum. As this zone may eventually be under the particularly strong influence of other factors, it is recommended to apply random balance to orthogonal test planning repeatedly as often as sufficiently good results will be obtained. The method presented under (Martin, 1980) yielded satisfying results for a stock keeping system of 15 storage goods at a computing time of about 3 hours by means of the computer EC 1020.

B. Hierarchic optimisation

For the M storage goods the partial mean optimum strategies (S_i^p, s_i^p) [i=1(1) M] are separately determined without regard to the capacity bound K_0, whereby the methods described in passage 2 and 4 respectively, are applied. For a stock keeping system of 14 storage goods the mean optimum order strategies were yielded by means of the search algorithm NS in combination with a statistic test. Without regard to the capacity bound nor to the increase of costs caused by this, the following estimation of costs is therewith yielded:

m=268.12, σ=12.37 (m –mean value, σ – standard deviation).

If the yielded unconditional mean optimum strategy does not comply with the specified auxiliary condition $\sum_{i=1}^{M} f_i S_i^p \leq K_0$, a second stage is carried out to determine the quadratic approximation of the costs of all storage goods to a sufficient vicinity of the optimum (S_i^p, s_i^p) by means of the orthogonal test planning (for two factors S_i, s_i):

$$\tilde{J}_i(S_i, s_i) = a_0^i + a_1^i S_i + a_2^i s_i + a_3^i S_i^2 + a_4^i s_i^2 + a_5^i S_i s_i.$$

For this purpose the search algorithms NS and S were combined with the orthogonal test planning, so that the quadratic

Table 8.1

Stock Keeping System (Müller, 1978)

Partition	k_B^0 / k_L	k_B^1 / k_L	k_F^1 / k_L	λ-	*T*	*s*	*S*	*J(s,S)*	*Method*
g					10	6.1	12.0	6.92	S
	1	0.01	0.5	0.3	10	6.1	13.0	6.91	BW
					10	7.2	12.6	6.93	NS
					—	5.0	14.4	6.89	T
					10	23.3	49.9	188.1[x]	S
					10	20.0	50.0	189.7[x]	NS
g	50	5	10	0.5	—	22.0	50.0	185.0[x]	T
					10	9.2	93.3	158.3	NS
					10	18.1	60.3	185.6	BW
					10	16.5	36.6	53.4	BW
g	10	1	5	0.3	10	17.0	34.0	53.3	NS
					—	19.8	34.0	52.9	T
					10	32.1	40.0	63.1	BW
d_r	10	1	5	0.3	10	25.7	38.9	63.3	NS
					—	22.2	41.9	62.4	T
					10	9.3	19.9	61.9	BW
d_l	10	1	5	0.3	10	8.5	27.1	62.3	S
					10	9.9	27.0	62.5	NS
					—	21.6	36.0	56.5	T
					10	3.3	20.2	21.9	BW
					10	0.4	16.5	22.0	S
e	10	1	5	0.3	10	2.3	14.8	21.6	NS
					—	1.0	17.0	21.3	T

g— Equipartition $R \in [0, 50]$
d_r—Triangular partition right-hand oblique $R \in [0, 50]$
d_l—Triangular partition left-hand oblique $R \in [0, 50]$
e—Exponential partition $E(R)= 7.2$
x—with auxiliary condition $S \leq 50$.

approximation of each optimum solution is additionally yielded in the vicinity of the optimum.

The exposed example showed with K_0=700 the available storage capacity to be insufficient for the unconditional mean optimum strategy, that means to be exceeded by 102.1 on the mean. This accordingly results in an increase of costs by 204.2 (c_L=2) on the mean. By the application of the very efficient regular search algorithm after Powell, the mean quasi-optimum order strategy (S_i^0, s_i^0) [i = 1 (1) M] was determined

$$J(S_i^0,\ s_i^0) = \min\left\{\sum_{i=1}^{M} \tilde{J}_i(S_i, s_i) \dot{+} c_L\left(\sum_{i=1}^{M} f_i S_i - K_0\right)\ \operatorname{sign}\left(\sum_{i-1}^{M} f_i S_i - K_0\right)\right\}.$$

It is obviously necessary to verify after the determination of S_i^0, s_i^0 [i = 1 (1) M], whether this strategy is within the range of validity of the partial quadratic models or not. The mean quasi-optimum order strategies, which were yielded is: the required storage demand is 700, the costs amount to m = 270.21, σ=14.03.

The computing time required to determine the optimum order strategies for all the 14 storage goods was 124 minutes, that required to determine the partial quadratical models by means of the orthogonal test planning was 21 minutes and that required to determine the quasi-optimum strategy was 14 minutes.

III

SCHEDULING ALGORITHMS IN MULTI-LEVEL PRODUCTION SYSTEMS

Introduction to Multi-Level Production Scheduling

We introduce the reader to a framework for multi-level systems by considering a system with four levels, 24 parts, and eight lines on which the parts can be produced. The framework can be used to evaluate scheduling algorithms for systems with any number of levels, parts, and production lines. It is currently operational at The Johns Hopkins University. Figures 8.2 to 8.4 are copies of computer outputs generated for this report for the four-level system from a programme called INVLEV.

Figure 8.1 illustrates some of the characteristics of the parts in our system. The first eight parts, at Level 1, are the finished products. The last four parts, at Level 4, are bought parts – for these only a purchasing schedule has to be provided. Parts at any level G, except those in the last level, may require for their

Part	*Level*	*Parts needed*	*Lines*	*Cost*	*Setup*	*Ship*
1	1	9, 13, 21, 22, 23, 24	1	250	450	10
2	1	10, 24	1, 2	50	100	25
3	1	11, 22, 33	1, 2	100	300	28
4	1	12, 21, 22, 23	1, 2, 3	200	350	20
5	1	12, 21, 22, 24	1	200	400	15
6	1	14, 24	1, 2, 3, 4	50	150	35
7	1	15, 23, 24	1, 2, 3, 4	100	250	40
8	1	16, 24	1, 2, 3, 4,	50	200	25
9	2	17, 21, 22, 23, 24	5, 6	100	400	10
10	2	20, 22	5, 6	30	200	35
11	2	17, 21, 24	5, 6	60	300	28
12	2	18, 21, 22, 23, 24	5, 6	120	400	35
13	2	17, 21, 22, 24	5, 6	75	300	10
14	2	19, 23	5, 6	30	200	35
15	2	19, 22, 24	5, 6	60	300	40
16	2	20, 24	5, 6	30	200	25
17	3	22, 23, 24	7, 8	30	200	48
18	3	21, 22, 23, 24	7	38	150	35
19	3	21, 22	7, 8	20	50	75
20	3	23	7, 8	8	100	50
21	4	—	—	6	60	238
22	4	—	—	4	60	351
23	4	—	—	1	60	311
24	4	—	—	3	30	371

Fig. 8.1 : Parts' Requirements, Costs, and Shipments

production parts at levels G+1, G+2, etc. For each part the figure also lists the lines on which it can be produced the cost of the part, the cost to set up a production run, and the average expected weekly shipments (in units of 100). The shipment of the finished products (parts 1 to 8) depend on external customers but those of the other parts are determined by internal scheduling.

The rate of production of a line depends on whether production is normal, a setup occurs, or overtime is authorised. For lines 1 to 4 the normal and setup rates are 10. The normal rate of lines 5 and 8 is 20, and the setup rate is 15. For lines 6 and 7 the corresponding rates are 25 and 20. The additional rate for overtime on all lines is 5.

Our production system includes numerous other characteristic that are usually encountered in real production systems such as lead time and shipping forecasts.

Production Scheduling

In this report the term production scheduling means the assignment of parts to production lines on every day of a planning horizon. For parts in the last level, the bought parts, the production schedule includes the purchased quantities and the days on which they are due. Mathematically the corresponding schedule is an array U(L, I) indicating the part that has to be

DAY	*L01*	*L02*	*L03*	*L04*	*P01*	*P02*	*P03*	*P04*	*P05*	*P06*	*P07*	*P08*
-1	1	2	7	6	1	2				4	3	
1	3	3	7	6			12			4	3	
2	7	3	4	7			2	3			14	
3	5	2	4	6		2		3	1	4		
4	5	2	4	6		2		3	1	4		
5	1	3	7	6	1			2		4	3	
6	8	3	7	7		2					34	1
7	8	2	8	7		2					4	13
8	8	2	8	6		2				4		13
9	5	3	4	6			2	3	1	4		
10	1	3	7	6	1		2			4	3	

Fig. 8.2 : Production Schedule of Lines and Parts in Level 1

produced on Line L, Day I. Figure 8.2 illustrates a portion of a production schedule for the parts and lines in Level 1 of the system described in Section 1.

Scheduling algorithms generate schedules meeting the following requirements:

(*a*) On a given day, a line is assigned to only one part, or it is idle. No fractional assignments are allowed.
(*b*) No part is assigned to a line on which it cannot be produced.
(*c*) One part may assigned to several lines on a given day.

A scheduling algorithm need not guarantee that all shipping requirements are met. For example, if insufficient production capacity is available then shortages inevitably arise. The total shortage for Part R is entered in the array I(R).

Our general framework allows the handling of numerous scheduling algorithms. Each algorithm is expected to return a scheduling array U(L, I) and a shortage array I(R). A costing routine is then used to evaluate the effectiveness of any scheduling algorithm.

(Ideally, one would wish to find U(L, I) and I(R) optimally by solving an appropriate mathematical programming problem. It is known, though, that such an approach leads to an NP complete problem [1]. Note that Reference [1] also gives a bibliography on mathematical programming approaches to production planning problems).

Two heuristic scheduling algorithms are currently incorporated in our framework. One of them, the LINE algorithm produces schedules similar to that in Figure 8.2 and the costs in Figures 8.3 and 8.4. The other, the DAY algorithm, is compared to the LINE algorithm in Section 5. Both algorithms use a lot-sizing algorithm to schedule the purchasing of the parts in the last level (the bought parts). This algorithm produces a schedule which minimises the total carrying and setup costs.

Both algorithms review the parts and lines level by level. First the schedule in Level 1 is determined. The shipping requirements for the parts in this level are known. The schedule in any Level G determines shipping requirements in Levels G+1, G+2, etc. The algorithms thus proceed from Level 1 to the last but one level, and then the lot-sizing algorithm mentioned above is used.

The DAY Algorithm

The Day algorithm produces a schedule by examining shipping requirements on a day-to-day basis, hence its name. On day I of the planning horizon, one part at a time is reviewed. If no shipments of the part are needed than the next part is reviewed. If a shipment is needed and there is sufficient inventory available, then the amount shipped is deducted from the inventory and the next part is reviewed.

If there is insufficient inventory for some Part R, then all lines on which the part can be made are checked. A line L which has available capacity is then scheduled (*i.e.*, U(L, I) = R), and the available inventory is updated accordingly. If inventory is still insufficient to meet the shipment, further lines are checked and, possibly, scheduled. If there still is need for more production, the same process is repeated for days I—1, I—2, ..., 1. If necessary, and if overtime is authorised, the whole procedure is repeated once again for the days and lines which have already been scheduled for Part R, and overtime production is added accordingly. Finally, if any shortages still exist then they are accumulated in the shortage array I(R).

The LINE Algorithm

This algorithm examines one line at a time, rather than one day at a time as the DAY algorithm does. For each Line L, every Part R that can be produced on it is selected. Dynamic Programming is then used to determine the optimal schedule U(L, I) for that part of line L during the whole horizon. This schedule minimizes the total carrying and setup costs. If insufficient capacity is available to meet all the requirements of the part, the remaining requirements are recorded, and an attempt is made to schedule them on the next appropriate line.

After all the lines have been scheduled, the remaining requirements for each Part R are recorded in the shortage array I(R). If overtime is authorized, the LINE algorithm attempts to reduce the amounts in I(R) by adding overtime production on the lines and days in which Part R had been scheduled by the Dynamic Programming procedure.

Carrying, Setup Shortage, and Overtime Costs

In this report we assume that there are five work-days in a week, and 50 work-weeks in a year. We also assume that the annual cost of carrying inventory is a percentage P of the part's cost.

The cost of starting a new production run is called the setup cost. That is, if a Part R is not produced on Line L on Day I—1, and is produced on this line on days I, I+1, I+2, etc., then one setup cost on Day I is incurred.

The assignment of shortage costs in inventory systems in general depends on whether shortages are backordered or not. In multi-level production systems this assignment is even more complex since production at any Level G causes demands for shipment in levels G+1, G+2, and so on. In the present framework we assume that shortages are overcome by an additional inventory which is made available at the beginning of the planning horizon. In our illustrative system the unit shortage cost is assumed to be nine times the unit cost of carrying inventory.

LEV	*PAR*	*DAY*	*BEG*	*PROD*	*SHIP*	*END*	*CAR/C*	*SET/C*	*SHO/C*	*OVE/C*	*TOT/C*
3	18	-4	15	25	0	40	0	0	615	0	615
3	18	-3	40	0	0	40	0	0	0	0	0
3	18	-2	40	0	0	40	0	0	0	0	0
3	18	-1	40	20	0	60	0	0	0	0	0
3	18	1	60	0	20	40	182	0	0	0	182
3	18	2	40	0	0	40	182	0	0	0	182
3	18	3	40	20	20	40	182	150	0	0	332
3	18	4	40	0	0	40	182	0	0	0	182
3	18	5	40	20	20	40	182	150	0	0	332
3	18	6	40	0	0	40	182	0	0	0	182
3	18	7	40	0	20	20	91	0	0	0	91
3	18	8	20	0	0	20	91	0	0	0	91
3	18	9	20	0	20	0	0	0	0	0	0
3	18	10	0	20	0	20	91	150	0	0	241

Fig. 8.3 : Inventory and Cost Details on Part 18.

Our present framework also makes a rather simplified assumption with regard to the method of charging for overtime production. It assumes that this cost is linearly dependent on the amount produced.

Some of the details on the inventory fluctuantions, production, shipments, and the corresponding costs of Part 18 during a planning horizon of 35 days are given in Figure 8.3. This figure shows how the various costs are computed and how the initial inventories are handled.

Computations similar to that in Figure 8.3 made for all parts in the system. A summary of these, for the first five days of the horizon, is given in Figure 8.4. The reader should be able to check some of the entries in the figure.

Sensitivity of Scheduling Algorithms and Options

Currently, a user may select the following options for costing a production system during the running of Programme INVLEV:

- ALG The scheduling algorithm. At present only the DAY and the LINE algorithms are available.
- SEQ The sequences (orderings) in which parts and lines are considered by the scheduling algorithm. Any consistent sequences may be specified.
- HOR The number of days in the planning horizon. Any number may be specified. However, shipments of the finished parts must be known during the entire horizon.
- TIM The length of the time of production. Either a normal (NOR) rate or overtime (OVE) may be specified.
- CAR The annual carrying cost percentage. Any per cent may be specified.

In Figure 8.5 we present the total costs of our illustrative system when two alternatives are selected for each of the above options. We discuss the significance of these results in the following sections.

(1) The DAY and LINE Algorithms : As one expects intuitively,

LEV	PAR	DAY	BEG	PROD	SHIP	END	CAR/C	SET/C	SHO/C	OVE/C	TOT/C
1	1	5	10	10	5	15	1200	450	0	0	1650
1	2	5	20	20	25	15	450	100	0	0	550
1	3	5	0	40	30	10	1080	900	0	0	1980
1	4°	5	15	30	15	30	2160	350	0	0	2510
1	5	5	15	20	15	20	1560	400	0	0	1960
1	6	5	20	40	35	25	630	150	0	0	780
1	7	5	20	40	40	20	1440	750	0	0	2190
1	8	5	20	0	20	0	480	0	0	0	480
2	9	5	0	20	10	10	840	400	0	0	1240
2	10	5	20	20	20	20	324	200	0	0	524
2	11	5	55	0	40	15	900	0	0	0	900
2	12	5	35	60	50	45	3096	1200	0	0	4296
2	13	5	10	0	10	0	360	0	0	0	360
2	14	5	40	15	40	15	378	200	0	0	578
2	15	5	30	80	40	70	1980	300	0	1900	4180
2	16	5	105	0	0	105	1890	0	1458	0	3348
3	17	5	20	45	20	45	792	200	0	0	992
3	18	5	60	40	60	40	912	300	615	0	1827
3	19	5	80	75	95	60	852	100	0	0	952
3	20	5	65	0	20	45	273	0	0	0	273
4	21	5	315	200	255	260	1004	120	0	0	1124
4	22	5	575	245	440	380	945	120	0	0	1065
4	23	5	375	340	300	415	246	120	0	0	366
4	24	5	445	330	355	420	720	90	32	0	842
4	24	5	2350	1670	1940	2080	24513	6450	2106	1900	34969

Fig. 8.4 : Inventory and Cost Summaries for Five Days

the LINE algorithm (which contains significant attempts at suboptimisation) gives lower total costs than the DAY algorithm (which does not).

The differences between the algorithms are especially noticable when comparing the results for carrying cost percentages of 20 and 30. Since the Dynamic Programming procedure in the

ALG	*SEQ*	*HOR*	*TIM*	*CAR*	*CAR/C*	*SET/C*	*SHO/C*	*OVE/C*	*TOT/C*
DAY	1	25	NOR	20	17436	6640	5760	0	29836
DAY	1	35	NOR	20	19806	6290	10080	0	36176
DAY	1	25	OVE	20	17571	6590	4730	1375	30267
DAY	1	35	OVE	20	18550	6650	6890	1375	33465
DAY	1	25	NOR	30	25966	6640	8640	0	41246
DAY	1	35	NOR	30	29110	6290	15120	0	50520
DAY	1	25	OVE	30	26090	6620	7095	1375	41181
DAY	1	35	OVE	30	27670	6620	10335	1375	46001
LIN	1	25	NOR	20	16433	6250	1368	0	24051
LIN	1	35	NOR	20	16928	6110	2520	0	25558
LIN	1	25	OVE	20	16219	6250	669	4650	27788
LIN	1	35	OVE	20	16549	6160	1425	4650	28785
LIN	1	25	NOR	30	23918	6740	988	0	31646
LIN	1	35	NOR	30	24692	6450	2538	0	33680
LIN	1	25	OVE	30	23820	6740	664	0	31224
LIN	1	35	OVE	30	24513	6450	2106	1900	34969
DAY	2	25	NOR	20	18841	5110	10080	0	34431
DAY	2	35	NOR	20	22129	5540	16380	0	44049
DAY	2	25	OVE	20	17324	5760	7200	1375	31659
DAY	2	35	OVE	20	19893	5850	11700	1375	38818
DAY	2	25	NOR	30	28150	5540	15120	0	48810
DAY	2	35	NOR	30	33268	5600	24570	0	63438
DAY	2	25	OVE	30	25832	5790	10800	1375	43797
DAY	2	35	OVE	30	29893	5970	17550	1375	54788
LIN	2	25	NOR	20	16440	4640	2376	0	23456
LIN	2	35	NOR	20	17836	4920	4392	0	27148
LIN	2	25	OVE	20	16456	4700	1882	4650	27689
LIN	2	35	OVE	20	17485	4920	3178	3275	28859
LIN	2	25	NOR	30	23808	6680	2964	0	33452
LIN	2	35	NOR	30	25458	5900	4752	0	36110
LIN	2	25	OVE	30	23800	6430	2424	1375	34029
LIN	2	35	OVE	30	24894	5900	3456	1375	35625

Fig. 8.5 : Sensitivity of Costs to Algorithms and Options

LINE algorithm minimizes carrying and set up costs. One expects somewhat more setups for 30 per cent as compared to 20 per cent.

In the DAY algorithm hardly any costs are considered and one should therefore expect no differences in the setup costs when comparing 20 per cent and 30 per cent carrying costs. The small differences that can still be noted are due to the lot-sizing algorithm for bought parts, which does consider costs.

(2) *Sequencing of Parts and Lines:* Both the DAY and LINE algorithms produce schedules which consider parts and lines in certain sequences. In the results of Figure 8.5 two different sets of sequences are used in Level 1 only :

Level	SEQ	Parts	Lines
1	1	1, 5, 2, 3, 4, 6, 7, 8	4, 3, 2, 1
	2	5, 1, 2, 3, 4, 6, 7, 8	1, 2, 3, 4

From Figure 8.5 we can see that although there is a relatively small difference in the sequences, the corresponding costs are quite different – 26 per cent in one case.

(3) *The Planning Horizon* : Two planning horizons are considered : 25 days and 35 days. (But note that all the costs are given for the first five days only). Invariably, the larger the horizon the more costly is the schedule. This does not seem to be an unexpected result. The DAY algorithm in particular is very sensitive to the length of the horizon.

For both algorithms the increase in costs is reflected mostly in the shortage costs. The longer the horizon the more difficult it is to meet the shipping requirements.

(4) *Normal and Overtime Production :* It will be recalled that both algorithms consider overtime only after normal production is scheduled, and then only if shortages occur. Thus, it is not surprising that whenever overtime is used the cost of shortages is reduced. Since shortages also affect the amount carried initially, the carrying costs are also reduced somewhat.

(5) *Carrying Costs :* In Figure 8.5 we consider two percentages of carrying costs per year: 20 and 30. Thus in comparing the results for these options one should expect an increase of 50 per

cent in the carrying costs and in the shortage costs, and a substantial increase of costs in general.

Conclusion

The framework presented in this profile is mainly intended as a planning tool for evaluating scheduling algorithms for multi-level production systems. The framework includes many of the elements, if not most, which exist in real production environments. In the following comments we mention a number of possible extensions that seem worth considering :

(1) The current DAY algorithm is extremely fast. It takes between 0.50 and 0.95 DEC-10 CPU seconds to produce each of the schedules for which the costs are given in Figure 8.5 Although the algorithm does not consider costs, the schedules that it produces are reasonably good. It can probably be greatly improved by the addition of heuristic routines which do consider costs. Our LINE algorithm is, of course, slower. It takes between 2.69 to 6.64 seconds to produce each schedule in Figure 8.5. The performance of the algorithm can, no doubt, be improved. Its running time can be speeded up, and one should also be able to include shortages and overtime in the optimisation phase. A related question is finding the optimal sequence of parts and lines in both scheduling algorithms. We have seen that a minor perturbation in the sequence leads to a great change in costs.

(2) Our current treatment of shortages may not be appropriate in some applications. When production capacities significantly exceed shipping requirements, then shortages will rarely occur. Whenever excessive shortages do occur the following approaches may be considered:

(a) Modifying shipping requirements. This option either postpones or sometimes even cancels shipments. If the option is exercised at some Level G, then the appropriate adjustments have to be made in levels G—1, G—2, etc.

(b) Authorisation of special overtime. Such extra overtime may include additional shifts and/or week-end production.

(c) On-line scheduling. The user is permitted to evaluate

on-line the options *(a)* and *(b)* and possibly others. Extensive and ingenious computer programming is required for the implementation of this approach.

(3) We have seen that when a 35-day horizon is used, as compared with a 25-day horizon, then the total costs increase. Since shipping forecasts are known to be notoriously inaccurate and subject to many fluctuations an interesting question arises: What is the optimal length of the planning horizon? We have used the first five days of a planning horizon for cost comparisons. This was done with assumption that during these five days the production schedule is not subject to change. In reality this assumption may not be valid. Another interesting question then arises : What is the optimal length of the period to be used for comparing scheduling alternatives?

(4) The constraints imposed on our scheduling algorithms do not include provisions for desired ending inventories. Thus both in the DAY and LINE algorithms inventories at the end of the planning horizon tend to approach zero. In some production environments this may not be appropriate. It should be relatively easy to include in an algorithm a desired minimum inventory for each part. But what should this minimum be? This, too, is an interesting optimisation problem for which no simple answer seems to be readily available.

IV

CONTROLLING PERISHABLE INVENTORIES

Introduction

The purpose of this section is to explore the potential for utilising a certain class of queueing models for determining operating rules to control the stocking of perishable goods.

In practice, many types of inventory items can be retained in stock only a limited amount of time, after which they can no longer be used to satisfy demand and must be discarded. Foodstuffs, blood, photographic film and drugs are just a few examples.

Recently, there has been a fairly considerable interest in the analysis of analytical models which result in optimal and sub-optimal ordering rules for perishable goods. Early unpublished work by Van Zyl (1964) gave the optimal order policy for a single product with a lifetime of two periods. This model was later generalised and extended by Nahmias (1975) and Fries (1975). Considerable additional work was reported by a number of researchers on both optimal order policies for more complex models and, variety of different types of approximations. A recent review article by Nahmias (1988) details the existing work in the fields and contains 75 references. A difficult and unsolved problem is determining suitable ordering policies for a fixed life commodity when inventory levels are reviewed continuously and there is a positive leadtime for placing an order.

This current section will describe the analogy between the perishable inventory problem and queueing models with customer impatience. We hope to show what specific results from queueing could be useful in the inventory context and how the queueing methodology might provide some clues for dealing with the unsolved continuous review problem mentioned above.

The Queueing-Inventory Analogy

Consider the following single server queue: customers arrive to a single channel system according to some stationary stochastic process, and proceed to queue up for service on a first come first served basis. If a customer has not completed service by the end of a fixed time, say L, he exits from the queue never to return.

If we identify the arrival of customers with the replenishment process, the total number of customers in the system with the level of inventory, the times of completion of service with times of demand and the impatience time with the lifetime of the fresh units, then the analogy is complete. However, this does not imply that the queueing results will automatically give operating rules for the inventory problem. On the contrary, the queueing models have only a somewhat limited utility in the inventory context, since in queueing it is generally assumed that the arrive rate is known and fixed, while in inventory this is the primary control variable.

Early work on inventory models with impatience is due to Barrer (1957) and Gnedenko and Kovalenko (1968) who treated the M/M/1 system with impatience. (Note that although Barrer's results appear to be correct, Gnedenko and Kovalenko point out that his method of analysis may not be entirely correct). Extensions of the results of these studies to more general systems are due to Finch (1960), Loris-Teghem (1972), Cohen (1969), Gavish and Schweitzer (1977) and Stanford (1979). Note that some of these models do not precisely fit into the analogy described above since in many cases it is assumed that the customer completes services once he enters even if his total waiting time plus service time exceeds L.

In most queueing systems, the stochastic process which specifies the total number of customers in the system is Markovian. That is, if one knows the number in the system at time t then the probabilistic evolution of the process beyond t is independent of the history prior to time t. In the inventory context, this would mean that the level of on hand (or on hand and on order) stock is Markovian.

However, when impatience is imposed on the system, the number of customers in the queue is no longer a Markov process. To analyse the queueing system in this manner would require keeping track of not only each customer individually, but the amount of time elapsed since each joined the queue. Fortunately, there is a single dimensional process that still remains Markovian when there is impatience. That process is the virtual waiting time process. The virtual waiting time is equivalent to the actual waiting time in a system in which the time of service are realised when customers arrive rather than when they enter service.

A closely related process is the age of the oldest unit in the queue, say A(t), which (if no other information is available) will also be Markovian. A typical realisation of the process A(t) is shown in Figure 8.6. Note that A(t) will increase at a unit rate and will jump downward at either times of demand (i.e., times of completion of service) or at times of outdating (i.e., times when customers exit from the queue due to impatience). The magnitudes of the jumps correspond to the times between successive arrivals.

The virtual waiting time process, say W(t), may have a typical sample path as pictured in Figure 8.7. The virtual waiting

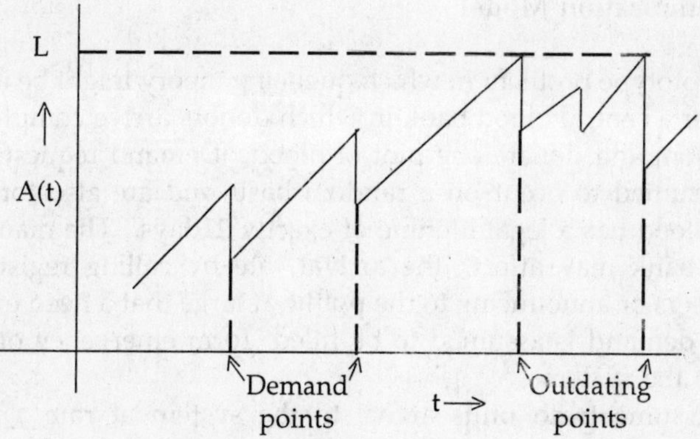

Fig. 8.6

time decreases at a unit rate and jumps at times of arrivals of customers. One can see that {L − W(t)} for an M/G/1 system has the same distribution as A(t) for a C/M/1 system, so that A(t) and W(t), are, in some sense, dual processes.

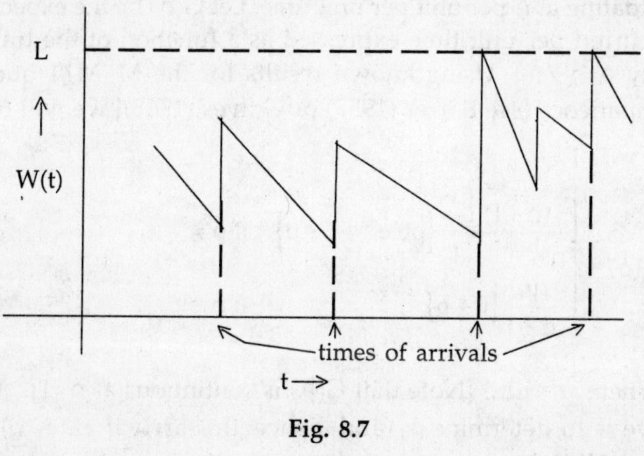

Fig. 8.7

Graves (1968) has analyzed the process A(t) directly to obtain various characteristics of interest for the perishable inventory problem [many of his results duplicate those of Barrer (1957) and others]. In the next section we will show how these results can be used to construct an optimisation model for a perishable inventory system.

An Optimisation Model

As a prototype problem in which queueing theory might be used, consider a central blood bank in which donors arrive completely at random and donate one pint of blood. Demand requests are also assumed to occur on a random basis and are also for one unit. Blood has a legal lifetime of exactly 21days. The manager of the bank may affect the arrival rate by calling registered volunteers or announcing to the public at large that a need exists. Excess demand is assumed to be filled form emergency orders outside the system.

Assume fresh units arrive to the system at rate λ and demand requests occur at rate μ. Suppose that the shelf life of new units is L. A common approach in managing such systems is to assume that stocking levels are chosen to meet some trade-off between shortages (under-stocking) and outdates (over-stocking). [See Jennings (1973) for a discussion of this type of methodology applied to blood banking.] Hence we will assume that there are known costs of stockout at p per unit per unit time and outdating at θ per unit per unit time. Let $G(\rho)$ be the expected cost incurred per unit time expressed as a function of the traffic intensity $\rho=\lambda/\mu$ Using known results for the M/M/1 queue with impatience [see Barrer (1957) or Graves (1968)] we will find that

$$G(\rho)=\begin{cases}\dfrac{(\rho-1)\mu}{\rho e^{\alpha(\rho-1)}-1}\left\{\rho\theta\, e^{\alpha(\rho-1)}+p\right\} & \text{if } \rho\neq \\ \dfrac{\mu}{\alpha+1}\{\theta+p\} & \text{if } \rho=\end{cases}$$

Where $\alpha=\mu L$. [Note that $G(\rho)$ is continuous at $\rho=1$]. The objective is to determine ρ (and hence the arrival rate λ) to minimise $G(\rho)$.

Differentiation gives $G'(0)=\mu e^{-\alpha}(\theta-p)-p$ so that a sufficient condition that $G'(0) < 0$ is that $p > \theta$. Since $G\infty=+\infty$, it is clear that the value of $\rho > 0$, say ρ^*, which minimises $G(\rho)$ solves $G'(\rho^*) = 0$. [It appears that G is strictly convex, so that the equation $G'(\rho^*) =0$ has exactly one root. However we have been unable to develop a proof of this result.]

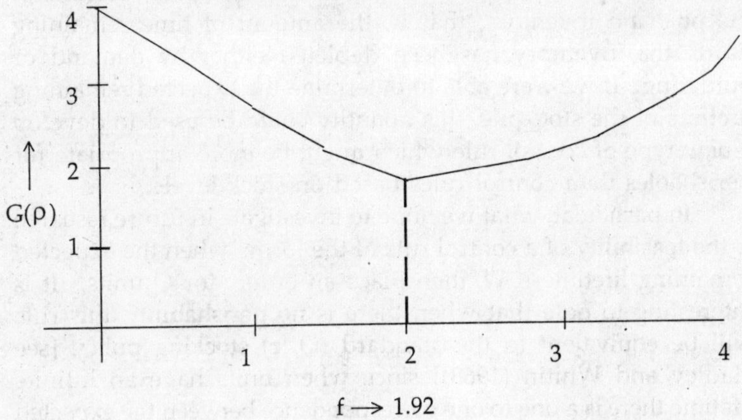

Fig. 8.8

As an example, suppose $\mu=1$, $L=1$, $\theta=1$, and $p=4$. For this case the function $G(\rho)$ is pictured in Figure 8.8.

The optimal $\rho^* = 1.92$ for the example. Note that in general the actual values of the shortage and outdate costs are not significant. In this case we are simply saying that the relative cost of shortages to outdates is 4 to 1.

This approach can be easily expanded to include procurement costs and holding costs. It can be extended to certain other cases—some results are known when the service distribution (*i.e.*, times between demands) is arbitrary. However, it should be recognised that these types of queueing models are only useful if items are resupplied on a one at a time basis. In most inventory problems, stock is replenished on a lot-sizing basis according to a specified control rule, such as an (s, S) policy. Hence, the queueing models are of only limited value and can be applied only when a rather special problem structure exists such as in the blood bank problem.

Directions for Further Work

That the virtual waiting time process gives sufficient information to analyze the queue with impatience suggests a rather intriguing approach to the inventory problem. In the inventory context we may think of the virtual waiting time as the virtual lifetime of the on hand inventory; that is, the amount of time remaining until the inventory has been depleted either by demand or outdating. If we were able to determine the expected remaining lifetime of the stockpile, this quantity could be used to develop a new type of control rule which might be more appropriate for perishables than control rules based on stock levels.

In particular, what we hope to investigate in future research is the feasibility of a control rule of the form: when the expected remaining lifetime ≤ W, then place an order for Q units. It is interesting to note that when there is no perishability, this rule will be equivalent to the standard (Q, r) stocking policy [see Hadley and Whitin (1963)] since when units have an infinite lifetime there is a one to one correspondence between the expected lifetime of the stockpile and numbers of units in inventory.

V

OPTIMAL ESTIMATION OF INTER-MACHINING INVENTORY LEVELS

Abstract

Effective scheduling relies on the accurate determination of the size and location of in-process inventory levels. In practice, in-process inventory levels may be determined either from estimates based on expected system behaviour or by directly measuring the inventory levels or by some combination of estimation and measurement. In this section the estimates to the states of the production system are combined together to form a best least squared error estimate. This is achieved using an extended Kalman filter. The use of the filter to determine the optimum choice of measurements to be taken is illustrated by the use of a numerical example.

Introduction

Actual production system behaviour results from the expected system behaviour together with the inherent random variations in the manufacturing process. These random variations degrade our knowledge of the system but it is possible to improve the accuracy of the estimation procedure by physically measuring the system. Measurement, though, has two disadvantages which limit its usefulness; firstly it is generally economically impractical to measure at every work station, and secondly the measurement itself is prone to error. Essentially therefore, we have two estimates of system behaviour. The first estimate is based on expected system behaviour and the second estimate is based on measurement at selected point. The problem is how to combine these estimates so as to produce a best least squared error estimate.

The powerful filtering techniques proposed by Kalman (1960) and Kalman & Bucy (1961), together with the state variable approach of control theory, are in fairly wide use in many fields. The possibility of using these techniques in production control is suggested by Koivo & Hendricks (1973). However actual applications are few: Tapiero (1977) derives the optimum inventory measurement interval and Stohr (1979) extends this to the multi-product inventory case.

In this section we also approach the problem by utilising the state variable approach of discrete control theory. But we treat the production system (manufacturing, inventory and delivery) as a whole. Initially we give the deterministic and stochastic system matrix equations which are capable of describing a wide range of production systems. We then revert back to the original problem, *i.e.* to obtain the best estimate of the state of the system given estimates based on expected system behaviour and estimates based on measurements of the system. We achieve this using a filter, capable of handing non-stationary systems, to optimally combine these estimates. This multi-level, multi-product filter is, in effect, a Kalman filter extended to incorporate deterministic inputs. The use of the filter is described by a numerical example.

State Variable Representation of Production Systems

A deterministic system can be expressed in the following form :

$$\underline{X}(N+1) = \underline{A}(N)\underline{X}(N) + \underline{B}(N)\underline{U}(N) \tag{3.1}$$

where $\underline{X}(N+1)$ is the n state vector for period N+1, and $\underline{X}(N)$ that for period N. $\underline{A}(N)$ is an n x n matrix and $\underline{B}(N)$ an n x m matrix, both defined at period N. The m vector $\underline{U}(N)$ indicate the system inputs. For a production control system these may be, for example, the work force level or the level of schedules.

The measurements of the deterministic system can be described by the equation :

$$\underline{Y}(N) = \underline{H}(N)\underline{X}(N) \tag{3.2}$$

where $\underline{Y}(N)$ is an h vector of the measurements and $\underline{H}(N)$ is an h x n matrix defined at period N. In view of possible random disturbances the deterministic system equations, (3.1) and (3.2), have to be amended to :

$$\underline{X}(N+1) = \underline{A}(N)\underline{X}(N) + \underline{B}(N)\underline{U}(N) + \underline{C}(N)\underline{W}(N) \tag{3.3}$$

$$\underline{Y}(N) = \underline{H}(N)\underline{X}(N) + \underline{V}(N) \tag{3.4}$$

$\underline{W}(N)$ and $\underline{V}(N)$ are vectors of purely random numbers having zero mean value with covariance matrices $\underline{Q}(N)$ and $\underline{R}(N)$ respectively. Matrices $\underline{A}(N)$, $\underline{B}(N)$, $\underline{C}(N)$ and $\underline{H}(N)$ are abbreviated to $\underline{A}$, $\underline{B}$, $\underline{C}$ and $\underline{H}$ respectively in the following sections.

System Estimates

We will consider two possible ways of obtaining estimates of the values of the state variables:-

(a) the first estimate, $\underline{X}_p(N)$, is obtained from the extrapolation of the present best estimate of the state vector to the next time period, using Eq. (3.3), with the noise $\underline{W}(N)$ taking its mean value of zero, so that :

$$\underline{X}_p(N+1) = \underline{A}\hat{\underline{X}}(N) + \underline{B}\underline{U}(N) \tag{4.1}$$

where $\underline{X}_p(N+1)$ is the estimate for time period N+1 and $\hat{\underline{X}}(N)$ is the 'best' estimate for time period N.

(b) the second independent estimate, $\underline{X}_r$, is obtained from measurements made on the system, with the value of $\underline{V}(N)$ taken to be the mean value of zero, so that from (3.4)

$$\underline{Y}(N) = \underline{H}\underline{X}_r \tag{4.2}$$

where $\underline{X}_r(N)$ is the estimate for the time period N, $\underline{H}$ is the measurement matrix, and $\underline{Y}(N)$ are the measured values of the system's state.

One way of reducing the system error is to combine these estimates, $\underline{X}_p(N)$ and $\underline{X}_r(N)$, and this process is described in the next section.

Multi-Dimensional Combination of System Estimates

Use of the Optimum Filter:

The multi-dimensional combination of the system estimates for a production system is achieved by an optimum filter given in Appendix 1. This optimum filter (in effect a Kalman filter extended to incorporate deterministic inputs) combines the estimates of the state of the system, $\underline{X}_p(N)$ and $\underline{X}_r(N)$ from Eqs. (4.1) and (4.2), into a 'best' estimate, $\hat{\underline{X}}(N)$.

The best estimate, $\underline{X}(N)$ is obtained by using the equation :-

$$\hat{\underline{X}}(N) = \underline{A}\hat{\underline{X}}(N-1) + \underline{BU}(N-1) + \underline{K}(N)\{Y(N) - $$

$$-\underline{HA}\hat{\underline{X}}(N-1) - \underline{HBU}(N-1) \quad (5.1)$$

Where $\underline{K}(N)$ is the Kalman gain matrix. It can be calculated as shown in Appendix 1. Equation (5.1) is shown diagrammatically in Figures 8.9.

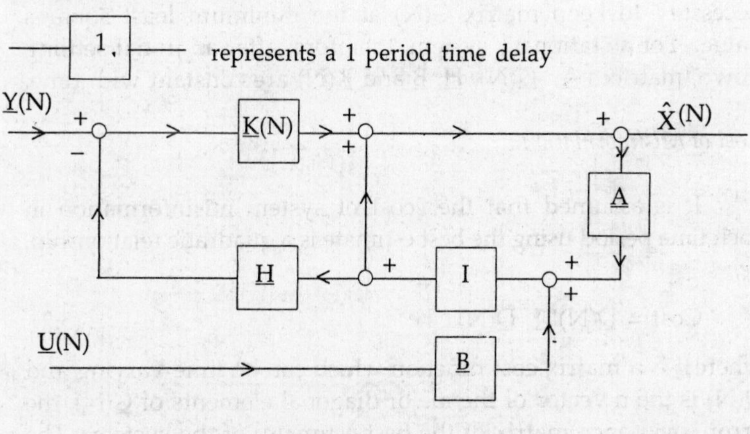

Fig. 8.9 : Optimum Filter

Matrices A, H, B can be made time varying. If measurements are not taken at every time period then either matrix H can be altered at different time periods to take into account the different measurements or else the error variance of the missed measurements can be increased to a very large number.

Essentially matrix K(N) operates to lower the best estimate error covariance matrix, G(N), to the minimum least squares from and a new best estimate is obtained using Eq. (5.1), taking as inputs the schedules, the measurements and the old best estimate. The order of events, therefore, in calculating the best estimate is as follows :

— Determine the system structure and errors and express these in the form of Eqs. (3.3) and (3.4), with the associated error covariance matrices Q(N) and R(N). The system structure and errors will be constant for a stationary system.

— Evaluate matrix K(N) as detailed in Appendix 1. If the system is stationary matrix K(N) attains a steady state within a few time periods.

— Substitute in the values of the schedules, measurements and the previous best estimate in (5.1) and, by the use of a computer programme, produce the value of the new best estimate of the system's state.

In a stationary system matrix K(N) tends to the steady state necessary to keep matrix G(N) at the minimum least squares value. For a stationary system, therefore, after an initial settling down, matrices A, G(N), H, B and K(N) are constant with time.

Cost of Misinformation :

It is assumed that the cost of system misinformation in each time period using the best estimate is a quadratic relationship, *i.e.:*

$$\text{Cost} = \underline{D}(N)'\ \underline{L}\ \underline{D}(N) \tag{5.2}$$

where L is a matrix cost function which can be time varying and D(N) is the n vector of the major diagonal elements of G(N), the error covariance matrix of the best estimate of the system. The prime symbol,' indicates the transpose of the matrix.

Example of the Use of the Optimum Filter

We will consider the production system described by Fig 8.10, with a manufacturing delay of 8 time periods and the orders being moved from the inter-matching stock after a 1 period delivery delay. This stationary systems can be expressed in the form of Eqs. (3.3) and (3.4). Matrix $\underline{C}$ is a constant unit identity matrix. The system extrapolation error variance is taken to be 1.0 for each stage, that is $\underline{Q}$(N) is a constant unit identity matrix. Initially we will take the 4 measurement positions to be Y1, Y2, Y3, and Y4 is deterministic with the error variance of the other measurements 0.5, and its is expressed as matrix $\underline{R}$.

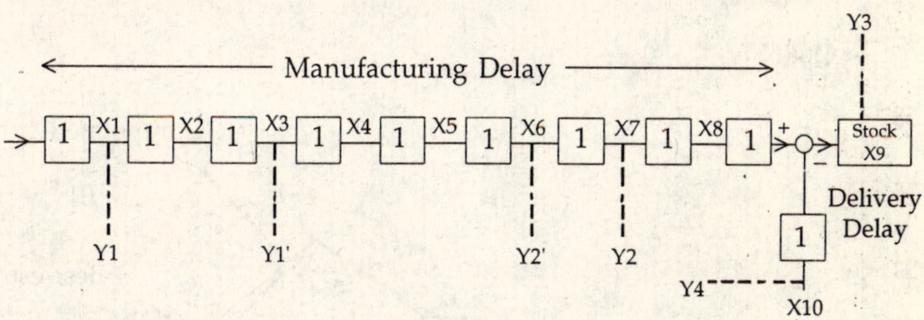

Fig. 8.10 : Optimum Filter

Starting with the assumed value for $\underline{G}$(N) taken to be $\underline{A}$(N), successive values of $\underline{K}$(N) are calculated by the interactive use of Eqs. (8.3) (8.4) and (8.5). Since the system is stationary both matrices $\underline{K}$(N) and $\underline{G}$(N) attain a steady state. The diagonal elements of $\underline{G}$(N) give the variance of the best estimate of the state variables. After several interations these were found to be:

X1	0.33	X6	5.33
X2	1.33	X7	0.46
X3	2.33	X8	1.46
X4	3.33	X9	0.43
X5	4.33	X10	0.0

As can be seen the error variance cascade along the system in the absence of any measurements. At the measuring points, (X1, X7, X9 and X10), the measurements lower the error variance of the best estimate. With matrix $\underline{K}$(N) evaluated, the values of the schedules, the system measurements and the best estimate $\hat{\underline{X}}(N-1)$ can be substituted in Eq. (5.1) and, using a computer programme, the value of the new best estimate of the state of the system, $\hat{\underline{X}}(N)$, can be produced.

One set of results for the stock level, X9, is shown in Figure 8.11. The 'Extrapolated Value' is the value obtained using Eq. (4.1) and the 'Measured Value' that obtained using Eq. (4.2). Since the measured values have a lower error variance than the extrapolated values, the values of the best estimate are allied more closely to the former.

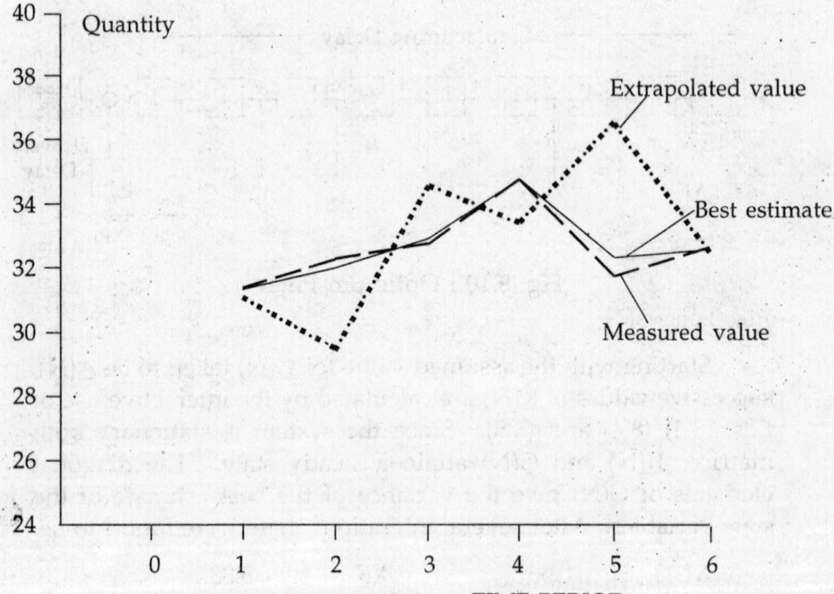

Fig. 8.11 : Stock Level.

If we take matrix $\underline{L}$ to be a unit diagonal matrix but with elements L(10,10) = 0.0 and L(9, 9) = 9.5 then the cost of misinformation, given by Eq. (5.2), can be calculated. To reduce the cost of misinformation then the positions of the measurements

Y1 and Y2 can be altered on a trial and error basis. The cost of misinformation is found to be a minimum when measurements Y1' and Y2' are taken.

The expected misinformation costs can be calculated for this system with different measuring configurations. The results, with misinformation cost matrix $\underline{L}$, are shown below :

Expected Misinformation Costs Per Time Period

1.	Measurements Y1, Y2, Y3, Y4, no optimum filtering	76.3
2.	" " " with optimum filtering	69.78
3.	" Y1', Y2', Y3, Y4 " " "	23.18

If the costs of taking each measurement were known, further analysis could be undertaken to produce both the optimum number and optimum choice of measurement.

Conclusion

The use of the filtering techniques is shown to reduce the cost of misinformation. Greater cost reductions can be achieved by an optimum selection of the measurement positions. In the simple example considered, the expected misinformation cost reduction using filtering techniques is about 8 per cent. However this is increased to about 70 per cent by an optimal choice of measurements.

Appendix 1—Optimum Filter

The full derivation of the basic Kalman filter is contained in Kalman (1960) and Kalman & Bucy (1961). The basic Kalman filter is used to obtain the best estimate of the state vector, $\underline{X}(N)$, using the equation :

$$\hat{\underline{X}}(N) = \underline{A}(N-1)\ \hat{\underline{X}}(N-1) + \underline{K}(N)\ \{\underline{Y}(N) - \underline{H}\ \underline{A}(N-1)\hat{\underline{X}}(N-1)\} \quad (8.1)$$

where $\hat{\underline{X}}(N)$ is the optimum linear estimate, $\underline{Y}(N)$ is the h measurement vector and $\underline{K}(N)$ the n x h Kalman gain matrix, both defined at time period N. $\underline{A}(N-1)$ is a n x n matrix defining the system.

With a deterministic input m vector $\underline{U}(N-1)$, (8.1) can be extended to :

$$\hat{\underline{X}}(N) = \underline{A}(N-1)\ \hat{\underline{X}}(N-1) + \underline{B}(N-1)\ \underline{U}(N-1) + \underline{K}(N)\{Y(N) -$$
$$- \underline{H}\underline{A}(N-1)\ \hat{\underline{X}}(N-1) + \underline{H}\underline{B}(N-1)\ \underline{U}(N-1)\} \quad (8.2)$$

The following equations, with nomenclature as in Eqs. (3.3) and (3.4), are used iteratively to determine matrix ($\underline{K}(N)$, the Kalman gain matrix :

$$\underline{P}(N) = \underline{A}(N-1)\ \underline{G}(N-1)\underline{A}(N-1)' + \underline{C}(N-1)\ \underline{Q}(N-1)\ \underline{C}(N-1)' \quad (8.3)$$

$$\underline{K}(N) = \underline{P}(N)\ \underline{H}'\ \{\underline{H}\ \underline{P}(N)\ \underline{H}' + R(N)\}' \quad (8.4)$$

$$\underline{G}(N) = \underline{P}(N) - \underline{K}(N)\ \underline{H}\ \underline{P}(N) \quad (8.5)$$

The prime, ′, indicates the transpose of the matrix. $\underline{G}(N)$ is the n x n error covariance matrix of the best estimate, $\hat{\underline{X}}(N)$. $\underline{P}(N)$ is the n x n error covariance matrix of the extrapolated estimate $\underline{X}_p$. The iteration is started by assuming an initial estimate of $\underline{G}(0)$ in (8.3) to calculate $\underline{P}(1)$. This is then substituted in (8.4) and (8.5) to obtain values of $\underline{K}(1)$ and $\underline{G}(1)$. The best estimate of the state, $\hat{\underline{X}}(1)$, can then be obtained from (8.2). The iteration can be repeated to give further values of $\underline{K}(N)$, $\underline{G}(N)$ and $\hat{\underline{X}}(N)$.

Bibliography

Barrer, D.Y. (1957), "Queueing with Impatient Customers and Ordered Service," *Operations Research*, 5, 650-56.

Cohen, J.W. (1969), "Single Server Queues With Restricted Accessibility," *Journal of Engineering Mathematics*, 3, 265-84.

Finch, P.D. (1960), "Deterministic Customer Impatience in the Queueing System GI/M/1," *Biometrika*, 43, 45-52.

Fries, B. (1975), "Optimal Order Policy for a Perishable Commodity with Fixed Lifetime," *Operations Research*, 23, 46-61.

Gavish, B. and Schweitzer, P.D. (1977), "The Markovian Queue with Bounded Waiting Time," *Management Science*, 23, 1349-57.

Gnedenko, B. and Kovalenko, I.N. (1968), *Introduction to Queueing Theory*, Israel Program for Scientific Translation.

Graves, S.C. (1968), "Simple Analytical Models for Perishable Inventory Systems," *Technical Report* No. 141, Operations Research Center, Massachusetts Institute of Technology.

Hadley, G. and Whitin, T.M. (1963), *Analysis of Inventory Systems*, Prentice-Hall.

Jennings, J.B. (1973), "Blood Bank Inventory Control," *Management Science*, 19, 637-45.

Loris-Teghem, J.(1972), "On the Waiting Time Distribution in a Generalized Queueing System With Uniformly Bounded Sojourn times," *Journal of Applied Probability*, 9, 642-49.

Nahmias, S. (1975), "Optimal Ordering Policies for Perishable Inventory – II," *Operations Research*, 23, 735-49.

Nahmias, S. (1980), "Perishable Inventory Theory : A Review," Submitted for Publication.

Stanford, R.E. (1979), "Reneging Phenomena in Single Channel Queues," *Mathematics of Operations Research*, 4, 162-78.

Van Zyl, G.J.J. (1964), "Inventory Control for Perishable Commodities," Unpublished Ph.D. Dissertation, University of North Carolina.

-

References

1. L. Gerencsér : Egy folyamatos nyilvántartásu sztochasztikus készletgzadálkodási modell ismertetése és érzékenysegi vizsgálata (introduction of a Continuous Reviewing Stochastic Inventory Model and Examination of its Sensitivity). MTA SZTAKI Közlémenyek, 10(1973).
2. M.J. Liberatore : The EQQ Model Under Stochastic Lead Time. Operations Research 27, pp. 391-396 (1979).
3. T. Kulesár Egy sztochasztikus késési idõs, folytonos készletallenórzéses költségoptimalizáló készletmodell (A Continuous Reviewing, Cost Optimization Inventory Model with Stochastic Lead Time). IX. Magyar Oparációkutatási Konferencia, Gyõr (1979).
4. A. Prékopa : Reliability Equation for an Inventory Problem and its Asymptotic Solutions. Colloquim on Appl. of Math. to Economics, Budapest (1963).
5. M. Ziermann : Készletgazdálkodasi és sorbanállási modellek, "Operációkutatás" (Inventory and Queuing Models, "Operations Research"), Chapter VI, pp. 309-312, SZÃMOK (1972).

[illegible]

[illegible] (19[illegible]) [illegible] Markets [illegible] Sciences [illegible] [illegible]

[illegible] (19[illegible]) [illegible]

[illegible] (19[illegible]) [illegible] in the [illegible] [illegible]

[illegible] Control of [illegible] Portfolios [illegible]

[illegible] (19[illegible]) [illegible] Research [illegible] Publication.

[illegible] (19[illegible]) [illegible] Portfolio [illegible]

Vanek [illegible] (19[illegible]) [illegible] Investment Control and [illegible] Commodities [illegible] University of North Carolina.

References

1. [illegible]

2. [illegible] Model [illegible]

3. [illegible]

4. [illegible]

5. [illegible]

Index